The Bishop's Bounty

compiled by

The Bishop's Bounty Cookbook Committee
Saint Mary's Parents Group, Inc.
Saint Mary's Training School for Retarded Children
Alexandria, Louisiana

featuring

Selected Recipes
and
Highlights of the life accomplishments
of
The Most Reverend Charles Pascal Greco

Cover Design and Illustration: Chuck Larson, Dallas, Texas
Cover and Text Calligraphy: Deborah A. Rediger, Dallas, Texas
Text and Illustrations: Gloria M. Allen, Marshall, Texas
Text Editor: Perre M. Magness, Memphis,
                               Tennessee
Promotional Materials: Carolyn Bullard, Dallas, Texas

Cookbook Committee:
Co-Chairmen: Cindy Ward, Dallas,Texas
             Gloria Allen, Marshall,Texas
    Members: Judy Read, Farmerville, Louisiana
             Venita Scott, Natchitoches, Louisiana
             Mary Ann Hawkins, Dallas,Texas

Second Printing–The Amicus Club, Alexandria, Louisiana

We sincerely thank these people for sharing their unique and out-
standing talents with us.

Additional copies of *The Bishop's Bounty* can be obtained by sending
$14.95 plus $2.00 for postage and handling to:

> *The Bishop's Bounty* Cookbook
> % The Amicus Club
> P.O. Box 5245
> Alexandria, Louisiana 71307-5245

For you convenience, order forms are included in the back of this
book.

First Printing–September, 1987   15,000 copies
Second Printing–July, 1988   10,000 copies

Copyright 1987

by
Saint Mary's Parents Group, Inc.
P.O. Drawer 7768
Alexandria, LA 71306

Library of Congress Catalogue Card #87-070591
ISBN #0-9618271-0-6

WIMMER BROTHERS
Memphis   Dallas

DEDICATION

The Most Reverend Charles P. Greco created St. Mary's Training School for Retarded Children as a garden into which young lives are transplanted. It is a safe, protected environment in which they are able to live, to flourish and to bloom into their fullest maturity, nurtured by the Sisters of Our Lady of Sorrows. Without the work and wisdom and watchfulness of these dedicated servants, the fullest harvest would not be realized. We come with our children to St. Mary's School, in bewilderment and pain. Here the healing and recovery begins, as our children set down roots and begin to grow.

We, the ever-widening circle of the families and friends of St. Mary's School, are partakers of the Bishop's Bounty as surely as are the children whom he loved. The Bishop's kind heart, gentle words, inspired vision, and determined labor have made possible the harvest. To his memory we dedicate these, our collective fruits.

St. Mary's Parents

ALL PROCEEDS REALIZED FROM THE SALES OF *THE BISHOP'S BOUNTY* COOKBOOK WILL BE PLACED IN THE ST. MARY'S PARENTS GROUP SPECIAL ENDOWMENT FUND AND THE AMICUS CLUB SPECIAL PROJECT FUND TO PERPETUATE THE EXISTENCE OF ST. MARY'S TRAINING SCHOOL FOR RETARDED CHILDREN, ALEXANDRIA, LOUISIANA.

ℬISHOP'S ℛESIDENCE

1805 JACKSON STREET
P. O. DRAWER 191
ALEXANDRIA. LA. 71301

CHARLES P. GRECO
Retired Bishop
DIOCESE OF ALEXANDRIA - SHREVEPORT

October 29, 1986

Heavenly Father, as we go to press with our new cookbook, published for the benefit of St. Mary's School for Retarded Children, we pray for your special blessing upon this cookbook.

May it bring knowledge of the art of cooking, with joy and happiness, to our school, to our special children, and to all who work with them.

And may all who use this cookbook receive the benefit of God's special blessing.

The Most Reverend Charles P. Greco

Bon Appetit!!

The Most Reverend Charles Pascal Greco

Born October 29, 1894

Ordained July 25, 1918

Consecrated February 25, 1946

Retired May 22, 1973

Died January 20, 1987

Supreme Knight–Virgil Dechant and
Supreme Chaplin–Bishop Charles P. Greco

KNIGHTS OF COLUMBUS

The fraternal order of the Knights of Columbus was founded by Father Michael J. McGivney in 1882. It is an organization of men who are at least eighteen years old and practice the Roman Catholic faith. Father Michael McGivney was the first Supreme Chaplain, his brother Msgr. John J. McGivney, the second, and their nephew Msgr. Leo M. Finn, the third. On January 14, 1961, following the death of Msgr. Finn, Bishop Charles P. Greco was elected to serve as the Supreme Chaplain, a position never before held by a bishop or anyone outside the immediate family of the founder.

Bishop Greco received exemption in the first three degrees of the Catholic fraternal society of the Knights of Columbus at ceremonies held May 25, 1919, one year after his ordination as a priest. He advanced to fourth degree on May 4, 1924. On July 1, 1954, he accepted the invitation to serve Louisiana State Knights of Columbus as their chaplain. On January 14, 1961, he became the Supreme Chaplain of the National Knights of Columbus and held an Honorary Life Membership in the society, serving as Supreme Chaplain until his death. As Supreme Chaplain, he became the spiritual leader of more than one-million knights worldwide.

In September, 1966, the Knights of Columbus honored Bishop Greco by presenting him with a triptych of three medallions commemorating the Papal visit to the United Nations.

ACKNOWLEDGEMENTS

We would like to express our deepest appreciation to:

Bishop Charles P. Greco for giving us permission to write this book and for sharing his most remarkable life story. We will always treasure the many visits and personal interviews.

The Knights of Columbus, especially the Supreme Knight, Virgil Dechant, who gave us their full support and encouragement.

The many friends of Bishop Greco who assisted us with this project.

Our dear friend, Marge Murrin, Bishop's faithful secretary, who assisted us in many ways.

Monsignor Joseph Susi, a close friend to Bishop, who helped us with Bishop Greco's story and encouraged along the way.

The Sisters of Our Lady of Sorrows, who have known and worked with Bishop for many years, caring for "Gods Special Children." Special thanks to Sr. Mary Antoinette, administrator of St. Mary's Training School, for relating many stories and inspiring us to continue our endeavors.

The Amicus Club of Alexandria, Louisiana, for assisting us in the continued efforts of this project.

All who have made this book possible by sharing their favorite recipes. In order to offer the widest variety of recipes and due to the lack of space, we regret we were not able to include all of the recipes submitted.

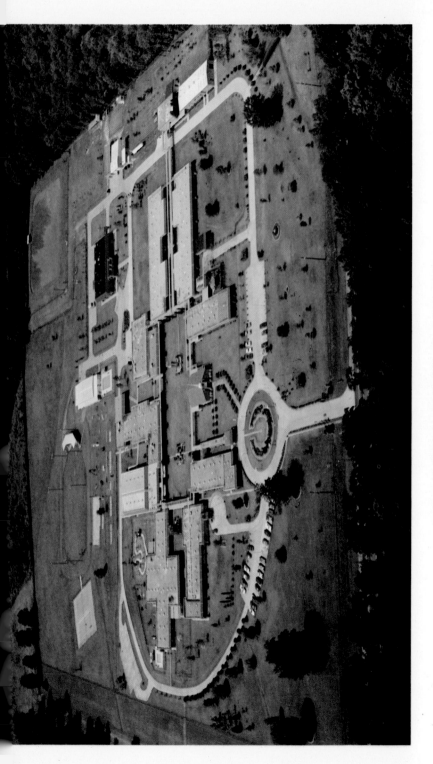

St. Mary's Training School for Retarded Children
Alexandria, Louisiana

TABLE OF CONTENTS

Bishop Greco learned to cook when he was just a young boy at home with his mother. "My mother was a marvelous seamstress and an excellent cook."

Cooking was an enjoyable diversion for Bishop from his busy schedule, and he took great pleasure in preparing special dishes for his friends and fellow priests.

Lemon Supreme Special

1 box lemon supreme cake mix	¾ cup cooking oil
½ cup sugar	1 cup apricot nectar
	4 eggs

Mix together the cake mix, sugar, oil and nectar. Add one egg at a time and beat thoroughly after each addition. Pour into a prepared bundt pan. Bake in 325 degree oven for 1 hour. Remove from oven and cool for 15 minutes before removing cake from pan. While the cake is still hot, brush with lemon glaze.

Glaze:
1 cup confectioners sugar   Juice of one lemon

Mix sugar and lemon juice until blended. Brush on hot cake.

Bishop Charles Pascal Greco, Alexandria, LA

Mascarpone

1 8-ounce package Philadelphia cream cheese	4 egg yolks
4 tablespoons sugar	5 tablespoons cherry liqueur
	Maraschino cherries

Let cream cheese come to room temperature and blend with sugar, egg yolks and liqueur. Pour into small dessert cups. Chill. When served, top with a marachino cherry.

Note: The Italian Mascarpone cheese, for which this dessert is named, is not available in this country. Philadelphia cream cheese is substituted.

Bishop Charles Pascal Greco, Alexandria, LA

Peanut Brittle

1½ cups sugar
½ cup white syrup

1½ cups raw peanuts
2 teaspoons soda

Bishop Greco says that cooking the syrup to the right consistency is the secret to making brittle. He makes his by bringing the sugar and syrup to a boil and cooking it for 7 to 8 minutes or until it reaches the hard ball stage; a ball is formed when a spoon of syrup is dropped into a cup of cold water. Then he adds the peanuts, preferably the small Spanish peanut, while the syrup is still over the flame and cooks for 10 minutes more or until "you can smell the peanuts cooking." Removing from the fire, he adds the soda and stirs well. Then he pours the mixture onto a buttered cookie sheet, tilting first one way and then the other, letting the brittle reach the desired thickness. When cold he breaks it into pieces.

Bishop Charles Pascal Greco, Alexandria, LA

Peach Cobbler

1 cup flour
2 teaspoons baking powder
1 cup sugar
1 cup milk

½ to 1 stick butter
1 16-ounce can sliced peaches, drained

Mix flour, baking powder and sugar; add milk and mix well. Melt butter in medium size pan, about 3 inches deep, then pour batter into pan. Drain the sliced peaches, spreading peach slices over batter. Bake in 350 degree oven for 45 to 50 minutes. The cake rises over the peaches, forming a crunchy, flavorful dessert.

Note: Fresh peaches may be substituted. Add extra sugar according to taste.
Bishop Charles Pascal Greco, Alexandria, LA

SACRED HEART CHURCH
Rodney, Mississippi

Bishop Greco was born October 29, 1894, the son of Frank and Camilla Testa Greco. He was baptized at Sacred Heart Church, Rodney, Mississippi, on the 30th of November, 1894, by Reverend P. Connally, with John T. O'Brian and Pepina Testa as sponsors.

In the 18th century, Rodney was called Gulf Petit. Later it was a thriving port, and once nearly became the capital of Mississippi. As early as 1844, Father Francis, a missionary priest, visited and baptized at Sacred Heart Church. In 1867, Father Charles Quehelberge built the present wooden Gothic building on one acre of land near the banks of the Mississippi River, and remained in Rodney for two years as its first and only resident pastor.

But around 1864, the Mississippi River changed its course, and Rodney gradually became a ghost town. In later years Sacred Heart became a mission of Port Gibson, Mississippi. The church was last used in 1957.

In 1969, the Diocese of Natchez-Jackson donated the property to the Foundation Society of Historical Monuments for preservation. The church was moved first to Port Gibson, and then to Grand Gulf Military Park, six miles northwest of the town, and completely restored.

Appetizers and Beverages

Sacred Heart Church
Rodney, Mississippi

Artichoke Balls

1 14-ounce can artichoke
  hearts
1 cup seasoned bread crumbs
2 eggs
2 tablespoons olive oil

2 tablespoons lemon juice
½ teaspoon garlic powder
2 tablespoons Parmesan
  cheese

Drain and mash artichoke hearts thoroughly. Add all remaining ingredients except Parmesan cheese and mix thoroughly. Refrigerate at least 4 hours or overnight. Form into balls and roll in Parmesan cheese. Serve cold or hot. If desired, heat in 400 degree oven approximately 10 minutes.

Mrs. William Hrapmann, New Orleans, LA

Artichoke Squares

4 eggs
4 tablespoons olive oil
6 green onions, chopped
2 cloves garlic, minced
1 14-ounce can artichoke
  hearts, drained and
  chopped

Salt and pepper to taste
½ pound Swiss or Cheddar
  cheese, shredded
Dash of Tabasco
¼ cup seasoned bread crumbs
1 teaspoon minced parsley
¼ teaspoon oregano

Preheat oven to 325 degrees. Beat eggs until frothy. In olive oil, sauté onions and garlic. Add eggs and all other ingredients. Bake in greased oblong pan for 25 to 35 minutes. Cool. Cut into 1½-inch squares. Reheat for approximately 10 minutes before serving. Yields approximately 24 squares.
Note: ½ pound crabmeat may be added for variation.

Judy Latuso, Baton Rouge, LA

Hot Spinach Squares

1 package spinach, thawed
2 eggs, beaten
1 cup milk
1 stick margarine, melted
1 pound Cheddar cheese,
   grated

½ cup chopped onion
1 cup flour
1 teaspoon salt
1 teaspoon baking powder

Drain and chop spinach. Combine eggs, milk and margarine. Add spinach and remaining ingredients and mix well. Bake in an 8 x 12-inch pan for 35 minutes at 350 degrees. Cool and cut in 1-inch squares. Yields 96.
Note: May be frozen and heated to serve at 350 degrees for 10 to 15 minutes.

Pat Hisel, Kankakee, IL

Husband: Robert Hisel
Knights of Columbus title: Supreme Director

Stuffed Mushrooms

12 large fresh mushrooms
3 tablespoons butter, melted
Salt and pepper to taste
¼ cup butter
⅓ cup finely chopped onion
1 tablespoon flour

½ cup whipping cream
   (unwhipped)
¼ cup chopped fresh parsley
¼ cup grated Swiss cheese
Kraft Parmesan cheese
   (green can)

Wash mushrooms, remove stems and set aside. Brush mushroom caps with the 3 tablespoons melted butter. Set stem-side up and lightly salt and pepper. Chop stems finely and place in saucepan with ¼ cup butter. Add onion and cook until tender. Stir in flour and mix until smooth. Add whipping cream and parsley. Fill mushroom caps with mixture. Sprinkle with Swiss cheese and repeat with Parmesan cheese. These may be made in advance and refrigerated. Warm in oven or microwave until cheese is melted. Serves 6.
Variation: Use less mushrooms and stuff artichoke bottoms.

Sondra Shine, Dallas,TX

Hot Cheese Squares

2 tablespoons flour
½ teaspoon salt
⅓ cup milk
2 eggs, beaten
½ pound sharp Cheddar
  cheese, grated

½ pound Monterey Jack
  cheese with jalapeño
  peppers, grated

Mix flour, salt and milk with beaten eggs; beat well. Add remaining ingredients and mix well. Pour into a flat, well-greased, 8 x 12-inch Pyrex baking dish and bake at 350 degrees for 35 to 45 minutes. Cut in small squares and serve hot.

Judy Read, Farmerville, LA

Swedish Meatballs

Meatballs:
6 pounds ground meat (beef
  with approximately ¼ pork)
6 slices stale bread soaked in
  milk
3 whole eggs, beaten
½ cup finely chopped parsley
½ cup finely chopped green
  onion tops

2 medium white onions, finely
  chopped
4 stalks celery, finely chopped
Garlic salt, black pepper, and
  salt to taste
Oil for frying

Mix all ingredients for meatballs and roll into bite-size balls. Fry in small amount of oil. Pour off excess oil.

Sauce:
2 large bottles barbecue
  sauce

2 cans cream of mushroom
  soup

Mix barbecue sauce and mushroom soup in a large saucepan. Add meatballs and simmer for 40 to 45 minutes. Makes about 400 small meatballs.

Peggy Allen, Ruston, LA

Sweet and Sour Meatballs

1 pound ground beef
6 slices white bread, soaked in
water, drained and mashed
½ medium onion, chopped
1 teaspoon salt
1 teaspoon chopped parsley
½ teaspoon pepper

1 teaspoon ketchup
1 teaspoon prepared mustard
2 eggs, beaten
1 clove garlic, crushed
1 14-ounce bottle ketchup
1 8 or 10-ounce jar grape jelly

Mix ground beef, bread, onion, salt, parsley, pepper, 1 teaspoon ketchup, mustard, eggs and garlic together. Shape into small balls. Deep-fry in 1 quart oil, until brown. Remove from oil and place on paper towel to drain. Place in deep dish. Serve with sauce.

Sauce:
Mix ketchup and jelly in saucepan over low heat. Stir often, until jelly is melted. Pour over meatballs. Serve warm with toothpicks. Yields 50 to 60 meatballs.

Ann Normand, Effie, LA

Braunschweiger Paté

1 16-ounce package
Braunschweiger
2 packages green onion dip
mix
1 teaspoon sugar
2 teaspoons water

2 3-ounce packages cream
cheese, softened
1 tablespoon milk
⅛ teaspoon Tabasco sauce
3 sprigs parsley, snipped
4 radishes, sliced

Mash softened braunschweiger with a fork. Combine dip mix, sugar and water. Blend well. Add softened cream cheese, milk and Tabasco. Blend then form into an igloo shape. Refrigerate until well chilled. Before serving garnish with snipped parsley and sliced radishes. Serve with assorted crackers or melba toast. Yields 8 servings.

Susan Cartier Willis, Austin, TX

Caviar Casserole

2 8-ounce packages cream
  cheese
4 tablespoons mayonnaise
4 tablespoons sour cream
Juice of 1 fresh lemon
¼ teaspoon Tabasco

1 teaspoon Worcestershire
  sauce
1 large jar Romanoff lumpfish
  black caviar
5 hard-boiled eggs, chopped
6 green onions, chopped

Blend cream cheese, mayonnaise, sour cream, lemon juice, Tabasco, and Worcestershire sauce together. (Use plastic blade if using food processor.) Put into mold (any shape desired) that has been greased with mayonnaise. Refrigerate overnight. Unmold and ice with caviar. Layer with chopped eggs and again with green onions. Serve with Carr's biscuits, Melba toast or homemade toast points.

Cindy Ward, Dallas, TX

Crab Zucchini Squares

4 cups sliced zucchini
1 onion, chopped
1½ cups grated Mozzarella
  cheese
1 7-ounce package frozen
  crabmeat

½ cup vegetable oil
3 eggs, lightly beaten
½ teaspoon oregano
1 teaspoon salt
½ teaspoon pepper
1½ cups Bisquick

Cut the zucchini lengthwise in half, then slice each half. Put the zucchini and chopped onion in enough water to cover and bring to a boil. Boil for about 3 minutes, or until onions are just transparent. Drain and cool a bit. Have the crabmeat thawed, drained and broken into small chunks. Combine the cheese, crabmeat, oil, eggs, seasonings and Bisquick and mix thoroughly. Add the zucchini and onion. Pour into a greased 9 x 13-inch baking dish and bake in a preheated 400 degree oven for 20 to 25 minutes (until a knife inserted in the middle comes out clean). Yields 2 to 3 dozen squares. Serve just warm.

Carol Wood, Dallas, TX

Crabmeat Mousse

1 can cream of mushroom
  soup
6-ounce package cream cheese
1 envelope gelatin
¼ cup water
½ cup finely chopped celery

½ cup finely chopped green
  onions
1 cup mayonnaise
1 can crabmeat
¼ teaspoon curry powder

Heat soup and cream cheese; stir until smooth. Add gelatin to cold water and let soften for 5 minutes. Stir and add to soup and cheese mixture. Add finely chopped celery and onions, mayonnaise, crabmeat and curry powder. Mix well. Pour into mold sprayed with Pam. Chill overnight. Unmold on plate. Serve with assorted crackers.

Jane R. Parnell, Newport, AR

Crabmeat Puffs

8-ounce package cream
  cheese, softened
1 stick butter, softened
8 ounces fresh crabmeat
  (or frozen)

½ teaspoon Worcestershire
  sauce
2 packages Pepperidge Farm
  poppy seed party rolls

Combine cream cheese, butter, crabmeat and Worcesteshire sauce. Split rolls and spread with mixture. Broil 5 minutes or until hot and bubbly.

Sunell Comfort, Cincinnati, OH

Raw Vegetable Dip

1 cup mayonnaise
1 small carton sour cream

1 package garlic dressing mix
2 teaspoons celery seed

Mix and let chill in refrigerator for 24 hours. Serve with raw vegetables of your choice. Very good with cauliflower, broccoli, carrots, cucumbers, squash and cherry tomatoes.

Melba Simmons, Bunkie, LA

19

Shrimp Mold

3 envelopes unflavored gelatin
½ cup cold water
1 can tomato soup
⅛ teaspoon baking soda
3 ounces cream cheese
1 cup mayonnaise

½ cup diced onions
½ cup diced celery
1½ pounds cooked and peeled
  shrimp, ground
Salt and pepper to taste

Dissolve gelatin in water. Combine soup, soda and cream cheese in a saucepan and heat until cheese is melted and well blended. Let cool. Add all other ingredients and mix well. Pour into desired mold and chill.

Elizabeth Ardoin, Alexandria, LA

Cracker Snackers

1 1-ounce package Hidden
  Valley Original Ranch-style
  dressing mix
¼ teaspoon dill weed
¼ teaspoon lemon pepper

⅛ teaspoon garlic powder
2 11-ounce packages oyster
  crackers
½ cup vegetable oil

Combine first four ingredients in a bowl. Add crackers and toss well. Drizzle oil over cracker mixture. Stir well. Place mixture in large paper bag. Fold bag to close and let stand for two hours shaking bag occasionally. Store in airtight container. Yields 11½ cups.

Lisa E. Sansom, Wetumpka, AL

Curry Dip

1 cup Hellmann's mayonnaise
1 tablespoon tarragon vinegar
1 tablespoon curry powder

1 tablespoon horseradish
1 tablespoon garlic salt

Mix ingredients well. Chill and serve with desired chips or crackers.

Jane Parnell, Newport, AR

Devil Sticks

1 loaf thin sliced bread	Garlic powder
1 stick melted butter	Red pepper
Mrs. Dash Seasoning	Grated Parmesan cheese

Preheat oven to 200 degrees. Trim crust from bread and cut each slice into four pieces. Place bread on baking sheet and brush with butter. Sprinkle desired amount of seasonings and cheese on bread slices. Bake in oven for 2 hours. Wheat, rye or white bread may be used.

Mary Frances Bowling, Jackson, MS

B-B-Q Pecans

2 tablespoons butter or margarine	2 dashes of hot sauce
¼ cup Worcestershire sauce	4 cups pecans halves
1 tablespoon ketchup	Salt to taste

Preheat oven to 325 degrees. Line jellyroll pan (10 x 15) with foil. In small saucepan, melt together all ingredients except pecans. Place pecans in mixing bowl and pour sauce over pecans. Stir well. Pour in single layer in pan. Bake for 20 minutes. Remove from oven and salt to taste. Pour onto paper towels to cool. Store in airtight container or plastic bag.

Deborah Watts, Lake Charles, LA

Spiced Pecans

1 egg white, slightly beaten	½ teaspoon nutmeg
1 tablespoon water	½ teaspoon cloves
3 cups pecan halves	½ teaspoon salt
½ cup sugar	1 teaspoon cinnamon

Beat egg white and water. Stir in pecans to coat. Mix all other ingredients and sprinkle over pecans, mixing well. Spread pecans on a lightly greased or foil-lined cookie sheet. Bake in 300 degree oven for 30 minutes. Stir twice during baking time to crisp and dry pecans.

Mrs. Earline Childers, Natchitoches, LA

Holiday Cheese Ball

2 8-ounce packages cream cheese (at room temperature)
1 8-ounce can crushed pineapple (unsweetened), drained
2 tablespoons grated onion
¼ cup chopped green bell pepper
¼ cup chopped red bell pepper
½ teaspoon Lawry's seasoned salt
¼ teaspoon Lawry's seasoned pepper
1 teaspoon Worcestershire sauce
¼ teaspoon Tabasco
1 cup chopped pecans, reserving ½ cup for final step

Thoroughly blend cream cheese, pineapple, onion, peppers, seasonings, Worcestershire sauce, Tabasco and ½ cup chopped pecans. Refrigerate several hours. Roll into ball and roll ball in the remaining ½ cup chopped pecans. Present on tray with doily surrounded with fresh parsley and a variety of crackers. A real Holiday treat!

Cindy Ward, Dallas, TX

Olde English Cheese Ball

8 ounces cream cheese
2 ounces Kraft Old English jar cheese
Dash of Worcestershire sauce
Dash of garlic powder
Dash of oregano powder
Dash of minced onion
Parsley and paprika for rolling

Soften cream cheese. Mix all ingredients and chill. When chilled, using hands form into a ball or log and roll in parsley and paprika.
Diana Smith, New Orleans, LA

Pepper Cream Cheese Ball

¼ cup cold butter, cut into
   3 pieces
2 small cloves of garlic
1 8-ounce package cream
   cheese, cut into 6 pieces

¼ cup fresh parsley
½ teaspoon salt
Coarsely ground peppercorns

In a food processor, blend butter and garlic with metal blade until garlic is finely minced, about 30 seconds. Add remaining ingredients except pepper. Process until parsley is minced. Shape mixture into flattened ball. Cover with pepper and chill several hours. Serve with assorted crackers.

Note: Butter and cream cheese must be COLD, otherwise they will not mix properly.

Judy Read, Farmerville, LA

Sausage Cheese Balls

1 pound hot sausage
1 pound Colby cheese, grated

¼ cup flour
3½ cups Bisquick

Combine sausage, cheese, Bisquick and flour. Knead thoroughly. Roll into 1-inch balls. Bake at 350 degrees 15 to 20 minutes or until brown. Easy to freeze. (May use Cheddar cheese.)

Aimee Maillet, Pearl River, LA
Mary Hodge, Dallas, TX

Cheese Nut Biscuits Columbus

1 cup soft butter or margarine
4 cups shredded sharp cheese
2 cups all-purpose flour

2 cups finely chopped nuts
1 teaspoon cayenne pepper
2 teaspoons salt

Thoroughly cream butter and cheese together. Then add other ingredients and mix well. Roll into long roll and refrigerate several hours. Slice into thin rounds. Place on slightly-greased cookie sheet and bake at 325 degrees for 20 minutes.

Lucille Schaider, La Porte, TX

23

Cheese Roll

2 pounds Velveeta Cheese
8-ounce package cream cheese
1 teaspoon garlic powder

1 teaspoon red pepper
1 cup chopped pecans
Paprika

Allow cheeses to stand until they reach room temperature. Thoroughly blend cheeses, garlic powder, red pepper and pecans. Form three balls. Roll in paprika (just enough to cover ball). Wrap in Saran wrap and chill overnight.

Sue Lamell

Ham Cream Cheese Roll

2 8-ounce packages cream
  cheese
1 teaspoon Worcestershire
  sauce
¼ teaspoon Accent

3 to 4 green onions, chopped
1 package thinly sliced ham,
  chop 4 slices, reserve 4
  slices

Blend all of the ingredients together, reserving 4 ham slices. Form mixture into a roll and cover with reserved ham slices. Chill. Slice when ready to serve.

Eileen Duke, Haughton, LA

Salmon Roll

8 ounces cream cheese,
  softened
2 teaspoons grated onion
¼ teaspoon salt
¼ teaspoon Liquid smoke
1 tablespoon lemon juice

1 teaspoon horseradish
1 15-ounce can salmon,
  drained
½ cup chopped pecans
¼ cup chopped parsley

Mix all ingredients together except the nuts and parsley and form into a ball. Roll in chopped pecans and parsley. Refrigerate. Serve with crackers.

Mrs. Henry DeBlieux, Sr., Natchitoches, LA

Mary Jane's French Loaf

½ cup butter
Garlic salt to taste
3-ounce can green chilies,
  drained

4 ounces Monterey Jack
  cheese, grated
½ cup mayonnaise
1 loaf French bread

Melt butter in saucepan and add garlic salt and green chilies. Mix cheese and mayonnaise and add to butter mixture. Cut French bread in half, lengthwise. Spread mixture on cut side of two lengths of bread. Place on cookie sheet and bake at 400 degrees uncovered for 20 minutes. Slice into serving pieces.

Mary Jane Robinson, Little Rock, AR

Miniature Pizza Appetizers

1 pound ground beef
1 pound hot bulk sausage
2 6-ounce rolls garlic cheese
1 6-ounce roll jalapeño cheese

½ teaspoon Worcestershire
  sauce
1 teaspoon oregano
2 loaves party rye bread

Cook beef and sausage in a heavy skillet until done; drain. Add cheese, Worcestershire sauce and oregano. Stir over low heat until cheese is thoroughly melted. Spread mixture on bread. Place on a cookie sheet and heat in 350 degree oven until hot.
Note: These may be made ahead and frozen before baking.

Judy Read, Farmerville, LA

Fruit Dip

1 stick butter, softened
1 box confectioners' sugar,
  sifted
2 or 3 tablespoons lemon juice

1 8-ounce carton sour cream
½ cup ground pecans
Mixed fruit of your choice

Cream butter and sugar together. Add lemon juice and sour cream, mixing with an electric mixer, blender or food processor. Stir in pecans. Slice and prepare fruit for dipping.

Carolyn Stanley, Ruston, LA

Hot and Spicy Mexican Dip

2 pounds Edam or Gouda
  cheese
1 pound hot pork sausage
½ cup chopped onion

¼ cup chopped green peppers
⅛ teaspoon ground allspice
1 can Ro-tel tomatoes with
  green chilies

Peel red wax from cheese and cut cheese into small wedges. Place in a deep casserole dish that has been sprayed with Pam. Brown sausage, drain and add onions, green peppers and allspice. Cook about 20 to 30 minutes on low heat until vegetables are tender. Pour over cheese and cover with Ro-tel tomatoes. Bake in a 350 degree oven for about 15 to 20 minutes or until cheese is hot and bubbly. Serve with large Frito dip chips.

Judy Read, Farmerville, LA

Broccoli Dip

3 10-ounce boxes frozen
  chopped broccoli (use 2
  boxes for dip)
Juice of one lemon
½ cup chopped green onions
½ cup chopped fresh parsley
½ cup chopped bell pepper
½ stick butter (more if
  desired)

1½ teaspoons Worcestershire
  sauce
¼ teaspoon red pepper
1 can cream of mushroom
  soup
1 6-ounce roll garlic cheese
  (or 8 ounces Velveeta
  cheese)
1 cup bread crumbs

Cook broccoli as directed on box, adding the lemon juice. Strain. Sauté onions, parsley and bell pepper in butter. Add Worcestershire sauce, red pepper, mushroom soup and cheese (diced for quicker melting) and blend well. Put cooked broccoli into a 2-quart casserole dish and pour sauce over. Top with bread crumbs and dot with butter. Bake for 30 minutes in 375 degree oven. Serves 12 as a casserole or a large group as a dip.

Glenda Lafleur, Ville Platte, LA

Cloud Nine Dip

8 ounces cream cheese
¼ cup sugar
1 teaspoon grated orange peel

Dash of ginger
1 7-ounce jar of Kraft
   Marshmallow Creme

Soften cream cheese to room temperature. With an electric mixer cream cheese and sugar. Add orange peel, ginger and marshmallow creme. Mix well. Serve with assorted fresh fruit slices.

Sister Helen, OLS, St. Mary's Training School

Resolution Hot Pea Dip

½ bell pepper
2 stalks celery
1 onion
1 teaspoon black pepper
2 tablespoons hot pepper
   sauce*
½ cup ketchup
1 tablespoon salt

3 chicken bouillon cubes
2 15-ounce cans black-eyed
   peas
1 15-ounce can tomatoes
1 clove garlic, pressed
1 teaspoon sugar
½ cup bacon drippings
3 tablespoons flour

Finely chop pepper, celery and onion, and place in a saucepan with black pepper, hot pepper sauce, ketchup, salt and bouillon cubes. Cook over low heat and stir until it reaches a simmer and the cubes have completely dissolved. Add the peas, tomatoes, garlic and sugar. Simmer for 30 minutes. Combine bacon drippings with flour, and stir into peas. Cook for 10 minutes more. Stir well and serve hot with corn chips for dipping. (You can transfer dip to chafing dish.)

This amount makes a very hot dip. Start out with 1 tablespoon and season to taste.

Shellie Futch, Farmerville, LA

27

Spinach Dip I

1 cup mayonnaise
1 cup sour cream
1 package Knorr's Vegetable
   Soup mix
1 small can water chestnuts,
   drained and chopped
4 green onions, chopped
   (optional)

1 16-ounce package frozen
   spinach, uncooked, thawed,
   and drained
1 hollowed out loaf Hawaiian
   Bread (optional)

Using a spoon, blend mayonnaise and sour cream until smooth. Add soup mix, water chestnuts, green onions and stir until well blended. Add spinach and mix well. Chill. Serve in hollowed out bread or in a bowl with chips and crackers.

Darlene LaGrange, Mandeville, LA

Variation: Same as above with the following changes: Use grated onion to taste, salt and pepper to taste, and two packages frozen chopped uncooked spinach.

Gloria Evans, Clarksdale, MS

Spinach Dip II

1 package chopped spinach,
   cooked and drained
½ cup chopped green onions
½ cup chopped fresh parsley
1 teaspoon lemon juice

1 8-ounce carton sour cream
1 cup Hellmann's mayonnaise
1 teaspoon dill seed or weed
Salt and pepper to taste

In a mixing bowl combine the spinach, onion, parsley and lemon juice. Add the sour cream, mayonnaise, and seasonings and blend well. Chill and serve with your favorite chips or crackers. If possible prepare a day in advance to enhance the flavor.

Darlene Cass, Dallas, TX

Shrimp Dip

1 8-ounce package cream
  cheese, softened
1 8-ounce carton sour cream
1 cup mayonnaise
¼ cup chopped onion
1 teaspoon Worcestershire
  sauce

1 tablespoon lemon juice
½ teaspoon garlic powder
Salt and pepper to taste
Dash Tabasco
2 4¼-ounce cans shrimp,
  chopped or ½ pound
  cooked shrimp

Combine cream cheese, sour cream and mayonnaise. Add the onion, Worcestershire sauce, lemon juice, seasonings and shrimp. Mix well. Refrigerate until chilled. Serve with chips or toasted bread rounds.

Cindy Broussard, Alexandria, LA
Bunny Laskowski, Houston, TX

Crab Dip

1 8-ounce package cream
  cheese, softened
2 tablespoons Worcestershire
  sauce
2 tablespoons lemon juice

1 bottle chili sauce
Horseradish to taste
2 6-ounce cans white crabmeat
Green onions, chopped
Fresh parsley, chopped

Mix cream cheese, Worcestershire sauce and lemon juice until smooth and well blended. Layer in the bottom of pie plate or a flat plate. Mix chili sauce and horseradish and layer over cream cheese. Top with crabmeat, then green onions and parsley, as desired. Chill before serving. Serve with assorted crackers.

Judy Read, Farmerville, LA

Clam Dip

½ pound bacon
2 8-ounce packages cream
   cheese
2 cans minced clams,
   reserving juice of one can

1 tablespoon hot sauce
4 green onions, chopped
1 tablespoon Worcestershire
   sauce

Cook bacon, drain and crumble. Blend bacon into cream cheese and add remaining ingredients. Pour into 1-quart microwave dish sprayed with Pam. Cook in microwave on high for 2 minutes. Stir. Cook on high for 2 more minutes. Serve with assorted crackers.

Audrey Morehouse, Alexandria, LA
Helen Dunn, Dallas, TX

Baked Minced Clam Dip

3 7½-ounce cans minced
   clams and juice
1½ teaspoons lemon juice
1 medium onion, minced
1 garlic clove, crushed
¾ teaspoon black pepper

½ cup margarine
1½ teaspoons chopped parsley
1½ teaspoons oregano
Dash cayenne pepper
1 cup bread crumbs
½ cup Parmesan cheese

Mix clams, juice and lemon together and simmer for 15 minutes. Add onion, garlic, pepper, margarine, parsley, oregano and cayenne pepper and simmer for 15 minutes more. Remove from heat, stir in bread crumbs, enough to make a spreadable consistency. Place in a small ovenproof dish. Sprinkle with Parmesan cheese. Bake in 400 degree oven for 20 minutes or until very hot. Yields 6 servings.
Note: Serve hot with Triscuits. Dish can also be frozen prior to baking.
Irene Crichton, Westtown, PA

Best Guacamole

3 large ripe avocados, pitted
  and peeled
2 tablespoons lemon juice
2 tablespoons sour cream
2 large tomatoes, chopped

4 to 5 green onions, finely
  chopped
Salt and pepper to taste
Dash of Tabasco

In large bowl mash avocados with fork. Add lemon juice, sour cream, tomatoes, and onions. Mix well. Season with salt and pepper to taste. Add Tabasco. Serve with chips.
Note: May serve as a salad on a bed of lettuce.

Donna Graham, Lyon, MS

Chili Con Queso

2 pounds Old English cheese
  or Velveeta cheese (or ½ and
  ½)
1 pod garlic, minced
1 large onion, finely grated

½ green pepper, chopped
2 tablespoons margarine
1 can Ro-tel tomatoes
1 small can evaporated milk

Melt cheese in top of a double boiler. Sauté garlic, onion and green pepper in margarine. Add to melted cheese. Add Ro-tel tomatoes and milk. Stir. Serve in a chafing dish with Fritos.
Note: Better the next day after flavors blend.

Marti Greenberg, Denton, TX

Layered Mexican Dip

1 16-ounce can refried beans
8 ounces guacamole dip
1 8-ounce carton sour cream
2 cups shredded Cheddar
  cheese

½ cup sliced black olives
4 to 6 green onions, chopped
2 medium tomatoes

In a shallow dish layer the above ingredients, beginning with refried beans and finishing with tomatoes. Chill until ready to serve. Dip with corn chips. I prepare this up to a day in advance. It looks so appetizing and is delicious. Very addictive!!

Charlotte S. Baham, New Orleans, LA

31

Ro-tel Sausage Dip

1 pound hot sausage
1 onion, chopped
1 bell pepper, chopped

2 10-ounce cans Ro-tel
   tomatoes
2 pounds Velveeta cheese

Brown sausage. Add onion and bell pepper to sausage and cook until tender. Drain off fat. Add tomatoes and cubed Velveeta cheese. Cook over medium heat until cheese has melted.

Nena Ventura Williams, Dallas, TX

Nacho Dip

8 ounces cream cheese,
   softened
8 ounces sour cream
10½ ounces jalapeño bean dip
1 1.25-ounce package chili
   seasoning mix
5 drops Tabasco

2 teaspoons chopped parsley
¼ cup taco sauce
1¼ cups shredded sharp
   cheese
1¼ cups shredded Monterey
   Jack cheese
Green onions, chopped

Combine softened cream cheese and sour cream; beat until smooth. Stir in bean dip, chili seasoning mix, Tabasco, parsley, taco sauce, ¾ cup sharp cheese and ¾ cup Monterey Jack cheese. Spoon into a 2-quart casserole that has been sprayed with Pam. Top with remaining cheeses and chopped onions. Bake at 325 degrees for 15 to 20 minutes. Serve hot with tortilla chips. Yields 3½ cups.

Mrs. Donna Graham, Lyon, MS

Lake Charles Dip

½ pint sour cream
Juice of ½ lemon
Dash of Tabasco
1 tablespoon mayonnaise

1 package Good Seasons
   Italian Salad Dressing mix
½ avocado, finely chopped
½ tomato, chopped

Mix all ingredients. Good Seasons Italian Salad Dressing mix is used dry. Serve immediately or chill if desired. Serve with chips or raw vegetables.

Doris Cartier, Austin, TX

Brandy Ice

1 pint French vanilla ice
  cream
1 jigger brandy
½ jigger Kahlua

½ jigger creme de cacao
Shaved chocolate
Pumpkin pie spice

Mix ice cream, brandy, Kahlua and creme de cacao in blender.
Serve topped with shaved chocolate and a dash of pumpkin spice.
Serves 4.

Jane Parnell, Newport, AR

Daiquiritas

Lime wedge
Salt
1 6-ounce can frozen limeade
  concentrate, undiluted

½ cup cold water
¾ cup light rum
⅓ cup tequila
Lime slices (optional)

Rub rim of cocktail glasses with lime wedge. Place salt in saucer;
spin rim of each glass in salt. Set glasses aside. Combine limeade
concentrate, water, rum and tequila in container of electric blender,
process well. Fill blender with ice and blend well until all is smooth.
Pour in glasses and garnish with lime slice if desired.

Terri Patterson, Farmerville, LA

Eggnog

1 gallon commercial eggnog
1 pint whipping cream
  (unwhipped)

1 quart brandy
½ gallon vanilla ice cream
Nutmeg

Mix eggnog, cream, brandy, and ice cream. Sprinkle with nutmeg
and serve immediately. Serves 16.

Harryette Shue, North Little Rock, AR

Coconut Eggnog

12 eggs, separated
1 15 or 16-ounce can cream
of coconut
1 3½-ounce can toasted
coconut flakes

8 cups milk
1 cup heavy cream or
whipping cream

About 2 hours before serving, in large bowl with mixer at high speed beat egg yolks and cream of coconut until thick and lemon colored (about 10 minutes). Reserve ¼ coconut flakes for garnish. In food processor with knife blade attached or in blender at medium speed, blend remaining coconut and one cup milk until pureed. Pour pureed coconut mixture into yolk mixture, cover and refrigerate. About 20 minutes before serving, in chilled 5 to 6-quart punch bowl, mix egg yolk mixture and remaining 7 cups milk until blended. In large bowl with mixer at high speed, beat egg whites until soft peaks form. With rubber spatula or wire whisk, gently fold beaten egg whites and whipped cream into egg yolk mixture. To serve sprinkle reserved toasted coconut over eggnog. Yields 18 cups.

Laura S. Scott, Natchitoches, LA

Party Punch

3 cups sugar
6 cups water
2 3-ounce packages mixed-
fruit Jello
1 46-ounce can pineapple
juice

1 quart orange juice (in
carton, not frozen
concentrate)
½ cup 100% pure Minute
Maid lemon juice
concentrate
2 1-liter bottles ginger ale

Boil sugar and water for 3 minutes. Add Jello. Cool slightly. Then add pineapple, orange and lemon juices. Mix well. Freeze mixture in half-gallon milk cartons. Set out of freezer for 2 hours before serving. Add a bottle of ginger ale for each carton of frozen punch mixture used. Punch is best when slushy but also good when thoroughly melted. Frozen mixture keeps well. Makes 50 servings.

Donna Ward, Farmerville, LA

Warm Apple Rum

3 ounces apple cider or juice   Slice of orange
1½ ounces dark rum   Few whole cloves
Cinnamon stick

Warm cider and add rum. Pour into mug or glass and garnish with cinnamon stick and orange slice stuck with cloves. Yields 1 serving.

Laura S. Scott, Natchitoches, LA

Spiced Tea Mix

1 7-ounce jar orange drink
   mix (Tang)
1 cup instant tea
2 3-ounce packages sweetened
   lemonade mix

1½ cups sugar
2 teaspoons cinnamon
½ teaspoon ground cloves

Mix all ingredients thoroughly. Store in airtight container. To prepare spiced tea, use 2 teaspoons mix to a cup of boiling water.

Mike Saucier, Alexandria, LA

Dixie's Spiced Tea

2 quarts boiling water
8 large family-size tea bags
3 tablespoons almond extract
4 cups Tang
1 cup raw sugar

3 tablespoons cinnamon
3 tablespoons nutmeg
1¼ teaspoons ground cloves
2½ gallons water
Mint leaves

Pour boiling water over tea bags and add almond extract, Tang, sugar and spices. Allow to steep several minutes. Add remaining 2½ gallons of water. Serve in tall glasses over crushed ice garnished with fresh mint leaves. Yield 3 gallons.

Dixie Harlan, Paris, TX

Minted Tea

4 cups boiling water
4 regular tea bags
1½ cups sugar
1 6-ounce can frozen orange
   juice concentrate, thawed
   and undiluted

1 6-ounce can frozen
   lemonade concentrate,
   thawed and undiluted
¾ cup chopped fresh mint
11½ cups water
Lemon slices (optional)
Fresh mint sprigs (optional)

Pour 4 cups boiling water over tea bags and cover. Let stand 12 minutes. Discard bags. Combine sugar, orange juice concentrate and lemonade concentrate in a saucepan; bring to a boil, stirring constantly. Remove from heat and add mint. Let stand 15 minutes. Strain mint from fruit mixture and discard mint. Combine tea and juice mixture and add 11½ cups of water. Serve hot, garnished with lemon slices and mint sprigs, if desired. Yields 1 gallon.

Vida Duke, Paris, TX

Wassail

2½ cups boiling water
¼ teaspoon allspice
¼ teaspoon nutmeg
¼ teaspoon cloves
6 tea bags

1 pint cranberry juice
¾ cup sugar
1½ cups water
½ cup lemon juice
½ cup orange juice

Pour boiling water over spices and tea bags. Let steep for 5 minutes. Strain and add remaining ingredients. Heat to boiling. Serve hot. Yields 8 to 10 servings.
Note: This is non-alcoholic, but the addition of rum will provide a welcome lift on a cold day.

Dorothy Staskey, Flagstaff, AZ

Husband: Paul J. Staskey
Knights of Columbus title: Supreme Warden

Banana Punch

5 bananas (blended)
1 large can concentrated
orange juice
46-ounce can pineapple juice

1 cup sugar mixed with 5 cups
warm water
1 quart ginger ale
½ gallon pineapple sherbet

Combine all ingredients except sherbet and chill about one hour. Just before serving fold sherbet into liquid mixture (in punch bowl). More ginger ale may be added if desired.

Lorraine Favors, Ponchatoula, LA

Cherry Valentine Punch

1 small package cherry Jello
¾ cup sugar
1 cup hot water
½ ounce almond extract

1 46-ounce can pineapple
juice
4 ounces lemon juice
1½ or 2 quarts ginger ale

Dissolve Jello and sugar in hot water. Mix all ingredients except ginger ale. Chill thoroughly. Just before serving, add chilled ginger ale. Serves 25. To change the color of the punch, substitute a different flavor of Jello.

Lucille Schaider, La Porte, TX

Sangria

1 6-ounce frozen limeade
1 6-ounce frozen orange juice
¼ cup brandy
1 750 ml. red wine (Gallo
Hearty Burgundy)

2 10-ounce bottles carbonated
water
Lime slices

Mix ingredients together and serve over ice. Serves 12.

Ann Comeaux, Baytown, TX

WHAT IS A BISHOP?

"...And Like a Shephed He Shall Lead His Flock..."

From the time of Saint Ignatius, the bishop has been the living and visible center, and effective principle of unity within the Church. "There is really one only flesh of Our Lord, one only cup to unite us in His blood, one only altar, as there is one only bishop..."(Ignatius, Philad. 4).

Canon Law describes bishops as successors of the Apostles. By divine institution they are placed over particular churches, which they rule with ordinary power under the power of the Pope. Bishops are members of an episcopal body, that, in union with the Pope, corporately shares a charge and mission for the universal church. To qualify for the episcopal office, a candidate must be born in lawful wedlock, be at least thirty years old, ordained a priest at least five years, and free from the bond of matrimony. He must possess the necessary qualities of character: integrity, prudence, piety, and zeal for souls; he should also be skilled as a theologian and canonist. Before taking possession of his office, he must make a profession of faith and take an oath of fidelity to the Holy See. In his own diocese, the bishop is the ordinary minister of the Sacraments of Confirmation and Holy Orders. As pastor of the diocese, he has the responsibility to lead his parishoners in the worship of God, to preach the Word of God and provide for the religious instruction of the faithful, especially the young. The bishop is, then, the high priest, the teacher, the shepherd of the faithful within the diocese.

Soups, Salads and Salad Dressings

Residence of Bishop Charles P. Greco
Alexandria, Louisiana

New England Clam Chowder

2 6½-ounce cans minced or
　baby clams
4 slices bacon
½ cup chopped onion
8 medium potatoes, peeled
　and cubed
2½ cups milk

1 cup light cream
3 teaspoons flour
½ teaspoon Worcestershire
　sauce
½ to 1 teaspoon salt
Dash of pepper

Drain clams reserving liquid and add enough water to clam juice
to make 2 cups of liquid. In a large soup pot fry bacon until crisp.
Remove bacon and reserve. Sauté onions in bacon fat until golden
brown. Add clam juice and potatoes. Cover and cook until potatoes
are tender (approximately 15 minutes). Add clams, 2 cups of milk
and cream. Blend ½ cup of milk with flour, forming a paste, and
stir into chowder. Boil for 2 to 3 minutes. Add Worcestershire, salt
to taste and a dash of pepper. When serving, top each bowl with
crumbled bacon if desired. Yields 6 servings.
Note: Excellent served on a cold, snowy New England night.

Mary Francis, Boston, MA

Three Potato Soup

3 medium potatoes
1 cup water
1 stalk celery, chopped
¼ teaspoon salt
2 green onions, sliced

1 large can evaporated milk
¼ cup margarine
1 teaspoon parsley flakes
Pepper to taste
Chopped green onion tops,
　as desired

Peel and cube potatoes. Place potatoes, water, celery, salt and 2
green onions in saucepan. Cover and cook on medium heat for 10
minutes or until vegetables are tender. Do not drain. Slightly mash
vegetables; then add milk, margarine, parsley and pepper. Garnish
with green onion tops. Yields 3½ cups.

Edna Polker

Gourmet Chicken Stock

12 cups cold water
1 chicken minus the liver
1 large onion, peeled and
    stuck with two cloves
2 leeks halved lengthwise
2 carrots
1 stalk celery with leaves

2 teaspoons salt
Cheesecloth and string
½ teaspoon thyme
6 sprigs fresh parsley
1 bay leaf
1 clove garlic

Place water and chicken in large kettle and bring to a boil. Skim the froth. Add onion, leeks, carrots, celery and salt. Make a bag by taking a square of cheesecloth and placing the thyme, parsley, bay leaf and garlic on the cloth and tying with string. Add the bag to the boiling mixture. Reduce heat, cover and simmer two hours. Remove chicken from kettle and remove the meat (meat may be saved for any desired purpose). Return the bones and skin to the water, cover and bring to a boil. Reduce heat and simmer two additional hours. Pour entire contents of kettle through a strainer and press hard on solids. Discard solids and chill stock. Remove fat. Yields 6 to 8 cups. Can be frozen in Ziploc freezer bags for future use.

Cindy Ward, Dallas, TX

Broccoli Cheese Soup

1 box frozen chopped broccoli
1 large onion, chopped
2 to 4 ribs celery, chopped
1 stick butter

1 can cream of chicken soup
1 can cream of celery soup
2 soup cans of milk
1 small jar Cheez Whiz

Cook broccoli according to package directions and drain. Sauté onion and celery in butter until tender. Put broccoli, onion and celery into soup kettle and add cream of chicken soup, cream of celery soup, milk and Cheez Whiz. Cook over low heat for about 30 minutes. Yields 6 to 8 servings.

Edgar Allen, Marshall, TX

Seafood Gumbo

⅔ cup flour
⅔ cup cooking oil
2 cups chopped onion
1 cup chopped celery
½ cup chopped bell pepper
½ cup chopped onion tops
4 cloves garlic, minced
¼ cup chopped parsley

2 quarts hot water
1 tablespoon salt
1 teaspoon cayenne pepper
2 pounds raw shrimp, peeled
1 pound crabmeat or 8 small
  whole crabs, cleaned
1 pint oysters, with natural
  liquid

Make a roux by mixing flour in cooking oil and cook with constant stirring until a dark caramel color. Add onions, celery and bell pepper to roux and cook for 10 minutes. Add onion tops, parsley and garlic and cook for 5 minutes. Add hot water, a little at a time, salt and cayenne pepper. Cook for 30 minutes, boiling down some of the liquid. Add shrimp, crabmeat (or whole crabs) and cook for 30 minutes. Add oysters with their liquid and cook for 20 minutes. Serve over rice adding filé as desired. Yields 8 to 10 servings.

Mrs. Mildred Pitre, Golden Meadow, LA

Husband: Easton J. Pitre
Knights of Columbus title: State Deputy

Potato Soup

8 to 10 Irish potatoes
4 cups water
3 chicken bouillon cubes
1 cup chopped onions
1 cup chopped celery
½ stick margarine
4 tablespoons flour

1½ cups milk
1 teaspoon parsley flakes
1 teaspoon white pepper
1 teaspoon garlic powder
1 teaspoon creole seasoning
  (optional)

Peel and dice potatoes. Place in water with bouillon cubes and boil until tender. Sauté onions and celery in margarine until tender; add flour to onions and celery and mix. Slowly add milk and stir until completely mixed and creamy. Add this to potatoes with constant stirring. Mix well. Add parsley flakes and seasonings. Cook over low heat for 20 minutes. Serves 12.

Becky Hebert, Natchitoches, LA

Crabmeat Bisque

2 7½-ounce cans king-crab
  meat
3 tablespoons butter or
  margarine
¾ cup finely chopped onion
4 cups milk
2 cups light cream

2 teaspoons salt
Dash of pepper
¾ cup sherry
⅓ cup unsifted all-purpose
  flour
Chopped parsley

Drain crabmeat; reserve liquid. Remove any cartilage from crabmeat. Melt butter in a 3-quart saucepan. Add onion, crabmeat and
reserved liquid; simmer 5 minutes. Meanwhile, heat milk with
cream until bubbles form around edge of pan. Stir into crab mixture along with salt and pepper. In small bowl, combine ½ cup
sherry with the flour, mixing well. Stir into crab mixture. Bring to
boiling; reduce heat, and simmer 20 minutes. Stir in remaining ¼
cup sherry. Sprinkle the bisque with parsley. Serve with toasted
salted crackers, if desired. Yields 2 quarts or 12 servings.
*Note: If preparing bisque a day in advance, omit last ¼ cup sherry, cover
and refrigerate. Reheat in top of double boiler or in saucepan set in pan of
hot water. Stir in ¼ cup of sherry just before serving.*
                                    Alice Williamson, Palmyra, NY

Baked Potato Soup

½ cup flour
½ cup butter
2 cups chicken stock,
  seasoned
2 cups milk
Salt and pepper to taste

2 large baked potatoes, peeled
  and cubed
1 cup grated Cheddar cheese
¼ cup crumbled bacon
3 tablespoons chives

Make roux with flour and butter. Add chicken stock and milk and
cook until thickened. Season with salt and pepper. Add cubed potatoes. Serve hot garnished with cheese, bacon and chives. Serves 4.
                                    Mary Anne Hawkins, Dallas, TX

French Market Soup

1 pound dried beans (mixed)
6 quarts water, divided
1 tablespoon salt
1 ham hock or ham scraps
2 bay leaves
Pinch of thyme
1 quart tomatoes
2 medium onions, chopped
2 cloves garlic, minced
6 ribs celery, chopped
1 bell pepper, chopped
Salt and pepper to taste
½ pound smoked sausage
½ of a large fryer
2 tablespoons chopped parsley
2 tablespoons chopped
   scallions

Wash and remove blemished beans. Drain. Place in a large pot and cover with water. Add 1 tablespoon salt and soak overnight. Drain beans. Add 3 quarts water, ham hock, bay leaves and thyme. Bring to a boil, cover and simmer for 2 hours. Add tomatoes, onion, garlic, celery, bell pepper and season with salt and pepper. Simmer uncovered for 1 hour and 30 minutes. Add sausage and chicken. Cook until chicken is tender. Remove chicken, bone and cut into chunks. Return chicken meat to soup. About 10 minutes before serving, garnish with parsley and scallions. For a thicker and creamier soup, mash beans. Yields 6 to 8 servings.

Ann Comeaux, Baytown, TX

Mushroom Soup

2 tablespoons butter
1 pound fresh mushrooms,
   thinly sliced
2 medium white onions,
   thinly sliced
3 garlic cloves, finely minced
1 tablespoon flour
1 bay leaf
⅛ teaspoon nutmeg
4 cups chicken broth
Generous sprinkling of fresh
   ground pepper
Dash of salt
½ cup cream

Heat the butter in a pan. Add mushrooms, onions and garlic and cook until tender, but do not brown. Sprinkle with flour. Add bay leaf, nutmeg, and chicken broth. Season to taste and simmer for 20 minutes, with frequent stirring. Place ingredients in a blender and purée. Return to pan, add cream and heat. Serve hot. Yields 8 servings.

Bunny Laskowski, Houston, TX

Oyster Soup a la Mildred

1 pound salt pork
3 cups water
¼ cup cooking oil
1 large onion, chopped
½ cup chopped shallots
1 bell pepper, chopped
1 can stewed tomatoes (or
  whole tomatoes)

Italian seasoning, as desired
1½ pints oysters, with their
  natural liquid
1 quart water (more or less)
2 ounces thin spaghetti,
  uncooked

Cut salt pork into cubes and boil in 3 cups water to remove salt. Drain and set aside. In cooking oil sauté onion, shallots and bell pepper until light brown. Add salt pork and stewed tomatoes, cooking for about 30 minutes. Add Italian seasoning or other seasoning to taste. Add oysters and their liquid and cook for 5 minutes. Add water and cook for 30 minutes or until liquid has cooked down slightly. Add spaghetti and cook for 15 to 20 minutes, adding more water as needed. The amount of water will determine the thickness of the soup as will the amount of spaghetti. Yields 6 servings.

Mrs. Mildred Pitre, Golden Meadow, LA

Husband: Easton J. Pitre
Knights of Columbus title: State Deputy

Chicken Soup

3-pound hen or turkey
5 cups water
4 ribs celery, chopped
4 whole carrots, scraped
Salt and pepper to taste

4 whole white onions, peeled
4 whole new potatoes, peeled
1 cup cooked peas
1 tablespoon chopped parsley

Place hen in large pot with water and vegetables. Cover and simmer until hen is tender. Remove hen and debone. Cut into cubes. Return to pot and simmer for 5 minutes. Pour into a tureen and add peas. Garnish with chopped parsley. Serves 4.

Nena Ventura Williams, Dallas, TX

45

French Onion Soup

3 tablespoons butter
1 tablespoon cooking oil
4 yellow onions (6 cups),
  thinly sliced
1 can Campbell's beef
  consommé
1 soup can water
2 cups homemade chicken
  stock or canned chicken
  stock

1 teaspoon salt
½ teaspoon sugar
3 tablespoons Gold Medal
  Wondra Pour 'n Shake flour
1 cup white wine
1 bay leaf
½ teaspoon sage
½ teaspoon white pepper

In a large soup kettle melt the butter with the oil; add the sliced onions and stir to coat with the butter. Cover the kettle and cook over moderately low heat for 15 to 20 minutes, stirring occasionally, until onions are tender and translucent. In a saucepan heat the beef consommé, water and chicken stock together. Uncover the soup kettle, raise the temperature to moderately high and stir in the salt and sugar. Cook onions for about 20 to 30 minutes, stirring frequently, until onions have turned an even deep golden brown. Lower the heat, stir in the flour and add a bit more butter if flour does not absorb into a paste with the onions. Cook slowly, stirring continually, for about 2 minutes to brown the flour lightly. Remove from heat. Pour in about a cup of the hot soup mixture stirring with a wire whisk to blend flour and soup. Add the rest of the soup mixture, wine, bay leaf, sage and pepper and bring to a simmer. Simmer slowly for 30 to 40 minutes and the soup is done! Garnish with fresh grated Parmesan cheese or Swiss cheese if desired. Serve with French bread and a dry white wine. Yields 6 cups.

Note: I use Vidalia, Georgia, onions or sweet Texas onions when they are in season.

Cindy Ward, Dallas, TX

Onion Soup

⅓ cup olive oil
6 cups thinly sliced onions
3 tablespoons flour
3 cans (10½-ounce each)
   condensed beef bouillon

3 soup cans water
6 slices French bread
1 cup grated Swiss cheese

In a large skillet or pot, heat oil. Add onions and sauté until golden brown. Stir in flour and cook for 2 to 3 minutes. Add beef bouillon and water. Bring to a boil, lower heat and simmer for 30 minutes. Toast the French bread and set in individual oven-proof soup bowls. Add the cooked soup and sprinkle the top with grated cheese. Bake in 375 degree oven for 10 minutes or until cheese is melted. Serve at once. Yields 6 servings.

Julia Van Tassell, North Haven, CT
Husband: William J. Van Tassell
Knights of Columbus title: Supreme Treasurer

Gazpacho

6 medium tomatoes
1 medium cucumber, peeled,
   seeded and finely chopped
1 medium onion, finely
   chopped
1 medium bell pepper, finely
   chopped
1 clove garlic, minced

1½ cups tomato juice
¼ cup olive oil
2 tablespoons vinegar
1 teaspoon salt
¼ teaspoon pepper
Few drops hot sauce
Croutons

Plunge tomatoes in boiling water for 30 seconds to loosen skin. Immerse in cold water. Slip off skin and coarsely chop tomatoes. In a large mixing bowl combine tomatoes, cucumber, onion, bell pepper and garlic. Add tomato juice, olive oil, vinegar, salt, pepper and hot sauce. Chill. Top with croutons when ready to serve. Yields 6 servings.

Note: Toasted bread crumbs can be substituted for croutons.

Edie Hellman, Mandan, ND
Husband: James Hellman
Knights of Columbus title: State Program Director
Honors: 1985 International Family of the Year

Pumpkin Potpourri

1 16-ounce can (2 cups)
  pumpkin (See note)
3 cups water
3 chicken bouillon cubes
½ teaspoon salt
½ teaspoon cinnamon
¼ teaspoon nutmeg
Dash pepper
1 cup raisins

1 10-ounce package Green
  Giant Rice Originals frozen
  long grain white and wild
  rice
2 tablespoons margarine or
  butter
½ cup chopped celery
½ cup chopped onion
1 2½-ounce jar sliced
  mushrooms, drained
2 cups half and half cream

In a large saucepan combine pumpkin and water and mix well. Stir in bouillon cubes, salt, cinnamon, nutmeg and pepper. Heat until bouillon cubes dissolve. Add raisins and rice and simmer. In skillet melt margarine and sauté celery, onions and mushrooms until tender. Stir vegetables into pumpkin mixture and simmer until hot and flavors have blended (about 15 minutes). Add cream before serving and heat until hot. This soup thickens as it stands. Yields 10 (1 cup) servings.

Note: Fresh pumpkin can be substituted for canned. Cut the meat of 1 small peeled pumpkin into 1-inch pieces. Add to boiling salt water. Cover and reheat to boiling. Cook about 30 minutes or until tender. Process in blender until smooth. I definitely recommend fresh pumpkin.

Carolyn Bullard, Dallas, TX

Tomato Soup

½ cup butter
½ cup flour
4 cups tomato juice

½ teaspoon white pepper
Salt to taste
2 cups milk

In saucepan melt butter and stir in flour. Add tomato juice, pepper and salt and simmer until thick. Add 2 cups milk and slowly heat to warm. Stir gently. Serves 4 to 6.

Janet Ward, Ennis, TX

Green Apple Salad

2 Granny Smith green apples
1 head raddicchio lettuce
1 head romaine lettuce

6 ounces Gorgonzola cheese
¼ cup sour cream
½ cup pine nuts, toasted

Slice apples and combine with bite-size pieces of lettuce. Mix together the cheese and sour cream leaving some chunks of cheese in the mixture. Pour over the lettuce and apple salad mixture. Toast the pine nuts in a 350 degree oven for several minutes until brown. Toss with the salad and dressing mixture. Serves 4.

Leigh Rachofsky, Dallas, TX

Lacy's Salad

1 can cherry pie filling
1 large can pineapple tidbits, drained
2 teaspoons lemon juice

1 can sweetened condensed milk
½ cup chopped pecans
Large Cool Whip

Mix pie filling, pineapple tidbits, lemon juice, milk and pecans. Fold in Cool Whip. Refrigerate until thoroughly chilled and firm. Serves 6 to 8.

Mrs. Mallie McLaughlin, Nashville, AR

Miss Harriet's Curried Fruit

1 can peach halves
1 can pear halves
1 can pineapple chunks
1 can apple slices

1 bottle sweet black cherries
1 tablespoon curry powder
¾ cup brown sugar
1 stick butter

Drain all fruit. Mix fruit together in a baking dish. Mix curry and sugar, then sprinkle mixture on top of fruit. Dot with butter. Bake in a 350 degree oven for 30 minutes. Serves 6 to 8.

Mrs. Martha P. McDermott, Biloxi, MS

Five Star Fruit Salad

½ package miniature
  marshmallows
½ can Angel flake coconut
1 8-ounce carton sour cream

1 small can crushed
  pineapple, drained
2 cans mandarin oranges,
  drained

Combine marshmallows, coconut, sour cream, pineapple and oranges. Cover and refrigerate overnight. Serves 6.
Pineapple chucks or tidbits may be used in place of crushed pineapple.

Carolyn Blanchard, Napoleonville, LA
Betty Slocum, Welsh, LA

Frozen Fruit Salad I

2 cups sour cream
1 ripe banana, sliced
1 small can crushed pineapple
¾ cup sugar

½ cup maraschino cherries,
  sliced
Juice of ½ lemon
½ cup chopped pecans

Combine all ingredients well and pour in glass dish that has been lightly greased with mayonnaise. Freeze. Cut into squares and serve on lettuce leaves.

Judy Latuso, Baton Rouge, LA

Frozen Fruit Salad II

1 20-ounce can Royal Anne
  cherries, pitted and halved
1 20-ounce can crushed
  pineapple
1 large package cream cheese

½ pint whipping cream,
  whipped
1 can Angel flake coconut
3 sliced bananas

Drain the cherries and pineapple, using the juice to whip into the cream cheese. Whip the whipping cream and add coconut and bananas. Add cherries, pineapple and cream cheese. Place in a pan that has been sprayed with Pam. Freeze for 24 hours. Cut into squares to serve. Yields 12 servings.

Bunny Laskowski, Houston,TX

Blueberry Salad

2 3-ounce packages
  blackberry Jello
2 cups boiling water
1 16-ounce can blueberries,
  drain and reserve juice
1 8¼-ounce can crushed
  pineapple, drain and
  reserve juice

8 ounces cream cheese
½ pint sour cream
½ cup sugar
½ teaspoon vanilla
½ cup chopped pecans

Dissolve Jello in boiling water. Measure juice and if not a cup, add water. Add juice to Jello. Add blueberries and pineapple to Jello and mix. Pour into a 2-quart flat pan. Refrigerate until firm. Combine cream cheese, sour cream, sugar and vanilla. Mix well. Spread over top of Jello. Sprinkle chopped nuts on top. Cut into squares and serve on lettuce leaf. Serves 10 to 12.

Mrs. Henry DeBlieux, Sr., Natchitoches, LA

Watergate Salad

1 20-ounce can crushed
  pineapple, undrained
2 small packages pistachio
  instant pudding mix
Green food coloring (optional)

Pecans (optional)
1 large Cool Whip
Miniature marshmallows
  (optional)

Mix pineapple with instant pudding mix, food coloring and pecans, if used. Fold in Cool Whip. Add marshmallows, if used. Refrigerate until serving time. Yields 10 to 12 servings.

Lynne Compton, Alexandria, LA

One Hour Fruit Salad

1 can peach pie filling
1 can crushed pineapple
1 can mandarin oranges

1 tablespoon Fruit Fresh
1 pint frozen strawberries
3 or 4 bananas, sliced

Combine all ingredients. Chill for one hour.
Note: May also be served as dessert.

Helen Owen, West Monroe, LA

Christmas Cranberry Salad

1 pound cranberries
1 large orange, seeded but not
   peeled
2 3-ounce packages red gelatin

2 cups boiling water
1 cup chopped pecans
1 15-ounce can crushed
   pineapple

Grind the cranberries with the orange. Dissolve gelatin in boiling water. Add other ingredients and pour into large greased mold. Chill until set. Unmold on lettuce, and top individual servings with Fluffy Mayonnaise or Miniature Cream Cheese Balls.

Fluffy Mayonnaise:
½ cup heavy cream

1 cup mayonnaise

Whip heavy cream until stiff, fold in mayonnaise, blending well.

Cream Cheese Balls:
Cream cheese

Chopped pecans

Using a melon-baller dipped in hot water, form cream cheese into small balls. Roll each in chopped nuts.

Mary West

Louisiana Jello Salad

1 can cranberry sauce
1 can water
2 3-ounce boxes black cherry
  Jello
8 ounces cream cheese,
  softened

½ pint whipping cream,
  whipped
1 small can crushed
  pineapple, drained
1 cup chopped pecans

In a saucepan, place cranberry sauce and water. Heat until cranberry sauce has melted. Dissolve Jello in hot cranberry sauce. Refrigerate until cool. Cream the softened cream cheese. Blend in the whipped cream and add pineapple and nuts. Blend cream cheese mixture into the cranberry-Jello mixture. Pour into mold. Refrigerate until firm before serving. Yields 6 to 8 servings.

Dot Sarver, Leesville, LA

Orange Congeal

2 3-ounce packages orange
  Jello
1 cup boiling water
1 small can orange juice
  (thawed and undiluted)

2 11-ounce cans mandarin
  oranges (do not drain)
1 20-ounce can crushed
  pineapple (do not drain)

Mix Jello and boiling water, stir until dissolved. Add all other ingredients. Pour into a 3-quart casserole dish and refrigerate until set. Serve on lettuce, top with mayonnaise. Yields 3 quarts.

Gloria Evans, Clarksdale, MS

Coke Salad

1 16-ounce can dark, pitted
    cherries, drain and reserve
    juice
1 large can crushed pineapple,
    drain and reserve juice
2 3-ounce packages black
    cherry Jello

2 3-ounce packages cream
    cheese, softened
1 cup mayonnaise
2 6½-ounce cokes
1 cup chopped pecans

Heat the fruit juice and dissolve Jello in hot juice. Add cream
cheese to Jello. Mix and put in blender and blend until smooth.
Add mayonnaise, Coke, fruit and pecans. Pour into a 3-quart mold.
Refrigerate until congealed. Serve on lettuce leaf topped with a dab
of mayonnaise. Yields 8 to 10 servings.

Gloria Evans, Clarksdale, MS

Gelatin Fruit Salad

1 3-ounce box of cherry
    gelatin
¼ cup boiling water
8 ounces cream cheese

1 can cherry pie filling
8 ounces crushed pineapple,
    undrained

Dissolve gelatin with ¼ cup boiling water. With electric mixer, beat
in cream cheese. Add pie filling and crushed pineapple (with juice).
Pour in 9 x 9 square dish. Refrigerate. When set, cut in nine squares
and serve on lettuce leaf. Serves 9.

Joanne Flinn, Branfort, CT

Husband: Ellis Flinn
Knights of Columbus title: Deputy Supreme Knight

Cranberry Salad I

2 3-ounce packages cherry
   gelatin
2 cups hot water

1 can whole cranberry sauce
1 pint sour cream
½ cup chopped pecans

Dissolve gelatin in hot water. Refrigerate until it begins to thicken. Remove from refrigerator and add cranberry sauce. Mix well and refrigerate until it begins to gel. Then add sour cream and nuts and mix well. Chill for several hours before serving. Yields 6 to 8 servings.

Mary Anne Hawkins, Dallas, TX

Cranberry Salad II

1 small can crushed pineapple
1 3-ounce package strawberry
   Jello
1 cup boiling water
1 1-pound can whole
   cranberry sauce

½ cup cold liquid (reserved
   pineapple juice and water to
   make ½ cup)
2 teaspoons lemon juice

Topping:
½ cup sugar
½ pint sour cream
½ teaspoon vanilla

1 8-ounce package cream
   cheese
½ cup chopped pecans

Drain pineapple, reserving juice. Dissolve Jello in hot water. While still warm, stir in cranberry sauce and mix until melted. Stir in ½ cup cold liquid, lemon juice and pineapple. Pour in 1½-quart bowl and chill until firm. Blend sugar, sour cream, vanilla, and cream cheese until smooth. Spread over Jello layer; sprinkle pecans on top. Refrigerate.

Note: This is very sweet and rich; may also be made without the topping.

Judy Read, Farmerville, LA

Pretzel-Strawberry Salad

Layer 1:
2 cups crushed pretzels   ¾ cup melted margarine
1 tablespoon sugar

Mix well and press into 9 x 13 x 2 pyrex dish. Bake 8 minutes at 350 degrees. Cool.

Layer 2:
1 cup sugar   1 small Cool Whip
2 8-ounce packages cream
  cheese

Cream all ingredients together thoroughly. Pour over layer 1 after it is cool.

Layer 3:
1 large strawberry Jello   2 10-ounce packages frozen
2 cups boiling water   strawberries

Dissolve Jello in water. Add frozen strawberries and mix well. Chill until thickened. Pour over layer 2. Chill. Serve in squares. Serves 20.

Vivian Mason, Houston, TX

Peach Cream

1 3-ounce package peach Jello   ⅛ teaspoon almond extract
1 cup hot water   1½ cups fresh peaches
2 tablespoons lemon juice   2 cups Cool Whip

Dissolve Jello in hot water. Add lemon juice and almond extract. Mix. Chill until mixture begins to thicken. Add peaches and fold in Cool Whip. Chill until set.

Helen Owen, West Monroe, LA

Velvet Peach Jello

1 29-ounce can sliced peaches   1 6-ounce package peach Jello
1 cup water   4 cups vanilla ice cream

Drain peaches reserving 1 cup liquid. Cut peach slices into cubes.
Heat peach liquid and water together to a boil. Add Jello and mix.
Add vanilla ice cream, stir, then add peaches. Pour into mold and
refrigerate until set. Serves 4.

Dot Sarver, Leesville, LA

Holiday Peach Mold

This must be prepared a day in advance!

Wesson oil for mold   8 ounces cream cheese
29 ounces canned Freestone   1 large package peach Jello
   peaches with juice (reserve   1½ cups boiling water
   ¼ cup of juice for dressing)   Desired fresh fruits

Oil one large mold or individual molds. In a blender combine
peaches, juice and cream cheese and blend well. In a bowl dissolve
the Jello in the boiling water. Add the blended mixture to the Jello
and mix well. Pour mixture into desired mold (individual molds
work well) and refrigerate overnight.

Dressing:
8 ounces sour cream   2 tablespoons powdered sugar
¼ cup juice reserved from
   peaches

Combine sour cream, peach juice and powdered sugar. Refrigerate. Serve peach mold on fresh lettuce leaf garnished with desired
fresh fruit. I prefer fresh raspberries and sliced kiwi. Top with
dressing. Serves 6 to 8. This is a beautiful holiday creation.

Ann Bradburn, Dallas, TX

Angel Salad

2 3-ounce packages cream
  cheese
2 packages lime Jello
2 cups hot water
1 small can crushed pineapple
  (drained)

3 cups diced celery
1 cup chopped pecans
1 2-ounce jar pimiento,
  chopped
½ pint whipping cream

Mix Jello and hot water; let cool. Mash cheese; add pineapple, celery, pimiento and nuts. Mix this into Jello and put in refrigerator until it begins to gel. Whip whipping cream and fold into Jello.

Gloria Allen, Marshall, TX

Sinful Salad

1 6-ounce package strawberry
  Jello
1 cup boiling water
3 medium bananas, mashed
1 cup chopped pecans or
  walnuts

2 10-ounce packages frozen
  strawberries, thaw and
  drain
1 20-ounce can crushed
  pineapple, drained
1 pint sour cream

Combine Jello and boiling water. Stir with a rubber spatula until Jello is completely dissolved. Cool. Add bananas, pecans, strawberries and pineapple to gelatin and stir until blended. Divide this mixture in half and pour one-half into an 8 x 12-inch pan. Refrigerate until set, about 1 hour, (keep the remaining half of the mixture at room temperature). Spread sour cream evenly over the partially set Jello. Pour remaining half of Jello over sour cream. Cover and refrigerate until set, about one and a half hours or overnight. Yields 12 servings.

Mrs. Jack Dietle

Very Special Chicken and Rice Salad

Prepare dressing in advance.

1 tablespoon Dijon mustard (Grey Poupon)	½ teaspoon salt
¼ cup white wine vinegar	¼ teaspoon white pepper
2 teaspoons sugar (to taste)	½ cup Wesson oil

Whisk together the mustard, vinegar, sugar, salt and pepper. Slowly add the oil a little at a time whisking briskly. Reserve for rice mixture.

Prepare the sauce for topping in advance.

1 cup Hellmann's Real Mayonnaise	2 tablespoons sour cream
8 ounces whipping cream (not whipped)	1 to 2 tablespoons strained fresh lemon juice (to taste)
	1 teaspoon tarragon

Combine all ingredients and refrigerate.

8 boneless, skinless chicken breasts	½ red bell pepper, chopped
2 cups raw Uncle Ben's Converted Rice	4 ounces chopped pimientos
	4 avocados, sliced (garnish)
½ green bell pepper, chopped	1½ cups fresh pineapple chunks (garnish)

Poach, bake or boil chicken breasts and shred or slice into large bite-size pieces. Prepare rice according to directions on box. While rice is still hot, add the green and red pepper and pimientos and toss with the Dijon dressing. Let stand to room temperature. Mound rice on large platter and cover with pieces of chicken. Top with sauce. Garnish platter with sliced avocados and pineapple chunks. Sprinkle with chopped fresh parsley, hard-boiled eggs, tomato and cucumber if desired. Serves 12.

Elaine Henrion, Dallas, TX

De-LITE-ful Chicken Salad

4 poached chicken breast
  halves
2 cups chicken stock
2 green onions, chopped
2 ribs celery, chopped
⅓ cup chopped pecans
½ cup seedless green grapes,
  halved

½ teaspoon salt
¼ teaspoon white pepper
½ teaspoon garlic powder
1 tablespoon Poppy Seed
½ cup plain yogurt
½ cup Miracle Whip Light
  Salad Dressing

To poach chicken breasts, place skinless, boneless breast halves in 2 cups chicken stock and bring to a boil. Reduce heat and simmer 7 minutes covered, turning once. Remove pan from heat and let stand 30 minutes. Chicken will be juicy and tender.

Cut chicken into bite-size pieces and combine with onions, celery, pecans, grapes and seasonings. Combine yogurt and Miracle Whip and stir into chicken mixture. Serve chilled on bed of lettuce or stuff fresh tomatoes. Yields 4 to 6 servings.

Note: You may substitute ¾ cup Hellmann's Real mayonnaise and ¼ cup whipping cream for the yogurt and Miracle Whip Light Salad Dressing. A bit more calories, however!

Cindy Ward, Dallas, TX

Taco Salad

1 pound ground beef
1 package taco seasoning mix
½ package dry onion soup
  mix
¾ cup water
½ head lettuce, shredded
1 tomato, sliced

1 onion, sliced
¼ cup chopped green pepper
½ cup sliced ripe olives
1 cup shredded sharp
  Cheddar cheese
Corn chips, crumbled

Brown beef, drain and sprinkle with taco seasoning mix and onion soup mix. Stir in water and simmer uncovered for 15 to 20 minutes. When ready to serve, gently toss meat, vegetables, cheese and chips until well blended. Serve immediately. Makes 4 servings.

A Friend of St. Mary's

Macaroni Salad

1 8-ounce package macaroni
  twists, cooked and drained
1 10-ounce box frozen green
  peas, thawed and drained
1 bunch green onions,
  chopped
¾ cup shredded cheese

1 2-ounce jar pimiento,
  minced
1 4.2-ounce can chopped black
  olives
1 cup finely chopped ham
½ cup Miracle Whip Salad
  Dressing

Mix first 7 ingredients together and fold into Miracle Whip Salad
Dressing. Chill. Yields 12 servings.

Mrs. Donna Graham, Lyon, MS

Pasta Salad

1 pound thin spaghetti
1 small bottle Viva Italian
  dressing
1 bell pepper, thinly sliced

½ bottle McCormick Supreme
  Salad Herbs
1 medium red onion, chopped
1 tomato for garnish

Cook, drain and cool spaghetti. Mix all ingredients except tomato.
Cover and let set in refrigerator overnight for full flavor. Garnish
with tomato when serving. Yields 12 servings.
*Note: Vegetables such as cauliflower, broccoli and carrots are very good to
use in this salad.*

Pat Hisel, Kankakee, IL

Husband: Robert Hisel
Knights of Columbus title: Supreme Director

Tuna Boats

1 6½-ounce can tuna, drained
1 stalk celery, chopped
1 hard-boiled egg, chopped
1 tablespoon sweet pickle
  relish

2 tablespoons mayonnaise
1 small green pepper
4 slices Cheddar or American
  cheese cut into triangles

Combine tuna, celery, egg, relish and mayonnaise. Cut green pepper into quarters lengthwise. Remove seeds and fill with tuna salad mixture. Top with a triangular piece of cheese for a sail. Rainy day fun lunch for kids! Recipe courtesy: The Cooking School, Dallas, Texas.

Katy Ward, Dallas, TX

Layered Sea Salad

1 8-ounce bottle bacon and
  tomato dressing
½ cup sour cream
2 cups or 8 ounces corkscrew
  noodles, cooked and
  drained

¼ cup chopped parsley
3 cups shredded lettuce
2 cups chopped cucumbers
1½ cups chopped celery
3 cups chopped tomatoes
1 pound boiled shrimp, peeled

Combine dressing and sour cream. Mix well. Chill. Combine noodles and parsley. Mix gently. In a shallow dish, layer lettuce, cucumber, noodle mixture, celery, tomatoes and shrimp. Chill. Just before serving, add dressing mixture and toss. Yields 8 to 10 servings.

Mrs. Donna Graham, Lyon, MS

Ice Green Salad

Salad:
1 head lettuce, broken
½ medium white onion,
   thinly sliced

½ cup chopped celery
2 ripe avocados, sliced

Combine salad ingredients. Peel and slice avocados just before serving. Serve with Bleu Cheese Dressing.

Bleu Cheese Dressing:
½ cup Wesson Oil
⅓ cup wine vinegar
4 ounces Bleu cheese,
   crumbled

½ teaspoon celery salt
½ teaspoon salt
Dash red pepper
1 clove garlic, pressed

Combine dressing ingredients in a jar and shake until well blended. Pour over salad and toss.
Note: The pale colors and subtle flavors make this quite a sophisticated salad. An excellent choice with prime rib and a hearty red wine.
                                  Mary Dee Soules, Conroe, TX

Cauliflower Supreme

1 head cauliflower
1½ cups Italian dressing
2 avocados
3 ounces cream cheese

Dash of onion salt
1 teaspoon lemon juice
Head of lettuce
1 teaspoon paprika

Steam cauliflower over boiling water until barely done. Drain. Pour Italian dressing over cauliflower. Cover and marinate overnight. Mash the avocados and mix with cream cheese. Add onion salt and lemon juice to cream cheese-avocado mixture. Place cauliflower stem down on lettuce leaves. Spread avocado sauce over it. Sprinkle with paprika.
Note: May be used as an appetizer.
                                  Mrs. Bernadine C. Laborde

Coleslaw Freezer-Style

1 cup vinegar	1 medium cabbage, grated
1 tablespoon celery seed	2 carrots, grated
½ cup water	1 bell pepper, finely chopped
2 cups sugar	1 tablespoon salt
1 tablespoon mustard seed	

Mix the vinegar, celery seed, water, sugar and mustard seeds together in a saucepan. Bring to a boil and boil for 1 minute. Remove from heat and cool. Mix the grated cabbage and carrots together. Add the bell pepper and salt to the cabbage. Let stand for 1 hour. Drain or squeeze all the liquid from the cabbage. Place in a bowl and add the boiled vinegar mixture to cabbage. Mix. Divide into serving containers. Seal and place in freezer until needed. Yields 6 to 8 servings.

Alta M. Wineland, Boyce, LA

Twenty-four Hour Salad

1 head shredded lettuce	8 ounces water chestnuts, drained
6 radishes, diced	
6 green onions, chopped	10 ounces frozen green peas, uncooked
5 ribs celery, chopped	
1 bell pepper, chopped	1½ cups salad dressing

Layer lettuce, radishes, onions, celery, bell pepper, water chestnuts and frozen green peas in large Tupperware bowl. Seal top with salad dressing. Cover and refrigerate overnight. Toss just before serving.

Becky Schaider, La Porte, TX

Seven Layer Salad

1 head lettuce, shredded
½ cup chopped celery
½ cup chopped onion
½ cup chopped bell pepper
1 large can green peas, drained or 1 package frozen green peas, cooked and drained

6 slices bacon, fried and crumbled
1 cup grated cheese, Swiss, Cheddar or Parmesan
1 to 2 cups Hellmann's Real Mayonnaise
2 tablespoons sugar (more if desired)

In a large bowl layer lettuce, celery, onion, pepper, and peas. Sprinkle crumbled bacon over peas. Sprinkle cheese over bacon. Combine mayonnaise and sugar and spread on salad completely sealing salad. Chill. Toss just before serving. Yields 8 to 12 servings. (A layer of cauliflower florets may be used if desired. Red or white onions may be used.)

Gwen Scott, Natchitoches, LA

Potato Salad

4 cups cooked and diced potatoes
½ cup sliced salad olives

¼ cup chopped celery
2 tablespoons chopped onions
2 hard-boiled eggs, chopped

Mix the above ingredients together in a large bowl. Set aside.

Seasoning:
¼ cup Wishbone Italian Dressing
1 teaspoon horseradish
½ teaspoon salt

¾ cup mayonnaise
2 tablespoons prepared mustard
Pepper to taste

Blend the above ingredients to form seasoning for salad. When blended, mix into potato mixture. Cover and refrigerate. Serve when chilled or if possible, refrigerate overnight to enhance the flavor. Yields 6 servings.

Mary Frances Bowling, Jackson, MS

Layered Salad

½ package (10 ounces)
  spinach, torn
Salt and pepper to taste
1 teaspoon sugar, halved
6 hard-boiled eggs, chopped
½ pound boiled ham, sliced
  julienne
1 small head iceberg lettuce,
  torn
1 package frozen sweet peas,
  thawed and drained (not
  cooked)

1 red Bermuda onion, thinly
  sliced
1 cup sour cream
1 cup real mayonnaise
½ pound thinly sliced Swiss
  cheese, sliced julienne
½ pound crisp fried bacon,
  crumbled

It is important to drain all ingredients well. Spread spinach in a
large bowl. Add salt, pepper and half of sugar. Add layer of eggs,
ham and lettuce. Sprinkle salt, pepper and remainder of sugar
over layer. Add layer of peas. Arrange onion rings on top of peas.
Mix sour cream and mayonnaise then pour over salad. Arrange
cheese strips on top. Cover with plastic wrap and refrigerate overnight. Before serving, sprinkle with bacon, but do not toss.
*Note: Tuna, crab or shrimp may be substituted for ham and bacon. Not all
of the spinach and lettuce is used; use according to preference.*
Ruth Turner, Palmyra, NY

Beet Salad

1 large can beets
½ cup beet juice
1 3-ounce package cherry
  Jello

1½ cups unsweetened
  grapefruit juice
½ cup finely chopped celery

Drain and dice beets into small cubes, reserving ½ cup beet juice.
Dissolve Jello in boiling grapefruit juice. When Jello has dissolved,
add beet juice. Refrigerate until partially congealed. Add beets and
celery. Mix well. Pour into a mold and refrigerate.
Mrs. Susan Cartier Willis, Austin, TX

Three Bean Salad

2 cups green beans
  (standard can)
2 cups yellow wax beans
2 cups red kidney beans
1 cup yellow whole kernel
  corn

½ cup finely chopped green
  pepper
¼ cup finely chopped
  pimiento
½ cup finely chopped onion

Dressing:
½ cup salad oil
½ cup cider vinegar
¾ cup sugar

1 teaspoon salt
½ teaspoon pepper

Drain beans and corn well; place in bowl. Add green pepper, pimiento and onion. Mix oil and vinegar with sugar, salt and pepper. Pour over bean mixture. Toss. Refrigerate. Much better after 3 or 4 days.

Amanda Greene, Marshall, TX

Cucumber and Onion Salad

3 cucumbers
1 large sweet onion
2 teaspoons sugar
2 tablespoons salad oil

½ teaspoon salt
½ teaspoon seasoned pepper
1 teaspoon celery seeds
1 cup vinegar

Peel and slice cucumbers and onions. Place in a bowl and sprinkle with sugar. Let set 15 minutes. Add remaining ingredients. Mix well. Cover and refrigerate.
Note: This salad will keep in the refrigerator for 2 to 3 days.

Venita Scott, Natchitoches, LA

Spinach Salad with Sweet-Sour Dressing

1 10-ounce bag raw spinach, rinsed, drained and refrigerated until crisp

1 16-ounce can bean sprouts, drained

1 8-ounce can water chestnuts, drained and sliced

8 strips bacon, fried crisp, drained and crumbled

4 hard-cooked eggs, cut in slices

Tear spinach into pieces. Combine spinach with remaining ingredients, tossing lightly but thoroughly. Toss again with enough Sweet-Sour Dressing to moisten all of the ingredients according to your taste. Yields 6 to 8 servings.

Sweet-Sour Dressing:

½ to 1 cup salad oil

1 tablespoon sesame oil

½ to ¾ cup sugar

¼ cup red wine vinegar (or white vinegar)

½ teaspoon salt

⅓ cup ketchup

2 tablespoons Worcestershire sauce

1 medium onion, grated or 1 teaspoon onion salt (omitting other salt)

Combine all of the ingredients and mix well. Refrigerate to chill before using.

Dixie Harlan, Paris, TX

Caddo Lake Coleslaw

1 large head cabbage, shredded

1 large onion, finely chopped

1 large carrot, grated

½ cup sweet pickle relish

6 tablespoons salad dressing

6 tablespoons sugar

Salt and pepper to taste

⅔ cup water

Mix all ingredients together and let set overnight.

Doc's Den, Caddo Lake

Spinach Salad

1 package fresh leaf spinach
1 head leaf lettuce
½ pound bacon, fried and
   crumbled

4 hard-boiled eggs, sliced
¼ pound fresh mushrooms,
   sliced

Combine all ingredients in large salad bowl.

Dressing:
1 medium onion
1 cup oil
¾ cup sugar
2 teaspoons Worcestershire
   sauce

⅓ cup ketchup
¼ cup vinegar

In a blender, blend onion and oil until dissolved. Add remaining ingredients and blend. Pour over salad and toss gently. Serves 8.

Anne Riesbeck, Hamden, CT

Husband: Charles P. Riesbeck, Jr.
Knights of Columbus title: Supreme Secretary

Vegetable Salad

2 cans French cut string beans
1 16-ounce can Le Sueur peas
½ onion, slivered
1 cup chopped celery

1 small jar pimiento, chopped
1 6-ounce can water chestnuts,
   sliced

Dressing:
¾ cup vinegar
½ cup oil

½ cup sugar

Drain and mix green beans and peas. Add slivered onion, celery, pimiento and water chestnuts. To prepare dressing, mix vinegar, oil and sugar. Pour dressing over vegetables and let marinate for 24 hours before serving. Yields 6 servings.

Mary Frances Bowling, Jackson, MS

Vegetable-Shrimp Medley

1 head cauliflower
2 or 3 stalks broccoli
1 package carrots
2 boxes fresh mushrooms
2 yellow squash
2 zucchini squash
1 pint cherry tomatoes

1 bunch green onions
1 red bell pepper
2 green bell peppers (may use
  any combination of the
  colored peppers)
3 pounds fresh cooked
  shrimp, peeled

Wash and chop, slice or cut above vegetables into bite-size pieces. Steam cauliflower, broccoli and carrots until vegetables are barely crisp. Do not overcook.

Marinade:
¼ cup fresh lemon juice
⅓ cup tarragon vinegar
⅓ cup white vinegar
½ cup Wesson oil
2 teaspoons Dijon mustard
2 teaspoons sugar

1 teaspoon salt
⅛ teaspoon cayenne pepper
2 tablespoons chopped fresh
  parsley
2 pods fresh garlic, pressed

Mix together all ingredients and pour over vegetables and shrimp. Let mixture stand in marinade for 24 hours, covered and refrigerated. Very colorful for entertaining. Yields enough for a party of 24 to 36 guests.

Sondra Shine, Dallas, TX

Chicken Salad Waldorf

1½ cups mayonnaise
½ teaspoon salt
2 teaspoons Worcestershire
3½ cups chicken chunks

2 cups diced red apples
1 cup diced celery
½ cup chopped walnuts

Combine all ingredients and mix well. Serve on lettuce leaf. Serves 6.
Note: Unpeeled apples make a colorful salad.

Laura S. Scott, Natchitoches, LA

Copper Pennies

5 cups or 2 pounds sliced
  carrots

1 medium onion
1 small bell pepper

Cook carrots in water until tender; drain and cool. Cut onions and bell pepper into round slices and mix with carrots.

Marinade:
½ cup salad oil
1 cup sugar
¾ cup vinegar
1 teaspoon prepared
  mustard

1 teaspoon Worcestershire
  sauce
1 teaspoon salt
1 teaspoon pepper
1 can condensed tomato soup

Combine ingredients and pour over vegetables. Cover and marinate for 12 hours. Drain before serving. The carrots will keep in the refrigerator for 2 weeks.

Donna Page, Dallas, TX
Mrs. Mallie McLaughlin, Nashville, AR

Black-Eyed Pea Salad

3 tablespoons white vinegar
4 tablespoons red wine
  vinegar
4 tablespoons oil
¼ cup sugar
½ teaspoon Lawry's seasoned
  salt
½ teaspoon Lawry's seasoned
  pepper

8 dashes Tabasco
½ cup chopped purple onion
½ cup chopped red bell
  pepper
½ cup chopped green bell
  pepper
4 15-ounce cans black-eyed
  peas, drained

Mix vinegars, oil, sugar, salt, pepper and Tabasco in a large, flat container that has a cover. Add onion, bell peppers and black-eyed peas. Cover, refrigerate and let stand several hours. Yields about 2 quarts. Keeps well in refrigerator for several days.

Cindy Ward, Dallas, TX

Home-Style Salad Dressing and Mix

Mix:

2 teaspoons instant minced onions

½ teaspoon Monosodium Glutamate

½ teaspoon salt

⅛ teaspoon garlic powder

1 tablespoon parsley flakes

Combine all ingredients. Mix well. Place in a foil packet or glass jar. Must be used within 6 months. Yields 2 tablespoons mix.

Salad Dressing:

1 recipe dressing mix

1 cup buttermilk

1 cup mayonnaise

Combine ingredients in a glass jar. Shake until blended. Chill before serving.

Note: To use as a dip recipe substitute 1 cup sour cream for buttermilk. Serve with fresh vegetables.

Dorothy Yutrzenka, Argyle, MN

Husband: Medard R. Yutrzenka

Knights of Columbus title: Supreme Director Emeritus

Dijon Dressing

1 tablespoon Dijon mustard
  (Grey Poupon)
¼ cup wine vinegar (red,
  white or balsamic)

2 teaspoons sugar (to taste)
½ teaspoon salt
¼ teaspoon white pepper
½ cup Wesson oil

Whisk together the mustard, vinegar, sugar, salt and pepper. Slowly add the oil a little at a time whisking briskly. Serve on any mixed green salad. Yields ¾ cup.

Cindy Ward, Dallas, TX

French Dressing

1 can Campbell's Tomato soup
¾ cup Wesson oil
½ cup vinegar
2 tablespoons sugar
1 teaspoon dry mustard

2 teaspoons salt
⅛ teaspoon cayenne pepper
Dash Worcestershire sauce
1 small onion, finely minced
1 clove garlic, finely minced

Combine all ingredients in a blender and blend well. Refrigerate. Yields ⅔ quart.

Dixie Harlan, Paris, TX

Basic French Dressing

1 cup oil	1 teaspoon salt
¼ cup vinegar	½ teaspoon dry mustard
¼ cup lemon juice	2 tablespoons honey

Combine all ingredients. Add black pepper for vegetable salads or poppy seed for fruit salads. Store in airtight container in refrigerator.

Bernadine Laborde

Green Mayonnaise

1½ cups mayonnaise	1 teaspoon finely chopped
2 tablespoons chopped parsley	tarragon
1 tablespoon finely chopped	1 teaspoon chopped dill
chives	

Pureé mayonnaise in blender; add herbs one at a time and blend thoroughly. Cover and let stand in a cool place at least 2 hours for flavor to mellow before serving. Serve over poached snapper.

Betty Bellamy, Marshall, TX

Sally's Homemade Mayonnaise

1 egg	1 tablespoon salt
2 cups Wesson oil	2 tablespoons Worcestershire
Juice of ½ lemon, strained	sauce
2 tablespoons French's	¼ to ½ teaspoon Louisiana
mustard	Hot or Tabasco sauce

Beat egg until frothy. Add oil slowly in small amounts beating constantly. Add the lemon juice and mix thoroughly. Add remaining ingredients and mix well. Pour in jar and refrigerate.

Sally Hamilton, Dallas, TX

Dressing for Fruit Salad

1 egg
1 cup sugar
4 tablespoons flour

1 6-ounce can pineapple juice
(or orange juice)
Dash of salt

Combine ingredients in saucepan. Cook over medium heat. Stir constantly to avoid sticking. Cook until thick. Pour into jar and refrigerate until cold. Pour over fruit.

Donna Ward, Farmerville, LA

Poppy Seed Dressing

½ cup sugar
1 teaspoon dry mustard
1 teaspoon salt
⅓ cup vinegar

1 tablespoon onion juice
1 cup Wesson oil
1 tablespoon poppy seed

In blender mix sugar, mustard, salt and vinegar. Add onion juice and mix again. Slowly add oil blending constantly on medium speed. Fold in poppy seed with spoon, do not blend. Store in refrigerator; keeps several weeks. Delicious on fruit salads of any kind, particularly grapefruit. Yields 1¾ cups. May be doubled.

Cindy Ward, Dallas, TX

Creamy Dressing

2 eggs
2 tablespoons sugar
2 tablespoons orange juice
2 tablespoons vinegar

2 tablespoons butter
2 cups sour cream
Dash of salt

In a saucepan mix eggs with sugar, orange juice and vinegar. Stir constantly until thickened. Remove from heat and stir in butter. Cool and fold in sour cream. Chill before serving over fruit salad. Keeps refrigerated several weeks in a tightly-sealed container.

Norma Russell

FATHER GRECO'S CAMP

In the 1930's Father Greco built a camp on Shell Beach for the young men of his diocese, where they would go often to fish and swim, and where he would cook for them. The house was built twelve feet above the water on pilings, driven in by a pile driver which the talented young priest constructed himself. Over the years, Father Greco was responsible for at least seventeen young men entering the priesthood.

Seafood and Fish

Father Greco's Camp
Shell Beach, Louisiana

Clam Sauce with Noodles

½ cup olive oil
¼ cup finely chopped onions
½ cup finely chopped celery
1 large carrot, finely chopped
3 6½-ounce cans minced
   clams

1 12-ounce can tomato paste
3 12-ounce cans of water
Salt and pepper to taste
1 large package fettucini
   noodles

Brown onions in olive oil. Add celery, carrots and clams. Continue to cook for 15 minutes. Add tomato paste and water to clam mixture and bring to a boil. Reduce heat and allow to simmer for 3 hours. Serve over noodles that have been cooked according to package directions. Yields 10 to 12 servings.

Sister Catherine Palazzi, St. Mary's Training School

Crabmeat au Gratin

1 stick butter
1 cup finely chopped onion
⅓ cup flour
1 13-ounce can evaporated
   milk
2 egg yolks, slightly beaten

1 teaspoon salt
½ teaspoon red pepper
¼ teaspoon black pepper
1 pound lump crabmeat
½ pound Cheddar cheese,
   grated

Melt butter in pan and sauté onion until very tender and clear. Add flour and gradually add milk. Add egg yolks slowly, stirring constantly. Add salt, red pepper and black pepper. Fold in crabmeat, mixing well. Divide mixture between six individual baking dishes and top with grated cheese. Bake in 375 degree oven for 15 to 20 minutes. Serves 6.

Lynn Fulbright, Marshall, TX

Pasta with Lump Crabmeat and Julienned Vegetables

Choose your favorite pasta and cook until al dente, slightly chewy.
Fresh is preferred. Set aside enough for 4 servings.

Scampi Butter: Mix the following ingredients in a small mixer until fluffy.

1 pound unsweetened butter (room temperature)	2 teaspoons Tony's Seasoning
	1 teaspoon white pepper
3 ounces brandy	3 dashes Worcestershire
3 ounces heavy cream	4 dashes Tabasco Sauce
1 teaspoon garlic powder (or fresh garlic)	1 teaspoon Sweet basil
	½ teaspoon English Thyme
1 teaspoon finely chopped shallots	Juice of 2 lemons

Julienned Vegetables: Slice these into matchstick sticks:

½ carrot peeled	1 small bell pepper
1 small summer squash	1 small yellow onion

Crabmeat:

½-1 pound Lump Crabmeat	1 cup White wine

Procedure:

In a sauté pan or skillet, place the white wine. Place carrots in wine and cook until tender. Add bell pepper and onion to simmer. Finally, add the squash. When all vegetables are tender but firm, add the pasta. Let the cooking liquid reduce until negligible. Add the lump crabmeat. Be careful not to break the chunks. When hot, add the Scampi Butter and toss carefully. The butter should blend smoothly. Garnish with fresh parsley and green onions.

Note: Bishop Greco on many occasions dined in this beautiful hotel in downtown Alexandria, Louisiana.

Jerry L. Miles, Sousa Chef, Bently Hotel, Alexandria, LA

Mammie's Baked Crab

1 stick butter
1 medium onion, finely
  chopped
2 ribs celery, finely chopped
1 6½-ounce can lump
  crabmeat
2 eggs, slighty beaten

1 teaspoon lemon juice
1 tablespoon Worcestershire
  sauce
1 tablespoon ketchup
½ cup cracker crumbs
Butter for topping

Melt butter in skillet and sauté onions and celery until very tender.
Add crabmeat and mix well. Add eggs and mix then add lemon
juice, Worcestershire, and ketchup. Mix all together very well. Divide mixture equally into 6 scallop shells. Sprinkle with cracker
crumbs and dot with butter if desired. Bake in 350 degree oven 15
to 20 minutes. Yields 6 servings.

Gloria Allen, Marshall, TX

Crawfish au Gratin

1 stick margarine
1 cup chopped onion
1 can cream of mushroom
  soup

1 pound peeled crawfish tails
  (or crabmeat)
Salt and pepper to taste
1 cup grated Cheddar cheese

Melt the margarine. Sauté onion in margarine until clear. Add
soup, crawfish (or crabmeat), seasonings and cook for 10 minutes.
Pour into a 1-quart casserole dish. Top with grated cheese. Bake in
350 degree oven for 30 minutes. Yields 4 servings.

Mrs. Louis Landry, Jr., St. Martinville, LA

Boiled Crawfish

6 gallons water
1 dozen lemons, quartered
10 onions, peeled
4 to 5 cloves garlic, peeled
1 pound box salt
4 ounces Tabasco sauce
10 3-ounce Zatarain's crab boil
  bags

12 small whole potatoes
12 ears of corn, shucked and
  cleaned
40 pounds live crawfish,
  purged and rinsed

On an outside burner place water in a large pot. Add lemons, onions, garlic, salt, Tabasco and 5 Zatarain's crab boil bags. Bring water to a boil. Add ½ of potatoes and corn. Boil for 15 minutes. Add ½ of live crawfish. Bring to a boil and boil for 10 to 15 minutes or until crawfish begin to float. Remove from boiling water, drain and place on a picnic table that has been covered with newspapers. Return water to a boil; add remaining crab boil bags and repeat boiling other ½ of potatoes, corn and crawfish. Serve butter for buttering corn and potatoes.

Sauce For Dipping:
6 ounces ketchup
Juice of ½ lemon

Dash of Tabasco sauce
Dash of horseradish

Prepare a dipping sauce for crawfish by mixing ketchup, lemon juice, Tabasco and horseradish. Peel and eat crawfish. Yields 8 to 12 servings.
Note: Prepare 3 to 5 pounds of crawfish per person.

                                        Earl Hebert, Natchitoches, LA

Crayfish Casserole

1 cup chopped onion
1 cup chopped bell pepper
1 cup chopped celery
1 stick margarine
1 can mushroom soup
1 can Cheddar cheese soup
1 pound crayfish tails, peeled
¼ cup parsley flakes

¼ cup chopped green onion
  tops
2 cups cooked rice
Salt and pepper to taste
Hot sauce to taste
Garlic powder to taste
1 4-ounce jar pimiento
½ cup bread crumbs

Sauté onion, bell pepper and celery in margarine until tender. Add mushroom and Cheddar cheese soup. Cook until heated thoroughly. Add crayfish tails, parsley, green onion tops and cooked rice. Cook for 5 minutes. Place in a 1-quart baking dish. Season to taste using salt, pepper, hot sauce and garlic powder. Garnish with a small jar of pimiento and bread crumbs. Bake in 350 degree oven for 30 minutes. Yields 4 servings.

Sadie DiStefano, Alexandria, LA

Crawfish Creole

1½ cups chopped green
  onions
1 bell pepper, chopped
3 sticks butter (not margarine)
2 8-ounce cans Ro-tel
  tomatoes, with chili peppers
1 12-ounce can tomato sauce

Salt
Black pepper
Tony Chachere's Creole
  Seasoning
Louisiana Hot Sauce
1½ to 2 pounds boiled
  crawfish tails, peeled

Sauté green onions and bell pepper in butter for 30 minutes on a low heat. Add cans of tomatoes and tomato sauce. Chop up the tomatoes while cooking. Season with salt, pepper, Tony's and hot sauce. Simmer for 30 minutes. Add crawfish tails and cook on medium heat until the crawfish are tender.

Peggy Long, Alexandria, LA

Crawfish Etouffée

1 large onion, chopped
3 ribs celery, chopped
½ bell pepper, chopped
6 green onions, chopped and
    reserve ¼ cup
1 stick butter
1 can cream of mushroom
    soup

1 soup can water
1 teaspoon salt
1 teaspoon pepper
1 teaspoon red pepper
1 teaspoon garlic powder
2 teaspoons paprika (optional)
2 pounds peeled and deveined
    crawfish tails

Sauté onion, celery, bell pepper and green onions in butter, cooking until onions are transparent. Add the soup and water. Bring to a boil, reduce heat and simmer for 10 minutes. Add seasonings and crawfish. Simmer, uncovered for 15 minutes. Add ¼ cup of green onions and simmer for 5 minutes. Serve over rice. Yields 4 to 6 servings.

Note: Paprika enhances the color of the gravy.

Venita Scott, Natchitoches, LA

Crawfish Jambalaya in Rice Cooker

2½ cups rice
1 10½-ounce can beef broth
1 onion, chopped
¼ cup chopped bell pepper
1 jalapeño pepper, chopped
1 4-ounce can mushrooms,
    drained and chopped
1 stick butter, melted

1 pound raw crawfish tails,
    chopped
1 8-ounce can tomato sauce
1 tablespoon parsley
    (optional)
1 tablespoon chopped onion
    tops (optional)
1½ teaspoons salt

Wash and drain rice. Place rice and all remaining ingredients into a rice cooker. Mix. Cook on rice cycle until cycle is complete (all liquid should be absorbed), then set rice cooker on warm cycle. Let warm for 30 to 40 minutes before serving. Use only an 8 or 10 cup rice cooker, do not double recipe. Yields 6 to 8 servings.

Note: If rice cooker is unavailable, cook all ingredients, except rice, in a dutch oven. Add cooked rice and continue to cook for 10 minutes before serving.

Glenda Lafleur, Ville Platte, LA

Crawfish Fettucini

3 medium onions, finely
   chopped
3 medium bell peppers, finely
   chopped
1½ cups butter
¼ cup flour
4 teaspoons parsley
3 pounds crawfish tails
1 pint half and half cream

1 pound Velveeta cheese, cut
   into pieces
2 teaspoons jalapeño relish
2 cloves garlic, chopped
Salt to taste
Red pepper to taste
1 pound fettucini noodles
Parmesan cheese, grated

Sauté onions and bell pepper in butter. Cook until tender. Add flour. Cover and cook 15 minutes, stirring often. Add parsley and crawfish, cover and cook 15 minutes, stirring often. Add cream, Velveeta cheese, relish, garlic, salt and red pepper to taste. Cook covered 30 minutes on low heat. Stir occasionally. Cook fettucini noodles. Mix crawfish mixture and fettucini in casserole. Sprinkle with Parmesan cheese. Bake in oven for 30 minutes at 350 degrees. Yields 6 servings. (May substitute a one pound box of Kraft jalapeño cheese for Velveeta cheese and jalapeño relish.)

Lorraine Medlin, Carencro, LA
Lorraine Tavors, Ponchatoula, LA

Seafood Cacciatore

1 tablespoon oil
½ cup chopped onion
1 pound cleaned shrimp
1 clove minced garlic
28 ounces whole tomatoes
8 ounces tomato sauce

1 bell pepper, cut in strips
⅛ teaspoon red pepper
½ teaspoon salt
½ teaspoon oregano
½ teaspoon basil
1½ cups Minute Rice

Place oil in a large saucepan and sauté onions, shrimp and garlic. When onions are transparent, add tomatoes, tomato sauce, bell pepper and seasonings. Bring ingredients to a full boil, stir in rice. Cover, remove from heat and let stand 5 minutes before serving. Yields 4 servings.

Edna Polker

Seafood Crepes

4 tablespoons butter
3 tablespoons minced shallots
1½ cups diced cooked shrimp
Salt and pepper to taste
¼ to ⅓ cup dry vermouth
2 tablespoons cornstarch
2 tablespoons milk

1½ cups heavy cream
White pepper to taste
¾ cup grated Swiss cheese
12 cooked Entre Crepes
  (prepared in advance)
Butter

Heat 2 tablespoons butter in an 8-inch skillet, stir in shallots, then shellfish. Toss and stir over moderately high heat for 1 minute. Season with salt and pepper, then add ¼ cup vermouth and boil rapidly until liquid has almost evaporated. Scrape shellfish into a bowl and set aside. Add ⅓ cup vermouth to skillet and boil rapidly until reduced to a tablespoon. Remove skillet from heat and stir in cornstarch mixture, cream, salt and white pepper. Simmer 2 minutes, stirring, then blend in ½ cup Swiss cheese and simmer one or two minutes longer. Blend half the sauce into the shellfish, then place a large spoonful (about 2 tablespoons) of the shellfish mixture on lower third of each crepe, and roll crepes into cylindrical shapes. Arrange the crepes closely together in a lightly buttered baking dish, spoon over rest of sauce, sprinkle with remaining ¼ cup Swiss cheese, and dot with bits of butter. Bake in upper third of a preheated 425 degree oven until bubbling hot and cheese has browned lightly. This recipe can be prepared ahead of time and refrigerated. Yields 4 to 6 servings.

Entre Crepes:
2 cups flour
½ teaspoon salt
4 tablespoons butter, melted

1 cup cold water
1 cup milk
4 large eggs

Sift flour and blend all ingredients with an electric mixer at high speed for 1 minute. Place 6 or 7-inch skillet on moderately high heat. Keep skillet lightly coated with oil. Heat skillet, remove from heat and add ¼ cup batter. Return to heat and cook one minute. Turn crepes and cook 30 seconds. Separate stack with waxed paper. Yields 12 to 15 crepes.

Barnett Greenberg, Denton, TX

Seafood Casserole with Parmesan Noodles

2 4.3-ounce packages Lipton
  Deluxe Parmesan Noodles
½ cup butter, melted
1 cup chopped celery
1 cup chopped onion
1 cup chopped green pepper
1 cup grated sharp Cheddar
  cheese
¼ cup grated Parmesan
  cheese
1 5-ounce can water chestnuts,
  drained and sliced

1 can cream of mushroom
  soup
1 can cream of shrimp soup
½ cup half and half cream
½ cup mayonnaise
2 pounds raw shrimp, boiled,
  seasoned and cleaned
½ pound flaked white
  crabmeat
½ cup dry white wine
Slivered almonds

Prepare noodles as instructed on package and set aside. To melted butter add celery, onion and pepper; sauté. Add cheeses and stir gently until melted. Add water chestnuts. Blend soups, cream and mayonnaise in large bowl. Stir until smooth. Add other ingredients and sautéed vegetables. Fold in noodles. Mix well. Turn mixture into 2-quart buttered casserole dish or individual ramekins. Sprinkle Parmesan cheese and almonds over top. Bake at 350 degrees for 30 minutes or until bubbly. Yields 12 servings.
Note: More half and half may be added if needed for moisture. Also, this dish freezes well, uncooked. Thaw and bake.
Mrs. Louis Reno, Natchitoches, LA

Seafood Casserole

2 large onions, chopped
1 large bell pepper, chopped
3 sticks butter
3 cans cream of onion soup
1 pound crawfish tails,
  cleaned
1 to 1½ pounds shrimp,
  cleaned

½ to 1 pound crabmeat
Jar of oysters
Salt and pepper to taste
6 cups cooked rice
½ cup bread crumbs

Sauté onions and bell pepper in butter. Add soup and cook for 20 minutes. Add seafood and seasonings and cook for 20 minutes. Add rice and stir. Place in a casserole dish. Top with bread crumbs. Bake in 350 degree oven for 45 minutes. Yields 10 to 12 servings.

Lorraine Medlin, Carencro, LA

Stuffed Oysters

½ cup chopped celery
1 cup chopped onion
2 tablespoons butter
1¼ cups oysters, chopped
2 hamburger buns
2 eggs

2 tablespoons flour
1 tablespoon parsley
1¼ cups crabmeat
20 large oysters
¼ cup bread crumbs
Oil for frying

Sauté celery and onions in butter until wilted. Add chopped oysters and let cook for 3 minutes. Soak buns in beaten eggs and add this to mixture. Now add bread crumbs, flour, parsley and crabmeat. Mix well. Let cool and then make 20 croquettes with this filling and place one oyster in the center of each croquette. Roll each in flour, dip in batter (recipe below), roll in crumbs and fry in deep fat until brown.

Batter:
1 egg, beaten
½ cup water

Salt and pepper to taste
¼ cup evaporated milk

Mix all ingredients together; ready to use.

A Friend of St. Mary's

Barbecued Shrimp

2 pounds large shrimp,
  headless and washed (leave
  shrimp in shell)
Black pepper to taste
½ pound butter
7 tablespoons Worcestershire
  sauce

½ teaspoon dry mustard
2 cloves minced garlic
Juice of 1 lemon
1 teaspoon liquid crab boil

Place shrimp (in shells) in single layer in oven-proof dish. Blacken with pepper. In a saucepan heat butter, Worcestershire sauce, mustard, garlic, lemon juice and crab boil. Pour over shrimp and place in 350 degree oven for 20 minutes. Serve in bowl. Serves 4.

Van Parkman, Columbia, MS

Shrimp Supreme

2 cups cooked shrimp,
  cleaned
2 tablespoons minced chives
2 tablespoons parsley
¼ teaspoon salt

⅛ teaspoon pepper
1 cup fine bread crumbs
4 individual baking shells
8 tablespoons butter

Combine shrimp with chives and parsley. Salt and pepper. Add bread crumbs. Mix well. Place into individual baking shells and top each shell with 2 tablespoons butter. Bake in 350 degree oven for 20 minutes. Yields 4 servings.

Ann Dechant, Hamden, CT

Husband: Virgil C. Dechant
Knights of Columbus title: Supreme Knight

Shrimp and Artichokes

½ pound fresh mushrooms,
    sliced
8 tablespoons butter
4½ tablespoons flour
¾ cup milk
¾ cup heavy cream
½ cup sherry
1 tablespoon Worcestershire

Salt and pepper to taste
1½ to 2 pounds shrimp, boiled
    and peeled
1 large can artichoke hearts,
    drained and chopped
½ cup Parmesan cheese
Dash of paprika

Sauté mushrooms in 3 tablespoons butter. Set aside. Over a low heat, stir cook, 5 tablespoons butter, flour, milk and cream until thick (do not boil). Then add sherry, Worcestershire sauce and season with salt and pepper. Combine mushrooms, shrimp, and artichoke hearts with sauce. Pour into a 3-quart casserole or into a large saucepan. Top with Parmesan cheese and sprinkle on paprika. Bake in 375 degree oven for 30 minutes. Serve in pastry shells or over toast points. Yields 6 to 8 servings.
Note: This dish was served at the 1979 Chi Omega State Day and was a Number 1 Gulf Coast treat.

Gloria Evans, Charksdale, MS

Shrimp and Fettucini

½ pound fettucini
2 tablespoons olive oil
2 green onions, minced
2 tablespoons butter
1 fresh tomato, peeled, seeded
    and chopped

1 teaspoon dried basil
2 tablespoons minced parsley
½ cup dry vermouth
1 pound raw shrimp, peeled
Salt and pepper to taste

Cook pasta in salted water until just done. Drain and toss with olive oil. Sauté onion in butter over a medium heat for 1 minute. Add tomato, basil, parsley, vermouth and shrimp. Bring to a boil. Reduce heat and simmer for 5 minutes. Add pasta to shrimp sauce and toss until pasta is hot. Season to taste. Yields 4 servings.

Bess Levell, Natchitoches, LA

Shrimp and Eggplant Casserole

1 large eggplant, cooked and
  drained
1 large bell pepper, chopped
1 large onion, chopped
1 can mushroom soup
½ cup grated cheese
1 egg, beaten
Dash of Accent
1 tablespoon Worcestershire
  sauce

½ teaspoon salt
¼ teaspoon red pepper
¼ teaspoon black pepper
½ can (1½-ounces) Parmesan
  cheese
1 pound peeled raw shrimp
1 cup cracker crumbs
2 tablespoons butter

Combine all ingredients except shrimp, cracker crumbs and butter. Mix well. Add shrimp to mixture and place in buttered casserole. Sprinkle with cracker crumbs and dot with butter. Bake at 350 degrees for 15 minutes; reduce to 300 degrees and bake 30 minutes longer. Serves 4.

Sadie DiStafano, Alexandria, LA

Fiery Cajun Shrimp

2 sticks butter, melted
2 sticks margarine, melted
3 ounces Worcestershire sauce
4 tablespoons ground black
  pepper
1 teaspoon rosemary

2 teaspoons Tabasco sauce
2 teaspoons salt
3 cloves garlic, minced
4 lemons, 2 juiced and 2 sliced
6 pounds raw shrimp (in shell,
  heads removed)

Preheat oven to 400 degrees. In a bowl mix all the ingredients except lemon slices and shrimp. Pour about ½ cup sauce mixture into bottom of a baking dish and arrange layers of shrimp and lemon slices until dish is filled. Pour remaining sauce over shrimp and bake uncovered for 30 minutes. Stir once or twice during baking time. Serve with French bread, generous napkins and a bowl for shells. Serves 8 to 10.

Rowena Brocato, Bunkie, LA

Shrimp and Rice Rockefeller

1 cup chopped onions
2 tablespoons butter
12 ounces raw shrimp, peeled
and cut in half
1 can cream of mushroom
soup
1 cup grated Swiss cheese
¼ cup sherry wine
3 cups cooked rice
1 8-ounce can water chestnuts,
drained and chopped

1 10-ounce package frozen
chopped spinach, cooked
1 tablespoon lemon juice
¼ cup grated Parmesan
cheese, divided
1 teaspoon salt
½ teaspoon red pepper
½ teaspoon black pepper

In 3-quart saucepan, sauté onions in butter. Add shrimp. Cook until pink. Stir in mushroom soup, Swiss cheese and sherry. Heat
thoroughly. Add cooked rice, water chestnuts, drained spinach,
lemon juice and 2 tablespoons Parmesan cheese. Add salt, red and
black pepper. Pour into greased, shallow 2-quart dish. Sprinkle remaining Parmesan cheese over top. Bake in 350 degree oven for
30 minutes.

Eileen Duke, Haughton, LA

Shrimp Casserole I

1 pound steamed, peeled
shrimp
1 small can flaked crabmeat
1 bell pepper, diced
1 small onion, grated
1 cup chopped celery
1 teaspoon salt

1 teaspoon pepper
1 tablespoon Worcestershire
sauce
1½ cups mayonnaise
1 can sliced water chestnuts
2 tablespoons butter
1 cup bread crumbs

Combine all ingredients, except butter and bread crumbs. Place
into a buttered casserole dish. Melt butter and add bread crumbs,
stirring until crumbs are lightly coated with butter. Sprinkle on top
of casserole. Bake in 350 degree oven for 30 minutes, or for 40
minutes if casserole dish was refrigerated before baking. Serve
over rice. Yields 6 servings.

Mrs. Helen Hurd, Atlanta, GA

Shrimp Casserole II

1 small bell pepper, chopped
1 small onion, chopped
1 stalk celery, chopped
1 clove garlic, minced
1 stick margarine
1 can cream of mushroom
  soup

1 pound shrimp, peeled
2 slices bread soaked in ½ cup
  of water
1 cup cooked rice
Salt and pepper to taste
½ cup bread crumbs

Sauté bell pepper, onion, celery and garlic in margarine until wilted. Add soup, shrimp and bread. Cook for 8 minutes. Add rice and season to taste. Cook for 3 minutes. Pour into a 9-inch baking dish. Top with bread crumbs. Bake in 350 degree oven for 30 minutes. Yields 6 servings.

Note: Crabmeat or crawfish can be substituted for shrimp.

Myrtle Girouard, Loureauville, LA

Shrimp and Sausage Jambalaya

2 yellow onions, chopped
1 stick butter
2 cans tomatoes
1 6-ounce can tomato paste
½ bell pepper, chopped
1½ ribs celery, chopped
6 teaspoons chopped, fresh
  parsley
4 garlic cloves, minced
½ pound Polish sausage links,
  sliced

3 cups cooked rice
½ teaspoon crushed cayenne
  pepper
Salt to taste
Fresh ground black pepper
2 pounds boiled shrimp,
  peeled
4 ounces Cheddar cheese,
  grated

Sauté onions in butter. Add tomatoes, tomato paste and stir until blended. Add bell pepper, celery, parsley, garlic and Polish sausage. Cook for 5 minutes. Stir in rice. Add cayenne, salt and black pepper to taste. Simmer for 20 minutes. Add shrimp and grated cheese. Cook until shrimp is hot and cheese has melted. Yields 8 servings.

Bunny Laskowski, Houston, TX

Shrimp Creole

⅓ cup oil
¼ cup flour
1 pound peeled, deveined
   shrimp
1 clove minced garlic
⅔ cup finely chopped green
   onions

2 tablespoons minced parsley
½ cup minced bell pepper
1 cup water
2 teaspoons salt
¼ teaspoon cayenne pepper
8 ounces tomato sauce

In large heavy skillet make roux by heating oil and flour, stirring constantly, until flour is a nutty brown color. Lower heat and add shrimp. Stir constantly about 3 minutes or until shrimp are pink. Add garlic, green onions, parsley and bell pepper. Cook 2 minutes longer, stirring. Raise heat; gradually add water, then remaining ingredients. Bring to a boil. Lower heat and simmer covered 20 to 25 minutes. Serve over cooked rice. May substitute 1 pound of cleaned crawfish tails for shrimp. Yields 4 servings.

Melba Simmons, Bunkie, LA

Shrimp in Wine Sauce

1 stick margarine, melted
½ cup olive oil
2 tablespoons Worcestershire
   sauce
Salt and pepper to taste

2 pounds peeled, deveined
   shrimp, "in shorts" (tips of
   tail left on)
1 cup sautene or white table
   wine

In a 9 x 12-inch baking dish place margarine, olive oil and Worcestershire sauce. Salt and pepper shrimp. Place in dish with sauce. Pour wine over shrimp. Bake in 350 degree oven for 15 minutes. Turn shrimp and continue to bake for 5 to 10 minutes or until shrimp turns pink. Yields 6 servings.

Joan Breaux, Loreauville, LA

Shrimp Marinade Supreme

3 pounds large shrimp (36/40 per pound)
Crab and shrimp boil (in bag)
1 hard-boiled egg, coarsely grated
1 cup mayonnaise
½ cup chili sauce
2 teaspoons paprika
2 tablespoons mustard with horseradish (Zatarain or another creole mustard)
¾ teaspoon celery salt
3 tablespoons chopped parsley
3 tablespoons grated onion
2 cloves garlic, pressed or grated
4 drops Tabasco
½ teaspoon fresh horseradish (optional)
2 teaspoons lemon juice

In a four-quart pan place water and shrimp-boil bag and heat to boiling. Add shrimp. Cover and boil shrimp 3 to 5 minutes. Do not overcook. Remove from heat, drain, set aside. When cool, peel and devein shrimp. Boil egg for 7 minutes and peel. Cool. Mix remaining ingredients in a large bowl. Stir in grated egg and shrimp. Cover tightly, refrigerate for 24 hours. Serve cold with Melba Toast rounds as an appetizer or serve with lettuce and tomato aspic. May also serve with fresh tomatoes as a salad. Use as a salad on wedges of iceberg lettuce. Yields 7 cups.

Mrs. Carroll Fay, Memphis,TN

Spicy Shrimp

1 large onion, thinly sliced
1 small jar ripe olives, sliced
½ cup olive or vegetable oil
¼ teaspoon dry mustard
Salt and pepper to taste
1 lemon, thinly sliced
1 cup lemon juice
½ teaspoon cayenne pepper
2 bay leaves
2 pounds boiled and shelled shrimp

Mix all of the above ingredients except the shrimp. Pour over shrimp. Mix. Refrigerate for at least 12 hours before serving. Yields 4 to 6 servings.

Bunny Laskowski, Houston, TX

Shrimp Stewart

¾ cup plus 2 tablespoons
  cooking oil
1 cup flour
1 bunch green onions,
  chopped
1 white onion, chopped
½ stalk celery, chopped

1 bell pepper, chopped
8 cups water
Salt and pepper to taste
1 pound shrimp, cleaned
2 cups rice
1 small roll jalapeño cheese

Make a dark brown roux by cooking ¾ cup oil and flour over medium heat, stirring constantly. Sauté onions, celery and bell pepper in 2 tablespoons cooking oil. Add roux and water to sauteéd vegetables and cook for 5 to 10 minutes. Add seasonings and fresh peeled shrimp and cook for 10 more minutes. Cook rice according to package directions. Serve shrimp over rice and top with melted jalapeño cheese. Yields 4 to 6 servings.

W. B. Stewart, Alexandria, LA

Shrimp Stuffed Peppers

6 green peppers
2 cups finely chopped cooked
  shrimp or crawfish
1 cup Hellmann's mayonnaise
1½ cups cooked rice

Salt and pepper to taste
1 8-ounce can tomato sauce
1 tablespoon soy sauce
1 teaspoon Worcestershire
  sauce

Remove top and scoop out center of green peppers. Then parboil in a small amount of water until just to the soft stage (about 5 minutes). Combine other ingredients. Stuff peppers and bake at 350 degrees for 30 minutes. Makes 6 servings. (Crawfish may be substituted for shrimp.)

Mrs. Joseph C. Ortis, Sr.

Baked Fish

Fish:

1 medium fish, filleted   2 lemons
   (speckled trout or redfish)   Water
Salt to taste   3 bay leaves
Black pepper to taste

Put the fish fillets in a shallow baking dish. Season both sides with salt and pepper. Squeeze the juice from one lemon over the fish. Add enough water to come up to the sides of the fish but not over the fish. Place 3 bay leaves and 1 lemon, quartered, in water. Cover with aluminum foil and bake for 45 minutes at 350 degrees.

Sauce:

2 sticks butter   2 tablespoons chopped parsley
1 small bunch green onions
   with tops, chopped

While the fish is cooking, melt the butter. Remove from heat and add green onions and parsley. After fish has cooked for 45 minutes, remove foil and add sauce to fish and baste. Cook uncovered for 15 minutes, basting frequently.

Carolyn Blanchard, Napoleonville, LA

Baked Fish Fillets

¼ cup butter   Juice of 1 lemon
3 pounds redfish fillets   2 tablespoons Worcestershire
1 teaspoon salt   sauce
1 teaspoon pepper   Dash of paprika
⅓ cup sherry

Place butter in baking dish and brown in 450 degree oven. Season fillets with salt and pepper. Place in baking dish with skin side down. Cook for 15 minutes or almost done. Mix sherry, lemon juice, Worcestershire and juice from baking fish. Pour over fish and sprinkle with paprika. Place in oven and bake for 5 minutes more or until done. Yields 6 to 8 servings. Red snapper fillets may be substituted for redfish fillets.

Susan Cartier Willis, Austin, TX

Citrus Baked Fish

1 onion, thinly sliced
2 pounds red snapper fillets,
   skinned
1 orange

1 lemon
1 stick butter
1 tablespoon parlsey

Place sliced onion in a single layer in a greased 9 x 12-inch baking dish. Place fillets in a single layer on top of onion. Squeeze juice from orange and lemon over fish. Dot with butter and sprinkle with parsley. Bake at 375 degrees for 20 minutes or until fish flakes with a fork. Broil quickly until brown. Do not overcook. Serves 4.

Nena Ventura Williams, Dallas, TX

Fish Fillet Papilotte

4 fillet of sole
½ stick butter
½ cup chopped scallions
¼ pound sliced fresh
   mushrooms
1 tablespoon flour
1 tomato, skinned and
   chopped

¼ cup lemon juice
4 tablespoons white wine
½ teaspoon oregano
¼ teaspoon salt
½ teaspoon white pepper
2 tablespoons sour cream

Place fish on lightly-buttered foil. Melt remaining butter and sauté scallions and mushrooms lightly. Add flour and tomato. Cook for 1 minute while stirring. Add remaining ingredients and stir. Spoon over fish. Wrap tightly. Bake in 350 degree oven for 35 minutes. Yields 4 servings.

Bunny Laskowski, Houston, TX

Blackened Redfish

1 tablespoon paprika	½ teaspoon white pepper
2 tablespoons salt	½ teaspoon black pepper
1 teaspoon onion powder	½ teaspoon thyme
1½ teaspoons garlic powder	½ teaspoon oregano
1 teaspoon red pepper	1 stick butter
1 teaspoon chopped parsley	6 1-inch thick redfish fillets

Mix all the spices into a bowl. Melt butter. Baste fillets with butter then dip into spice mixture. Place a large heavy skillet on a high flame. When skillet is very hot, put fillets into skillet and cook 3 to 4 minutes on each side. If fillets tend to stick, place 1 tablespoon of butter in skillet. Yields 6 servings.

Keith Patin, Lafayette, LA

Mustard Battered Fried Fish

Mustard Batter:

⅓ cup prepared mustard	2 teaspoons fresh lemon juice
⅛ teaspoon Lawry's seasoned salt	1½ teaspoons Worcestershire
	4 or 5 drops Tabasco
⅛ teaspoon lemon-pepper marinade	⅛ teaspoon black pepper

Mix above ingredients to make a batter for coating fish. Yields enough batter for 1 or 2 pounds of fish pieces.

Frying Fish:

2 teaspoons pepper	1 recipe of mustard batter
2 teaspoons salt	3 cups corn meal
1 to 2 pounds fish pieces	Cooking oil

Salt and pepper fish. Liberally coat each fish piece with mustard batter. Roll in corn meal. Place oil in frying pan and heat to 425 or 450 degrees. Drop coated fish into oil and fry until golden brown. Yields 4 to 5 servings.

Foster Madeley, Conroe, TX

Poisson de Theophile
(Fish of Theophile)

½ cup oil
4 tablespoons flour
1 cup (or more) chopped
  onions
1 cup (or more) chopped
  celery
4 garlic cloves, minced
15 ounces tomato sauce

4 cups water
2 tablespoons Worcestershire
  sauce
Crushed red pepper
Black pepper
Fresh fish (2 pounds),
  deboned

Combine oil and flour in large iron pot; cook until golden brown to make roux. Sauté onions, celery and garlic in roux. Add tomato sauce, water and Worcestershire. Add red pepper and black pepper to taste. Cover and cook over low heat for 40 minutes. While sauce is cooking, prepare fish. Cut deboned fish into 1-inch squares. Salt fish heavily and let set until sauce is done. Add fish and cook another 30 minutes. Serve over rice. Yields 6 to 8 servings.
Note: Catfish, bass or any fish large enough to fillet may be used.

Theophile N. Scott, Natchitoches, LA

Broiled Trout

1 6 to 8-ounce trout fillet
Flour

Sherry wine
Juice of one lemon

Dust fillet lightly with flour and place in a broiling dish. Cover with sherry wine and small amount of water and lemon juice. Cook in 400 degree oven until done. Serve with vegetables.
Note: Herbie K. Smith was a hunting companion of Bishop Greco and Bishop was often a patron in his restaurant.

Chef Dick Betar, Herbie "K's" Restaurant, Alexandria, LA

T. C.'s Bass Fillets

2 pounds fresh bass fillets
1 cup flour
1 teaspoon paprika
1 teaspoon salt
1 teaspoon pepper
1 cup beer
Kettle of hot cooking oil

Cut bass fillets into large bite-size pieces. Blend flour, paprika, salt, pepper and beer into a batter. Dip pieces of fish into batter and drop into hot cooking oil. Cook until pieces of fish rise to the top, about 2 to 3 minutes. Serve immediately. Yields 4 servings.

T. C. Hamilton, Dallas, TX

Tuna Florentine

2 10-ounce packages frozen chopped spinach, thawed
2 tablespoons instant minced onion
12½ ounces tuna, drained
6 hard-boiled eggs, sliced
2 cans cream of mushroom soup
Salt and pepper
1 cup sour cream
¼ cup melted butter
2 cups soft bread crumbs

Squeeze spinach to remove excess liquid. Spread evenly in a greased 2-quart casserole. Sprinkle with onion, tuna, and eggs. Mix soup, seasonings and sour cream. Pour mixture evenly over eggs. Mix butter and bread crumbs and sprinkle evenly over top. Bake at 350 degrees for 30 to 35 minutes or until golden brown and bubbly.

Kim Boystel, Suffolk, England

Tuna Noodle Crisp

4 ounces uncooked noodles
⅓ cup chopped onion
2 tablespoons chopped green
  pepper
1 can Cheddar cheese soup
½ cup milk

1 tablespoon chopped
  pimiento
1 teaspoon salt
⅛ teaspoon pepper
1 6½-ounce can tuna

Cook noodles in boiling salted water until done. Drain and reserve. Sauté onion and pepper in Crisco until tender. Stir in soup, milk, pimiento, salt and pepper. Bring this mixture to a boil. Add cooked noodles and tuna. Place into a lightly-greased 1½ to 2-quart casserole dish. Bake in 350 degree oven for 25 to 30 minutes. Yields 4 servings.

Susan Cartier Willis, Austin, TX

Chopstick Tuna

1 can cream of mushroom
  soup, undiluted
¼ cup water
1 3-ounce can chow mein
  noodles

1 cup sliced celery
½ cup salted, roasted cashews
¼ cup chopped onion
1 6½-ounce can tuna
Dash of pepper

Combine soup and water; add ½ chow mein noodles, celery, cashews, onion, tuna and pepper. Toss lightly. Place in ungreased 10 x 6 x 1½-inch baking dish. Sprinkle remaining noodles over top. Bake in 375 degree oven for 15 minutes or until thoroughly heated. Yields 4 to 5 servings.
Note: Can garnish with mandarin orange slices.

Ann Comeaux, Baytown, TX

STAR OF THE SEA
Pineville, Louisiana

One of the attractions for visitors to Maryhill is the *Star of the Sea*, a ninety-six foot ship designed and built by Bishop Greco. It took Bishop, his yardman, and chauffeur some five years during the late 1950's to build the *Star of the Sea*. "I always had an attraction for ships. As a young boy in New Orleans, I would spend hours watching the ships pass through the harbor," the Bishop said. When he built Maryhill Camp in 1951, he envisioned a ship on a small body of water near the camp. "It would be a place for the children to walk around and for adults to sit and relax." With this in mind, he began to draw the plans for this ninety-six foot ship, with an upper and lower deck and two stacks; on the bow would be an American flag, indicating where it was going, and on the stern an Italian flag, indicating from whence it came. The name *Star of the Sea* honors the Blessed Mother.

The ship gives much pleasure to visitors today. In 1986, it was completely restored to its original beauty by the Knights of Columbus.

Poultry, Game and Stuffings

"Star of the Sea"
Pineville, Louisiana

Baked Chicken Salad

1 6-ounce can sliced
  mushrooms, drained
1 cup thinly sliced celery
½ cup chopped onion
1 to 2 tablespoons butter
2 to 3 cups cubed cooked
  chicken (may use 3 cans
  canned chicken)
1 can cream of chicken soup
1 cup chicken broth

½ cup mayonnaise (low cal)
½ cup sour cream (low fat
  yogurt may be substituted)
1 tablespoon lemon juice
1 cup cracker crumbs
½ cup slivered almonds,
  toasted
6 to 8 ounces grated American
  cheese

Sauté mushrooms, celery, and onions in butter until tender. Mix chicken, soup, broth, mayonnaise, sour cream, lemon juice, ½ cup cracker crumbs and almonds. Add to sautéed ingredients and mix well. Put into large casserole and top with grated cheese and ½ cup cracker crumbs. Bake at 400 degrees for 30 to 35 minutes or until well heated and cheese is melted. Serves 6 to 8.

Dixie Harlan, Paris, TX

Crunchy Hot Chicken Salad

3 cups cooked chicken,
  deboned, skinned and
  chopped
1 can cream of chicken soup
1 cup water chestnuts, sliced
⅔ cup mayonnaise
½ cup chopped celery

½ cup chopped onion
½ cup sour cream
1 8-ounce can crescent rolls
⅔ cup shredded cheese (Swiss,
  American or Monterey Jack)
½ cup almonds, thinly sliced
3 tablespoons butter, melted

Combine chicken, soup, water chestnuts, mayonnaise, celery, onion and sour cream. Pour into ungreased baking dish or casserole. Separate crescent rolls and lay over chicken mixture. Sprinkle cheese evenly on top. Mix almonds and butter; sprinkle evenly on top. Bake at 375 degrees for 25 minutes. Serves 6.

Donna L. Gay, Little Rock, AR

Chicken Almondine

Salt and pepper to taste
4 chicken breasts, halved
Flour for dredging and gravy
Oil for frying
1 tablespoon butter

Paprika
Water or chicken broth
1 small can sliced mushrooms
1 small package slivered almonds

Salt and pepper chicken. Dip in flour. Brown in oil until crust forms, then transfer chicken to pan that has been greased with butter. Sprinkle paprika on chicken. Cover and cook until tender, basting with juices in pan. Uncover and cook until brown. Remove the chicken from the pan and keep warm. Add water or broth, salt, pepper and flour to drippings in the pan to make a gravy. Add mushrooms and slivered almonds to gravy and serve over the chicken. Yields 4 to 6 servings.

Marti Greenberg, Denton, TX

Artichoke and Chicken Casserole

4 tablespoons margarine
1 tablespoon cooking oil
1 fryer, cut in parts
½ pound fresh mushrooms, sliced
1 tablespoon flour
1 can cream of chicken soup
1 cup dry white wine

1 cup water
½ cup cream
1 teaspoon salt
¼ teaspoon pepper
1 14-ounce can artichoke hearts, drained
6 green onions, chopped
2 tablespoons chopped parsley

In a large frypan, place margarine and oil; heat until margarine melts. Add chicken and cook turning after about 10 minutes. Remove chicken and place in casserole dish. In same frypan sauté mushrooms for 5 minutes. Stir in flour and add soup, wine and water. Simmer about 10 minutes or until sauce thickens. Stir in cream, salt and pepper; pour over chicken. Bake uncovered at 350 degrees for 60 minutes. Remove from oven and mix in artichoke hearts, green onions and parsley. Return to oven and bake approximately 5 minutes longer. Yields 4 to 6 servings.

Dora Medica, Alexandria, LA

Lemon Chicken

4 chicken breasts	½ cup dry, white wine
¼ pound butter	¼ cup lemon juice
2 tablespoons vegetable oil	4 tablespoons chopped parsley
Pinch of thyme	Salt and pepper to taste
2 tablespoons flour	

Freeze chicken breasts, just a little, to make them stiff. Then slice each into 3 thin slices. Melt butter in skillet with oil. Mix thyme into flour; dredge chicken in flour. Brown on both sides. When they are brown, drain on paper. Then add wine, lemon juice, parsley, salt and pepper to skillet and mix. Place breasts into baking pan, pour lemon mixture over them and bake for 15 minutes at 350 degrees. Yields 2 to 4 servings.

Diane Smith, New Orleans, LA

Chicken Bundles

4 chicken breasts, boned and skinned	1 egg, beaten
	2 tablespoons milk
4 fresh spinach leaves, washed and large part of stem removed	1½ cups crushed herb-seasoned bread stuffing
	¼ cup Parmesan cheese (canned)
4 sticks Mozzarella cheese (2 x ½-inches)	½ teaspoon paprika

Flatten chicken breasts and place one spinach leaf on each. In center of leaf place one stick of cheese. Roll chicken breast and secure with toothpicks. In bowl combine egg and milk. In another bowl combine stuffing, Parmesan and paprika. Dip chicken bundle into egg mixture and roll in dry mixture, coating well. Place in 9 x 13-inch baking dish. Bake at 350 degrees for 1 hour or until done. Serve with Bearnaise Sauce. (See Index.) Yields 4 servings.

Anita White, Kilgore, TX

Rolled Chicken

½ cup finely chopped fresh
   mushrooms or 1 3-ounce
   can chopped mushrooms,
   drained
2 tablespoons butter
2 tablespoons flour
½ cup light cream
¼ teaspoon salt

Dash of cayenne pepper
1½ cups shredded sharp
   Cheddar cheese
6 to 7 deboned chicken breasts
Salt to taste
All-purpose flour
2 eggs, slightly beaten
¾ cup fine bread crumbs

Cook mushrooms in butter about 5 minutes. Blend in flour, stir in cream. Add salt and cayenne pepper, cook and stir until mixture becomes very thick. Stir in cheese, cook over very low heat, stirring constantly until cheese is melted. Turn mixture into pie plate, cover, chill thoroughly about 1 hour. Cut the firm cheese mixture into 6 to 7 equal portions. Shape into short sticks. Remove skin from chicken breasts. To make cutlets place each piece of chicken, deboned side up, between two pieces of Saran Wrap. Working out from the center, pound with wooden mallet to form cutlets. Peel off Saran Wrap. Sprinkle meat with salt. Place a cheese stick on each chicken breast, tucking in the sides, roll chicken jellyroll-style. Press to seal. Dust the chicken rolls with flour, dip in slightly beaten egg, roll in fine dry bread crumbs. Cover and chill chicken rolls thoroughly, at least 1 hour. About an hour before serving fry rolls in deep hot fat (375 degrees), 5 minutes or until crisp and golden-brown. Drain on paper towel. Place rolls in shallow baking dish and bake at 325 degrees 30 to 45 minutes. Yields 6 to 7 servings.

Laura Scott, Natchitoches, LA

Stuffed Chicken Breasts

1 small onion, chopped
½ green pepper, chopped
½ pound fresh mushrooms,
   sliced
1 cup plus 1 tablespoon butter
½ teaspoon Worcestershire
   sauce

Pinch of sage
Salt and pepper to taste
1 cup cooked white rice
1 cup cooked wild rice
8 chicken breasts
Juice of 1 lime
1 tablespoon paprika

Sauté onions, green pepper and mushrooms in 1 tablespoon butter until tender. Add Worcestershire sauce, pinch of sage, salt and pepper. Stir in rices to make a stuffing. Stuff the chicken breasts by lifting skin, stuffing, then securing the skin. Arrange chicken in a shallow baking pan. Melt 1 cup butter and add lime juice and paprika. Use this sauce to baste the chicken while baking. Bake in 350 degree oven for 1 hour with frequent basting. Yields 8 servings.

Kathleen Waguespack, Napoleonville, LA

Chicken Cordon Bleu

6 whole chicken breasts,
   deboned
Salt and pepper to taste
6 slices ham

6 slices Swiss cheese
1 stick butter
1 cup bread crumbs
Paprika

Pound deboned chicken breast until flat. Salt and pepper; place 1 slice of ham and 1 slice of Swiss cheese on each breast. Roll and secure with toothpick. Melt butter in pie plate or casserole dish. Mix 1 cup bread crumbs and paprika in another container; roll each chicken breast first in butter then crumbs. Place in a buttered baking dish and bake at 350 to 400 degrees for 45 minutes until brown and tender. If chicken browns too fast, cover with foil. Good served with wine cream sauce. Yields 6 servings.

Note: Dish may be prepared ahead of time and stored in refrigerator.

Gloria Evans, Clarksdale, MS

Stuffed Chicken Crab Rolls

4 whole chicken breasts, split, boned and skinned
3 slices bread, toasted
⅓ cup mayonnaise
1 teaspoon lemon juice
½ cup chicken bouillon
Dash of hot sauce
⅔ cup finely chopped celery
⅔ cup finely chopped green onion
¾ cup melted butter, divided
¼ teaspoon basil, marjoram, thyme and pepper
½ teaspoon seasoned salt
1 cup fresh flaked crabmeat
⅓ cup shredded Swiss cheese
2 tablespoons chopped parsley
⅓ cup flour
Paprika

Place each ½ chicken breast on waxed paper and flatten to ¼ inch. Tear bread into small pieces and place in mixing bowl. Combine mayonnaise, lemon juice, bouillon and hot sauce. Pour over bread. Sauté celery and onions in ½ of butter. Add bread mixture. Stir in seasonings, crabmeat, cheese and parsley. Mix well. Place equal portion on each chicken breast. Fold long sides of chicken over stuffing. Roll up and secure with toothpicks. Dredge each roll in flour, dip in remaining butter. Place in long baking dish. Sprinkle with paprika. Bake in 350 degree oven for 45 minutes to 1 hour. May sprinkle fresh chopped parsley over top before serving if desired. Yields 4 servings. Should be served with Bearnaise Sauce. (See Index.)

Gloria Allen, Marshall, TX

Tracy's Favorite Chicken and Rice

4 to 6 chicken breasts
Seasoning salt
1 cup uncooked rice
1½ cups water
1 package onion soup mix

Sprinkle chicken with seasoning salt. In 3-quart shallow casserole place uncooked rice, then place chicken on top of rice. Mix water with soup mix and pour over chicken. Cover and bake at 350 degrees for 1½ hours. Yields 4 to 6 servings.

Marti Greenberg, Denton, TX

109

Chicken Kiev

6 chicken breasts, skinned,
and deboned
Accent
Salt to taste
White pepper to taste
1 tablespoon minced chives
1 tablespoon minced shallots

¼ pound butter
Seasoned flour
2 eggs, slightly beaten
1 cup toasted, fine bread
crumbs
2 cups clarified butter
1 tablespoon peanut oil

Preheat oven to 350 degrees. Pound chicken breasts until thin, being careful not to tear or split the flesh. Sprinkle with Accent, salt and white pepper. Combine chives and shallots. Cut the butter into 6 strips and place one strip on each chicken breast, along with 1 teaspoon of the chive-shallot mixture. Roll each breast tightly and secure with string. Dredge each portion with seasoned flour, dip into beaten eggs and coat with bread crumbs. Heat clarified butter and oil and brown chicken breasts. Transfer to a baking dish and bake at 350 degrees for 15 minutes. Drain and serve with Sour Cream Sauce (See Index).

Bunny Laskowski, Houston, TX

Chicken Delight

1 jar dried chipped beef
6 chicken breasts
6 strips bacon
2 cans cream of chicken soup

12 ounces sour cream
6 ounces cream cheese
Dash of Tabasco

Preheat oven to 300 degrees. Line a 9 x 12-inch pan with chipped beef. Wrap breasts of chicken with bacon strips and lay on top of chipped beef. Place chicken soup, sour cream and cream cheese in a saucepan. Heat and stir until dissolved. Pour mixture over chicken. Sprinkle Tabasco over chicken; cover with foil. Bake for 2 hours. Yields 6 servings.

Martha Meador, Clinton, MS

Chicken and Rice

2 sticks margarine
2 chickens, cut up
Salt and pepper to taste
Dash of Lawry's seasoned salt
1 pound rice, uncooked
1 can cream of mushroom
   soup

1 can cream of chicken soup
1 can cream of celery soup
2 small cans mushroom slices
1 mushroom can water

Preheat oven to 275 degrees. In large roaster, melt butter, dip each piece of chicken in butter and set aside. Season chicken to taste. In roaster, mix remaining ingredients. Then place chicken on top of rice mixture. Cover roaster. Bake 2½ hours. Yields 6 to 12 servings. *Note: This dish can be frozen. Reheats well in oven or microwave. Sprinkle a little water over rice when reheating to add moisture.*

Deborah T. Watts, Lake Charles, LA

Chicken Rice Divan

1 fryer, cut into pieces,
   deboned and skinned
2 tablespoons oil
1 cup water
1 tablespoon wine (optional)

1 package frozen broccoli
   spears
1 can cream of chicken soup
1½ cups cooked rice
Parmesan cheese to taste

Brown chicken in oil until tender, turning once. Combine water, wine, broccoli and soup and pour over chicken in skillet. Bring to a full boil. Remove from heat and serve over rice. Sprinkle with cheese as desired. Serves 4.

Lucille Schaider, La Porte, TX

Chicken Spectacular

1 package Uncle Ben's long
  grain wild rice
3 cups cubed cooked chicken
1 small can water chestnuts,
  sliced
1 can cream of celery soup,
  undiluted
1 small jar pimiento, minced
1 medium onion, chopped
1 large can French style green
  beans, drained
1 cup mayonnaise
1½ cups grated cheese
Grated almonds

Cook rice as directed on package. Drain. Combine rice, chicken, water chestnuts, soup, pimiento, onion, beans, mayonnaise and 1 cup of grated cheese. Place in a lightly-greased oblong casserole dish. Bake in 350 degree oven for 20 minutes. Remove and top with remaining cheese and grated almonds. Return to oven and bake for 10 minutes. Yields 8 to 10 servings.
Note: This was served at the St. Francis Cabrini Style Show Luncheon in 1985.

Santina Brocato, Alexandria, LA

Divine Chicken Casserole

1 medium bunch fresh
  broccoli
3 cups diced cooked chicken
1 can cream of chicken soup
  (undiluted)
2 tablespoons water
¼ cup mayonnaise
2 teaspoons fresh lemon juice
¼ teaspoon ground black
  pepper
2 tablespoons melted butter
½ cup seasoned bread crumbs
¼ cup shredded cheese,
  Cheddar or Parmesan

Wash broccoli and remove large leaves and tough part of stalks. Cut stalks lengthwise into quarters. Steam broccoli 10 to 15 minutes until crisp but tender and drain thoroughly. Place broccoli in a 12 x 8-inch baking dish and cover with chicken. In a small bowl combine soup, water, mayonnaise, lemon juice and pepper. Mix well and pour over chicken. Mix melted butter, bread crumbs and cheese and sprinkle over soup mixture. Bake in a preheated 350 degree oven for 25 minutes or until mixture is hot and bubbly. Serves 4 to 6.

Elena Roberts, Dunedin, FL

Chicken and Wild Rice Supreme

½ cup chopped onion
1 stick margarine
½ cup chicken broth
4 tablespoons cornstarch
1½ cups half and half cream
1 6-ounce box Uncle Ben's
   white and wild rice

6 ounces mushrooms, sliced
3 cups boiled, chopped and
   deboned chicken
1 tablespoon parsley
½ teaspoon salt
¼ teaspoon pepper

Sauté onion in margarine. Set aside. Slowly heat chicken broth, then add cornstarch and cream. Stir cook until thick. Cook rice according to package directions. Mix onions, sauce, rice, mushrooms, chicken, parsley and seasonings. Place in a 2 or 3-quart casserole. Bake in 325 degree oven for 30 minutes. Yields 8 to 10 servings.
Note: Sliced pimiento, blanched almonds or water chestnuts make an excellent garnish.

Sheila Fyfe, Lula, MS

Chicken Spaghetti

1 4 to 5 pound hen
1 cup diced green pepper
3 cups diced onion
3 cups diced celery
1 clove garlic, finely chopped
1 stick margarine
1 can tomatoes
1 cup chicken stock
1 can tomato paste

Salt and pepper to taste
1 tablespoon chili powder
1 tablespoon Worcestershire
Tabasco to taste
1 can English peas
1 can mushrooms
⅔ pound bag Italian style long
   spaghetti

Cook hen in salted water until tender. Remove from stock and save 1 cup stock. Remove chicken from bone in small pieces. Sauté green pepper, onions, celery and garlic in margarine in large dutch oven. Add tomatoes, chicken stock, tomato paste and seasonings. Cook slowly for 1 hour. Add chicken, peas, mushrooms and cooked spaghetti. Yields 12 to 15 servings.
Note: Better made the day before serving. Can be frozen.

Irene T. Roberts, Newport, AR

113

Chicken Manicotti

8 manicotti shells
1 10¾-ounce can creamy
   chicken mushroom soup
½ cup sour cream
2 cups chopped, cooked
   chicken
1 4-ounce can sliced
   mushrooms, drained

¼ cup chopped onion
2 tablespoons butter
¼ cup warm water
½ teaspoon chicken bouillon
1 cup shredded Cheddar
   cheese

Cook manicotti shells as directed on package, omitting salt. Drain and set aside. Combine soup and sour cream, mix well. Combine half of soup mixture and chicken. Mix well. Reserve remaining soup mixture, set aside. Stuff manicotti shells with chicken mixture. Place in a greased 12 x 8 x 2-inch baking dish. Sauté onions and mushrooms in butter in a large skillet until tender, set aside. Combine water and bouillon granules, stirring until dissolved. Add to reserved soup mixture, mixing well. Pour soup mixture into mushroom mixture, mixing well. Spoon mixture over manicotti. Bake uncovered at 350 degrees for 15 minutes. Sprinkle with cheese and bake an additional 5 minutes. Yields 4 to 6 servings.

Joyce V. Stanford, Plain Dealing, LA

Herbal Chicken

3 tablespoons butter
1 3½-pound chicken, cut up
½ teaspoon garlic salt
¼ teaspoon tarragon

½ teaspoon mixed dried herbs
   (Italian seasoning)
Cracked pepper

Heat butter in large skillet at medium heat (about 250 degrees). When butter is melted, coat each piece of chicken with butter on all sides. Mix all seasonings together and sprinkle half on chicken. Cover and cook for 10 to 12 minutes. Turn chicken and sprinkle with remaining seasonings. Cover and cook until done (about 10 to 12 minutes more). Yields 4 to 5 servings.

Barnett Greenberg, Denton, TX

Three-Cheese Chicken Casserole

1 8-ounce package wide egg
noodles
3 quarts water
2 tablespoons salt
1 teaspoon Wesson oil
3 tablespoons butter
½ cup chopped green bell
pepper
½ cup chopped celery
1 can cream of chicken soup
½ cup milk

1 6-ounce jar whole
mushrooms
¼ teaspoon black pepper
1 12-ounce carton small-curd
cottage cheese
1 3 to 4 pound hen, boiled,
deboned, and cut up
10 ounces grated Cheddar
cheese
½ cup grated Parmesan
cheese

In large kettle place noodles in water, salt and oil. Cook 12 to 15 minutes then drain and set aside. Melt butter in skillet and sauté bell pepper, celery and onion until tender. Add chicken soup, milk, mushrooms and black pepper. In a large baking dish begin layering with noodles, cover with ½ of soup mix, ½ cottage cheese, ½ chicken, ½ Cheddar cheese. Repeat and top with Parmesan cheese. Bake at 350 degrees for 45 minutes. Yields 8 servings.

Edgar Allen, Marshall, TX

Sour Cream Chicken

Salt and pepper to taste
8 chicken breasts, deboned
1 tablespoon parsley flakes
1 stick butter
2 eggs, lightly beaten

1 cup Italian bread crumbs
1 cup Parmesan cheese
4 green onions, chopped
1 can sliced mushrooms
2 cups sour cream

Salt and pepper chicken breasts. Lay flat; sprinkle with parsley. Divide ½ of the butter into equal portions and place one portion on each breast. Roll up and secure with a toothpick. Dip in lightly beaten eggs, roll in combined bread crumbs and cheese. Brown in butter. Remove chicken and place in casserole dish. Sauté onions and mushrooms in pan in which chicken was browned. (May need to add more butter.) Add sour cream and heat thoroughly. Pour over chicken and bake in 325 degree oven for 45 minutes or until chicken is tender. Serves 8.

Mrs. Madge Marshall, Pineville, LA

Easy Chicken and Dumplings

1 fryer, cut into pieces	½ teaspoon baking powder
1 medium onion, chopped	1 tablespoon vegetable
2 ribs celery, chopped	shortening
Salt and pepper to taste	1 egg yolk
1 cup flour	¼ cup broth or milk
¼ teaspoon salt	1 egg, hard-boiled

Boil the chicken in water seasoned with onion, celery, salt and pepper. Remove the chicken from the stock. Make the dumplings by mixing flour, salt, baking powder and shortening together. Add egg yolk and mix well. Add broth or milk to make the dough. Roll the dough on a floured surface until thin. Cut into squares. Lay the squares on waxed paper for 30 minutes or more to dry. Bring the chicken stock to a boil. Drop in dumplings. Add hard-boiled, chopped egg and milk if desired. Return the chicken to the pot. Cover and cook for approximately 5 minutes or until dumplings are tender.

Lorine Kordsmeier, Morrilton, AR
Husband: William Kordsmeier
Knights of Columbus title: State Membership

Miss Martha's Cajun Tamale Pie

2 dozen spicy, Cajun hot tamales (preferably Miss Martha's)	1 16-ounce can tomato sauce
	1 4-ounce can chopped ripe olives, drained
1 3-pound chicken, boiled, deboned and shredded	2 tablespoons chili powder
1 onion, chopped	1 14-ounce can cream style corn
1 clove garlic, minced	½ pound Cheddar cheese, grated
½ green pepper, chopped	
2 tablespoons vegetable oil	

Line an 11 x 15-inch baking dish with tamales. Cover with a layer of chicken. Sauté onion, garlic and green pepper in oil and add to combined tomato sauce, olives, corn and chili powder. Pour this mixture over chicken and top with grated cheese. Bake at 300 degrees for 1 hour or until cheese is bubbly. Serves 6 to 8.

Martha Shoffner, Little Rock, AR

Mere's B-B-Q Chicken

2 3-pound fryers, cut in half
3 medium onions, sliced thin

Salt and pepper to taste
Water

Tuck a slice of onion under each wing and a slice under each leg. Salt and pepper to taste. Place in roaster, skin side up, with enough water to cover the bottom of the pan. Bake in 350 degree oven for ½ hour then turn and bake for another ½ hour. Remove from oven and prepare sauce.

Sauce:
3 tablespoons butter
1½ cups tomato juice
¼ teaspoon cayenne pepper
2 teaspoons salt
¼ teaspoon black pepper
¼ teaspoon powdered
  mustard

4½ teaspoons Worcestershire
  sauce
1 bay leaf
1 teaspoon sugar
¾ cup cider vinegar
3 cloves garlic, minced

Mix all of the ingredients and simmer for 10 minutes. Pour ½ of the sauce in roaster. Turn fryer halves skin side up and pour remaining sauce on top of chicken. Return to oven and bake at 350 degrees for 1 hour, with frequent basting. Yields 4 servings.
Note: This original recipe won 1st prize in a cooking contest in New Orleans, Louisiana.

Carol Morgan, Dallas, TX

Oven Fried Chicken

1 fryer, cut into pieces
Salt to taste
Pepper to taste

Garlic powder to taste
¼ cup cooking oil
¾ cup Italian bread crumbs

Season chicken pieces with salt, pepper and garlic. Dip chicken pieces in oil and then roll in bread crumbs, coating each side. Place chicken on a lightly greased baking sheet. Bake, turning once, in 375 degree oven for 40 to 45 minutes or until chicken can easily be pierced with a fork. Yields 4 servings.

Dora Medica, Alexandria, LA

Chicken Stew

1 chicken
4 cups water
1½ sticks margarine
½ cup flour
1 cup chopped onion
½ cup chopped bell pepper
1 cup chopped celery

Garlic powder to taste
Red pepper to taste
Salt to taste
Black pepper to taste
2 cans cream of chicken soup
½ cup chopped green onion
  tops

Place chicken in large saucepan with water and boil until tender. Remove chicken, reserving broth. Cool, debone and cut chicken into large cubes. Make a roux using 1 stick of margarine and flour, stirring constantly until golden brown. Sauté onions, bell pepper and celery in ½ stick margarine. Add sautéed vegetables, chicken, seasonings, soup and roux to broth. Simmer until done and thickened. Add green onions the last five minutes of cooking. Serve over rice. Serves 6.

Becky Hebert, Natchitoches, LA

Chicken Fajitas

3 pounds chicken breast
  meat, cooked
8 flour tortillas
1 tablespoon cooking oil
1 medium onion, sliced
2 bell peppers, sliced

1 teaspoon Liquid Smoke
Juice of half a lemon
Guacamole
Sour cream
Picanté sauce or
  pico de gallo

In advance: poach, bake or boil the chicken meat and cut into strips. Wrap flour tortillas tightly in foil and place in 350 degree oven for about 20 minutes. Heat oil in skillet over medium heat and add onion and pepper slices, Liquid Smoke and lemon juice. Stir and cook until the onion and pepper slices are tender. Keep warm in skillet. When ready to serve add the chicken strips to mixture in skillet and heat thoroughly. Serve with tortillas, guacamole, sour cream and picanté sauce or pico de gallo. Yields 4 to 6 servings.

Dana Martinez, Dallas, TX

Chili Chicken Casserole

4 cups cooked white rice
1 chicken, boiled, deboned
   and chopped
1 can cream of chicken soup
1 can green chilies, chopped
3 cups Cheddar cheese,
   shredded

3 cups Monterey Jack cheese,
   shredded
1 can pitted black olives,
   sliced

Place one half of the rice in the bottom of casserole dish. Top with one half of the chicken, soup, chilies, Cheddar cheese, Monterey Jack cheese and olives. Repeat the same procedure until all ingredients are used and olives are the last layer. Bake 1 hour and 15 minutes at 350 degrees until bubbly and cheese is melted.

Stephanie Schaider, La Porte, TX

King Ranch Chicken

1 large fryer or 6 chicken
   breasts
1 large onion, chopped
1 bell pepper, chopped
1 large bag of Doritos
Stock from chicken
½ pound Cheddar cheese,
   grated
1½ teaspoons chili powder

Garlic salt to taste
1 10½-ounce can cream of
   chicken soup
1 10½-ounce can cream of
   mushroom soup
1 10-ounce can Ro-tel
   tomatoes with green chilies,
   chopped

Boil chicken, debone and cut in small pieces. Reserve stock. Butter a 3½-quart casserole dish. Combine chicken, onion and bell pepper in mixing bowl. Layer chicken mixture alternately with Doritos that have been dipped in hot chicken stock just long enough to soften. Make three or four layers of each. Top with grated cheese, sprinkle with chili powder and garlic salt. Separately, mix cream of chicken soup with ½ cup chicken stock and pour over casserole. Repeat with cream of mushroom soup, top with Ro-tel tomatoes. Do not stir. Bake at 350 degrees for 35 to 45 minutes. Serve hot with tostadoes. Yields 4 to 5 servings.

Jackie Stonestreet, Dallas, TX

119

Mexican Chicken

1 fryer or 1 package chicken
  breasts
1 small onion, chopped
1 can cream of mushroom
  soup
1 can cream of chicken soup

1 can Ro-tel tomatoes, diced
½ pound bag Doritos
1 pound Velveeta cheese,
  grated

Boil and debone chicken. Combine onion, soups and Ro-tel to-matoes. Pour Doritos in a greased 13 x 9-inch pan. Layer chicken over Doritos and pour soup mixture over chicken. Sprinkle cheese over top. Cover with foil. Bake at 350 degrees for 1 hour.

Brenda Gray, Farmerville, LA

Chinese Chicken

¾ cup chopped onion
½ cup chopped celery
1 garlic clove, chopped
1 can cream of mushroom
  soup
¼ cup sherry wine
1 small can mushrooms, sliced

1 can water chestnuts, sliced
6 boneless chicken breasts
Salt and pepper to taste
Flour as needed
Butter as needed
1 package frozen Chinese
  pea pods

Brown onions, celery and garlic in small amount of butter. Add soup, sherry, mushrooms and water chestnuts. Bring to a boil. Salt and pepper chicken and coat with flour. Brown in butter. Place chicken in a baking pan or casserole dish then pour hot mixture on top. Bake in 350 degree oven for 40 minutes. Put frozen pea pods over chicken during last 10 minutes of baking time. Yields 4 to 5 servings.

Note: Can be prepared in advance. Do not add pea pods until preparing to serve. Good served with Fried Rice Cantonese Style. (See Index)

Marti Greenberg, Denton, TX

Island Broiled Chicken

½ cup Kikkoman soy sauce
¼ cup water
⅓ cup salad oil
2 tablespoons instant minced
    onion
⅛ teaspoon red pepper
2 tablespoons sesame seeds

1 tablespoon sugar
1 teaspoon ground black
    pepper
½ teaspoon instant minced
    garlic
2 broiler/fryer chickens,
    halved or quartered

Combine the soy sauce, water, oil and seasonings together. Put marinade and chicken into a large bowl with a tight-fitting lid. Cover and let marinate in the refrigerator for 12 hours or longer, with occasional turning. Broil chicken over hot charcoal, turning and basting frequently with marinade, for 45 minutes or until done. Yields 8 servings.

Note: Chicken will be dark, but very good. This is also a good marinade for steaks.

Mrs. Jean Sain Wilkirson, Jackson, MS

Spicy Chinese Chicken

4 pounds of cut-up chicken
2 cloves garlic (minced)
½ teaspoon black pepper
1 teaspoon sugar

½ teaspoon ground cloves
½ teaspoon cinnamon
¼ cup soy sauce

Place chicken in a foil-lined pan. Mix next 5 ingredients and pour over the chicken. Let stand for 1 hour. Pour soy sauce over chicken and mixture and bake at 325 degrees for 45 minutes to 1 hour or until tender and brown. Serves 6.

Tish Rodriquez, Alexandria, LA

Fried Turkey

20 ounces Italian dressing
10 ounces Worcestershire
  sauce
2 tablespoons soy sauce
5 tablespoons salt
8 tablespoons garlic powder

8 tablespoons onion powder
1 tablespoon celery salt
1 tablespoon black pepper
2 cups red pepper
1 13-pound turkey
4 gallons cooking oil

To prepare marinade, mix dressing, sauces and all of the spices together in a large container. Place defrosted and cleaned turkey in bowl with marinade. Place in refrigerator and let marinate for 48 hours, basting frequently. To fry, preheat oil to 325 degrees using a candy thermometer. Fry for 40 minutes or three minutes per pound. The turkey will be light brown, darker with hotter oil, but very moist and tender. Serves 12 to 15.

Allison and Gwen Scott, Natchitoches, LA

Baked Dove

12 fresh doves
Salt and pepper
12 jalapeño peppers

12 strips bacon
12 toothpicks
3 tablespoons butter

Rinse doves in cold water and pat dry. Salt and pepper freely. Slice jalapeño peppers in half and remove seeds. Place one jalapeño in the cavity of each dove. Wrap each dove in a strip of bacon and secure with a toothpick. Melt butter in iron skillet and brown doves on each side. Remove from skillet and place in baking dish that just fits the quantity to be baked.

Sauce:
1 can cream of mushroom
  soup

5 cloves garlic, pressed
1 can beer

Combine all ingredients in a saucepan and bring to a boil. Simmer about 10 minutes. Pour over doves. Bake at 250 degrees for 2 hours. Yields 4 servings.

T. C. and Sally Hamilton, Dallas, TX

Basic Wild Duck

1 wild duck	1 rib celery, chopped
Salt	½ cup butter, melted
1 apple, chopped	½ cup chicken broth
½ onion, chopped	½ cup Port wine

Clean and wash duck. Cover duck with mixture of ½ vinegar and ½ water and soak in the refrigerator overnight. Remove duck from refrigerator and rinse, then lightly salt inside and outside. Mix apple, onion and celery together and stuff in cavity of duck. Place duck in oven dish breast-side up. Combine butter, broth and wine and pour over duck. Cover and bake in 350 degree oven for 2½ hours. Turn and cook breast-side down for 20 minutes.

Note: Overnight soaking is not required but helps to remove some of wild taste. Serve with wild rice and Mandarin Orange Sauce (See Index) or sauce of your choice.

Anita A. White, Kilgore, TX

Delicious Duck Casserole

3 cups duck meat, cooked and chopped	1½ cups duck broth
½ cup margarine	1½ cups half and half cream
½ cup chopped onion	1 tablespoon chopped parsley
¼ cup flour	6 ounces cooked wild rice
4 ounces sliced mushrooms, drained	1½ teaspoons salt
	¼ teaspoon pepper
	Slivered almonds

Melt margarine in pan and sauté onion. Stir in flour. Add mushrooms. Mix and stir in duck broth. Add meat, cream, parsley, cooked rice and salt and pepper. Mix. Place in 2-quart greased casserole and sprinkle almonds on top. Place covered casserole dish in 350 degree oven and cook for 20 minutes. Remove and uncover. Return to oven and bake uncovered for 10 minutes. Yields 4 to 6 servings.

Note: This recipe is also delicious made with a hen or chicken.

Mrs. Donna Graham, Lyon, MS

Roast Wild Duck

2 wild ducks, cleaned
Heavily-salted water for
  soaking
Salt and pepper to taste
2 small onions, peeled
2 small potatoes, peeled
½ cup cooking sherry,
  sauterne or Chablis

½ cup water
2 strips bacon
2 teaspoons poultry seasoning
¼ cup melted butter
½ teaspoon garlic powder or
  1 pod fresh garlic, pressed

Soak clean ducks in heavy salt water for 3 hours. Rinse and pat dry. Salt and pepper freely. Insert one small onion and one small potato in cavity of each duck. Mix cooking wine and water in measuring cup. Put ducks in roasting pan and pour wine-water mixture over ducks. Lay a strip of bacon on breast of each duck and sprinkle ducks with poultry seasoning. Cover with foil and bake at 350 degrees for 2 hours. Combine melted butter and garlic in small saucepan. Remove foil and baste duck with garlic butter mixture. Bake an additional 20 minutes. Serves 2 to 4 people depending on size of ducks.

Note: This is a very special recipe given to me years ago by my friend, Lytle Nichol of Memphis, Tennessee, an avid hunter and excellent cook.

Cindy Ward, Dallas, TX

Quail with Mushroom Gravy

Salt and pepper to taste
6 quail, cut in half
½ or 1 stick butter or
  margarine
3 tablespoons flour

½ pound fresh mushrooms,
  sliced
2 cups chicken broth
½ cup sherry (pale dry)

Salt and pepper quail halves. Brown in butter (do not flour). Remove, drain and place in a casserole dish that has been sprayed with Pam. Add flour to butter and blend. Add mushrooms, broth and sherry. Cook until smooth. Pour over quail. Bake in 350 degree oven for 1 hour. Serve over rice with gravy. Yields 6 servings.

Note: This is equally delicious with cornish hens or chicken breasts. To increase number of servings, just double or triple the recipe.

Gloria Evans, Clarksdale, MS

Pheasant and Artichokes

6 pheasant breasts
Bacon
¾ cup cream, divided
Flour
Salt, pepper and paprika
   to taste

½ cup butter
1 cup Madeira or Port wine
1 6-ounce can artichoke
   hearts, drained
Wild rice

Remove skin from breasts. Roll a piece of bacon around each breast. Dip in cream and dredge in flour. Salt, pepper and paprika to taste. In a baking dish melt the butter and sauté the breast lightly. Add the wine, cover with foil and bake at 325 degrees for 1 hour and 30 minutes, or until tender. Remove breasts from dish and set aside. Add ½ cup cream to the sauce remaining in dish, add artichoke hearts and stir, cooking until thoroughly heated. Pour over pheasant and serve with wild rice.

Amanda Greene, Marshall, TX

Grilled Venison Tenders

2 venison tenderloins
1 cup dry red wine
1 cup wine vinegar
1 cup water
1 clove garlic, sliced
1 teaspoon fresh crushed
   peppercorns

1 bay leaf
½ cup soy sauce
½ cup Worcestershire sauce
½ cup vegetable oil
2 teaspoons Lawry's lemon
   pepper seasoning

Place tenderloins in an enamel or porcelain dish. Combine the red wine, vinegar, water, garlic and crushed peppercorns and pour over the tenderloins. Marinate for at least 6 hours. Drain and discard the vinegar solution. Combine the soy sauce, Worcestershire sauce and vegetable oil and pour over the tenderloins. Let the tenderloins marinate in this mixture for 2 hours, turning occasionally. Drain the marinade and sprinkle the tenderloins with lemon pepper seasoning. Place tenders on grill and cook 4 to 8 minutes on each side, depending on size. Meat is best medium rare. Slice the tenders thin and serve immediately. Serves 4 to 6.

Cindy Ward, Dallas, TX

Mother's Turkey Dressing

Corn bread:

½ cup shortening	3 teaspoons salt
2 cups flour	2 cups yellow corn meal
1 tablespoon sugar	4 eggs, beaten
8 teaspoons baking powder	2 cups milk

Place shortening in pan and melt. Combine all other ingredients together and blend. Pour into pan containing melted shortening. Bake in 400 degree oven for 25 minutes or until brown.

Dressing:

Neck and giblets from turkey	1 cup chopped fresh parsley
4 cups water	2 teaspoons black pepper
2 cups chopped celery	2 teaspoons thyme
1 cup chopped green onions	2 teaspoons sage
1 cup chopped onion	2 teaspoons poultry seasoning
½ stick butter	2 teaspoons marjoram
4 slices bread, toasted	Salt to taste
1 recipe of cooked corn bread	

To make broth, boil turkey neck and giblets in 4 cups of water until tender. Sauté vegetables in butter. Crumble toast and corn bread into a large bowl, adding sautéed vegetables and seasonings to crumbled bread. Mix and add enough giblet broth to make mixture very moist (if giblet broth is not enough liquid, use chicken broth or chicken bouillon cubes). When mixed, pour into a greased 9 x 13-inch baking pan. Bake in 400 degree oven for 20 minutes or until dressing is heated thoroughly. Serve as a side dish with turkey. Yields 8 to 10 servings.

Vivian Mason, Houston, TX
Variation: Add 2 beaten eggs, 2-4 chopped hard-boiled eggs, and one can sliced water chestnuts.

Irene T. Roberts, Newport, AR

Corn Bread Dressing

1 pound ground meat
1 pound bulk sage sausage
6 chicken bouillon cubes
6 cups hot water
1 stalk celery, chopped
6 onions, chopped
½ cup parsley flakes

¼ teaspoon red pepper
1 pan corn bread, baked
1½ teaspoons poultry
  seasoning
1½ teaspoons black pepper
6 eggs, well beaten

Brown meat and sausage in large heavy pot. Dissolve bouillon in hot water. Add bouillon liquid, celery, onions, parsley and red pepper to meat. Simmer for 30 to 45 minutes. Crumble baked corn bread and add ⅔ of the meat mixture. Add remaining seasonings and eggs. Mix well (should be consistency of thick corn bread batter). Pour into large greased casseroles or baking pan. Bake in 400 degree oven for 30 to 40 minutes. Serves 20 to 24.
Note: Extra meat mixture can be frozen. Serve dressing with giblet gravy.
Melba Simmons, Bunkie, LA

Giblet Gravy

1 turkey neck
1 turkey gizzard
1 turkey liver
3 cups water
½ teaspoon black pepper

½ teaspoon salt
½ teaspoon cayenne pepper
2 teaspoons cornstarch
2 hard-boiled eggs, chopped

Place giblets into a saucepan with water. Boil until giblets are tender. Remove, cool, debone and cut into small pieces. Return to broth. Add seasonings. Reduce heat to a simmer. Add chopped boiled eggs. Mix cornstarch with a small amount of broth or water to form a smooth paste. Add to broth and continue to simmer until broth begins to thicken (gravy consistency).
Note: Serve over corn bread dressing.
Venita Scott, Natchitoches, LA

Oyster Dressing

½ loaf French bread
2 dozen fresh oysters,
reserving liquid
1 onion, chopped
1 bell pepper, chopped
2 stalks celery, chopped

½ teaspoon thyme
¼ teaspoon garlic powder
1 stick butter
1 egg, beaten
Bread crumbs

Soak French bread in oyster water. Over low heat, sauté the vegetables and seasonings in butter until tender, approximately 15 minutes. Add oysters, bread mixture and egg. Mixture should be moist. Pour into a greased casserole and top with bread crumbs and pats of butter. Bake in 350 degree oven for about 20 minutes or until lightly brown. Yields 8 to 10 servings.

Mrs. William Hrapmann, New Orleans, LA

Sage Dressing

½ cup chopped onions
½ cup chopped celery
2 tablespoons chopped parsley
4 tablespoons bacon drippings
3 cups stale bread, toasted
and cubed

1 egg, beaten
Salt and pepper to taste
½ teaspoon nutmeg
2 teaspoons sage
1 teaspoon poultry seasoning
1 cup hot water

Sauté onion, celery and parsley in bacon drippings. Add bread cubes, egg, salt and pepper to taste, nutmeg, sage and poultry seasoning. Pour hot water over mixture. Mix well. Loosely pack into cavity of fowl. Bake in 375 to 400 degree oven until fowl is tender and brown and dressing is cooked.

Note: If seasoned bread crumbs are used, you will not need as much seasoning as recipe has listed.

Chris Williams

South Louisiana Rice Dressing

1 cup chopped onion
1 cup chopped green
  onion tops
1 cup chopped bell pepper
1 clove garlic, minced
½ stick butter
2 pounds ground meat
2 cups chopped chicken
  giblets

1 cup water
1 can cream of mushroom
  soup
1 can cream of chicken soup
5 cups cooked rice
1 envelope dry onion
  soup mix
Salt and pepper to taste

Sauté onions, bell pepper and garlic in butter. Cook ground meat and chicken giblets until tender. Add remaining ingredients. Season to taste. Cook for 20 minutes over medium heat. Remove from heat and cover. Let stand 20 minutes. Yields 24 servings.

Pam Faul, Patterson, LA

Wild Rice Stuffing

1 cup wild rice or ½ brown
  and ½ wild rice
2 cups chicken broth
4 tablespoons butter, divided
1 medium onion, chopped
½ pound mushrooms,
  washed and sliced

1 rib celery, finely chopped
¼ cup chopped bell pepper
2 tablespoons chopped parsley
¼ teaspoon Italian seasoning
¼ teaspoon black pepper
Salt to taste

Cook rice in chicken broth until done (may need to add small amount of water). When done, stir in 2 tablespoons butter with a fork. In large skillet sauté in 2 tablespoons butter, onion, mushrooms, celery and bell pepper. Cook until crispy tender. Add parsley and continue to cook until onion is clear. Fold rice into mixture, add Italian seasoning, pepper and salt.
Note: Stuff into cavity of pheasant, ducks or bird of choice. Serve with currant, fruit or cream sauce.

A Friend of St. Mary's Training School

MARYHILL
Pineville, Louisiana

In the late 1940's, the Knights of Columbus of Louisiana were investigating a state youth program. About this same time, Bishop Greco was developing plans for a diocesan summer camp for children. He realized that such an undertaking, on a large scale, would be very costly and funds were limited. Subsequent discussions with the Knights and his contagious enthusiasm for the project gave birth to the summer camp for children from throughout the state.

The summer of 1951, Maryhill opened to 853 campers and by 1954, attendance had risen above the 3,000 mark. The camp includes many buildings: a chapel, pavilion, cabins, infirmary and dining hall. A lake was built between the camp grounds and the chapel, and it is on this body of water that Bishop Greco built his ship, *Star of the Sea*.

Shortly after the opening of Maryhill Camp, a seminary was established on the grounds. The seminary was in operation for several years, but is now closed and the buildings have been converted into retreat facilities for the diocese.

Meats

Maryhill Chapel
Pineville, Louisiana

Marinated Brisket

5 to 6-pound brisket
Meat tenderizer
Garlic salt
Celery salt

2½ tablespoons Liquid Smoke
¼ cup Worcestershire sauce
1 cup Hickory Smoke Bar-B-Que sauce

Sprinkle brisket with meat tenderizer, garlic salt and celery salt. Combine Liquid Smoke, Worcestershire sauce and Bar-B-Que sauce. Pour over brisket. Marinate in refrigerator for 24 hours. Bake in a covered casserole dish, in marinade, at 250 degrees for 5 to 6 hours. Yields 6 to 8 servings.

Melba Simmons, Bunkie, LA

Grillades (with Grits)

2 to 3 pounds beef tenderloin
   or veal
1 tablespoon vegetable oil
1 tablespoon flour
1 onion, chopped
1 clove garlic, minced
4 sprigs thyme, minced
2 bay leaves

1 green bell pepper, chopped
4 sprigs parsley, chopped
2 medium-sized tomatoes,
   chopped
2 cups dry red wine
Salt and pepper to taste
½ cup or more cooked grits
   or rice, per person

Have beef tenderloin or veal sliced in medallions about ¼-inch thick. Brown meat lightly in oil and remove from skillet. Add flour, onion, garlic, thyme, bay leaves, bell pepper, and parsley to the oil in skillet and brown thoroughly to make a dark roux. Add tomatoes and wine and simmer about 30 minutes. A small amount of water may be added if roux becomes too thick. Add meat; season with salt and pepper and simmer about an hour or until meat is tender. Serve over grits or rice. Serves 6.

Carol C. Morgan, Dallas, TX

New England Boiled Dinner

3 to 4 pounds roast beef
Salt and pepper to taste
1 large onion, quartered
6 cups water

2 turnips, quartered
1 package carrots, halved
1 cabbage, quartered
4 to 5 potatoes, quartered

Salt and pepper meat. In a large covered roaster, place roast, onion and water. Cover and cook for 3 hours. Add turnips, carrots and cabbage and simmer for 2 hours. Add potatoes and continue to cook for 1 hour. Yields 6 to 8 servings.
Note: Ham can be substituted for beef.

Connie Schram, Bellingham, MA

Sour Cream Beef Stroganoff

¼ cup fat or margarine
2 cups chopped onion
1½ pounds lean boneless
   chuck, cut into 1½-inch
   strips
2 tablespoons flour
8-ounce can tomato sauce

1 cup water
2 teaspoons salt
Dash of pepper
½ cup canned, sliced
   mushrooms, drained
¾ cup sour cream

Sauté onions in fat until yellow. Remove onions from pan and reserve. Add beef to pan and slowly brown. When beef is brown, sprinkle with flour and blend. Add tomato sauce, water and seasonings. Cover and simmer for 1 hour, stirring occasionally. Add cooked onions and simmer for ½ hour or until meat is tender. Add mushrooms and stir in sour cream. Cook for 5 minutes longer. Yields 6 servings.
Note: Serve over hot rice.

Delphine Zydzik, Russellville, AR
Husband: James L. Zydzik
Knights of Columbus title: State Deputy

Meat Pies

1 pound ground chuck
1 onion, chopped
1 bell pepper, chopped
  (optional)
2 tablespoons tomato paste
Juice of 1 lemon

8 ounces sour cream
Ground cinnamon to taste
Salt and pepper to taste
2 10-ounce cans flaky biscuits
Oil to fry pies

Brown meat and onion and drain. Add bell pepper, tomato paste, lemon juice, sour cream, cinnamon, salt and pepper and stir well. Place in refrigerator until cold. On a floured board, roll the dough of 2 biscuits to form a 4 to 5-inch circle. Place small portion of filling on each circle of dough. Fold over and crimp edges with fork to seal. Place on tray and freeze pies until ready to fry. Fry in hot oil.

Mrs. Donna Graham, Lyon, MS

Stuffed Cabbage Rolls
(Holishkes)

2 pounds beef chuck, ground
¾ cup cooked rice or kasha
2 eggs
¼ cup grated onion
⅓ cup grated carrot
½ teaspoon salt
20 to 24 large green cabbage
  leaves

½ cup cider vinegar
¼ teaspoon sour salt (citric
  acid crystals)
¾ cup firmly packed dark
  brown sugar
1 8-ounce can tomato sauce

Mix meat with rice, eggs, onion, carrot and salt. With sharp knife carefully slice off the back of the tough rib of each cabbage leaf, keeping surface of leaf in one piece. Pour boiling water over cabbage leaves and let stand until wilted. Drain. Place a ball of meat about the size of a small plum at one side of the leaf. Roll the cabbage tightly around the meat to enclose the filling completely. Place filled rolls in a heavy Dutch oven or deep saucepan. Mix remaining ingredients together and add to saucepan. Cover and simmer for 50 minutes to 1 hour. Add water if necessary to prevent sticking. Makes 8 to 10 servings.

Mrs. Dina Scokin, Dallas, TX

Green Pepper Steak

1 pound chuck or round steak
¼ cup soy sauce
1 clove garlic (minced)
½ teaspoon ground ginger
¼ cup salad oil
1 cup sliced green onions

1 cup green peppers (cut in 1-inch squares)
2 ribs celery (sliced)
1 tablespoon cornstarch
1 cup water
2 tomatoes (cut in wedges)

Cut beef into ⅛-inch strips. Combine soy sauce, garlic and ginger. Add beef; toss and set aside. Heat oil in large frying pan or wok. Add beef and toss over high heat until brown. Cover; lower heat and simmer for 30 to 40 minutes or until tender. Raise heat; add onions, peppers and celery and toss for 10 minutes. Mix cornstarch with water. Add cornstarch mixture to pan. Stir; cook until thickened. Add tomatoes and heat thoroughly. Serve over cooked noodles or rice. Yields 4 servings.

Marguerite Robin, Alexandria, LA

Creamy Green Enchiladas

1 pound lean ground meat
1 teaspoon salt
1 large onion, chopped
8 ounces Cheddar cheese, grated
1 can cream of chicken soup, undiluted
1 small can Pet milk

1 8-ounce jar Cheez Whiz
1 envelope green onion dip
1 4-ounce can chopped green chilies, drained
1 2-ounce jar chopped pimientos, drained
12 corn tortillas

Combine beef, salt and onions in a skillet and cook until onions are tender. Drain drippings and stir in Cheddar cheese. Set aside. Combine soup, milk and Cheez Whiz in double boiler. Place over low heat, stirring until cheese is melted. Add the envelope of onion dip, green chilies and pimientos and blend well. Set aside. Dip tortillas one at a time in hot oil for about 1 to 2 seconds to soften. Spread meat mixture on tortillas and roll tightly. Place the rolled tortillas in a 9 x 13 x 2-inch baking dish and pour cheese sauce over tortillas. Bake at 350 degrees for 30 minutes. Serves 6 to 8.

Gloria Allen, Marshall, TX

135

Chili

2½ pounds ground chuck
2 cups chopped onion
1 green pepper, chopped
2 cloves garlic, crushed
3 tablespoons chili powder
1½ teaspoons dried oregano
1 teaspoon crushed red
 pepper
2 teaspoons cumin
1 teaspoon dried basil

1 tablespoon sugar
2 teaspoons salt
¾ teaspoon pepper
2 1-pound cans whole
 tomatoes, undrained
2 8-ounce cans tomato sauce
1 6-ounce can tomato paste
1 or 2 1-pound cans kidney
 beans, drained

In large pot brown beef. Drain. Add onion, green pepper, garlic, chili powder, oregano, basil, red pepper and cumin. Mix well. Simmer about 5 minutes, stirring occasionally. Stir in sugar, salt, pepper, tomatoes, tomato sauce and paste. Mix well. Break up tomatoes with fork. Cover and simmer slowly for 1 hour. Add beans; simmer covered for 10 minutes. Yields 12 servings.

Mrs. Donna Graham, Lyon, MS

Mexican Casserole

½ pound Velveeta cheese
 (20 slices)
1 package (12) soft tortillas
1½ pounds ground beef
1 medium onion, chopped
1 tablespoon chili powder

Garlic salt to taste
1 can pinto beans
1 can cream of chicken soup
1 can Ro-tel tomatoes with
 green chilies

Preheat oven to 350 degrees. Slice cheese into 20 slices. Butter 10 x 14-inch pan. Line bottom with 6 tortillas. Sprinkle with raw ground beef, onion and seasonings. Pour on pinto beans with juice. Lay cheese slices on top of beans. Cover cheese with remaining 6 tortillas. In bowl, mix together cream of chicken soup and Ro-tel tomatoes. Pour on top of casserole. Cover with foil. Bake 1 hour at 350 degrees. Let stand a few minutes before serving. Yields 8 servings.

Note: 1 can of tomatoes with ½ jalapeño pepper cut up may be substituted for Ro-tel tomatoes with chilies, makes it not quite so hot. This dish freezes well.

Nancye Zwink, Houston, TX

Layered Enchiladas

2 pounds ground sirloin
1 onion, chopped
½ green pepper, chopped
¼ teaspoon coriander
½ teaspoon chopped garlic
10-ounce can chili without
  beans
⅛ teaspoon hot pepper sauce

¼ cup picanté sauce
1 teaspoon Worcestershire
  sauce
1 tablespoon chili powder
½ cup chopped ripe olives
12 to 15 tortillas, quartered
2 cups grated Cheddar cheese

Sauté sirloin, onion and bell pepper together. Drain excess fat from sirloin. Add remaining ingredients except tortillas and cheese.

Sauce:
½ cup melted butter
2 tablespoons flour

1½ cups milk
2 cups sour cream

In a small saucepan combine butter and flour, mixing well. Slowly add milk and cook until thickened and smooth. Cool and then add sour cream. Spread a little of the sauce in the bottom of a 9 x 13-inch baking dish. Place half of the quartered tortillas over the sauce. Follow by layering half of the meat mixture, half of the white sauce and half of the cheese. Repeat layers. Bake in 375 degree oven for 20 minutes. Yields 6 to 8 servings.

Nancy Haynes, Dallas, TX

Chinese Barbequed Spareribs

⅓ cup soy sauce
3 tablespoons vinegar
1 tablespoon sugar
1½ cups beef broth
⅓ cup honey

2 tablespoons sherry
1 teaspoon ginger
2 cloves garlic, minced
2 racks of ribs

Combine ingredients and pour over ribs. Marinate ribs in refrigerator overnight. Place on rack and roast in 350 degree oven for 1½ hours, basting frequently with sauce. Serves 4 to 6.

Mrs. Marti Greenberg, Denton, TX

Classic Lasagna

2 large onions, chopped
2 tablespoons oil or butter
4 pounds ground chuck
Salt and pepper to taste
2 tablespoons dried Italian
  seasoning
3 pods garlic, finely chopped
Tabasco to taste
2 16-ounce cans tomatoes,
  chopped (reserve ½ cup
  juice)

1 6-ounce can tomato paste
4 packages sliced Mozzarella
  cheese
1 large carton small-curd
  cottage cheese
1 3-ounce can Kraft Parmesan
  cheese
1 large package lasagna
  noodles (cook as directed
  on package)

Sauté onions in butter or oil until translucent. Add ground chuck and cook until meat is browned. Season with salt and pepper, Italian seasoning, garlic and Tabasco. Add chopped tomatoes with juice (remembering to reserve ½ cup juice) and tomato paste to meat mixture and blend well. Cook 30 minutes until meat sauce has thickened. In a 17 x 12 x 2-inch pan pour ½ cup juice over bottom of pan. Next place a layer of noodles followed by a layer of meat sauce, 2 packages of sliced cheese and the carton of cottage cheese. Repeat the layering process using first the noodles, followed by the meat sauce, 2 packages of cheese and top with the can of Parmesan cheese. Cover with foil and bake in a 375 degree oven for 45 minutes. Uncover and bake an additional 15 minutes. Serves 12 to 16.

Edgar Allen, Marshall, TX

Meatballs and Spaghetti

Sauce:

1 medium onion, chopped	2 tablespoons sugar
3 cloves chopped garlic	1 teaspoon sweet basil
2 tablespoons olive oil	Salt to taste
1 14½-ounce can of tomatoes	Pepper to taste
chopped	2 cups water
3 cans of tomato sauce	

To make sauce: Sauté onions and garlic in olive oil. When golden brown, add tomatoes and tomato sauce. Stir in sugar, basil, salt, pepper and water. If too thick, add more water. While sauce is cooking, make the meatballs.

Meatballs:

5 crackers (soaked in water	1 clove chopped garlic
and then drained)	1 tablespoon chopped parsley
1½ pounds ground beef	½ cup Parmesan cheese
4 eggs	Salt and pepper to taste

Meatballs: Squeeze all the water out of the crackers. To crackers add ground meat, eggs, garlic, parsley, and cheese; salt and pepper to taste. Roll into meatballs. Place on slightly greased cookie sheet and cook in oven until brown. Then add meatballs to sauce and simmer for at least 4 hours on medium heat.
Note: Serve over spaghetti.

Annie Giordano, Alexandria, LA

Real Italian Meatballs and Spaghetti

Meatballs:

3 pounds ground beef,
  veal or pork
1 cup chopped green onions
1 large jumbo onion,
  chopped
2 cups chopped celery

1 cup chopped bell pepper
5 cloves garlic, finely chopped
4 whole eggs
½ cup chopped parsley
1 cup bread crumbs or
  oatmeal

Sauce:

1 stick butter
1 cup chopped green onions
2 jumbo onions, chopped
1 cup chopped celery
2 cups chopped bell pepper
½ cup chopped parsley
5 cloves garlic, finely chopped
2 tablespoons Italian dry
  seasoning

1 2½-pound can whole Italian
  tomatoes
3 6-ounce cans tomato paste
3 8-ounce cans tomato sauce
5 cups water
1 tablespoon sugar
Salt and pepper to taste

Mix all meatball ingredients together well. Roll into 1½ to 2-inch balls. Sauté in olive oil or cooking oil until brown. Set aside. In a large iron pot, melt butter and sauté next 7 ingredients for approximately 30 minutes. Then add whole tomatoes. Cook slowly 1 hour. Add tomato paste and tomato sauce, 5 cups water and sugar. Salt and pepper to taste. Let simmer on low for 2 hours. Then, add meatballs and let simmer another 45 minutes to 1 hour on low. Serve over spaghetti, with grated Romano cheese.

Note: This recipe was passed to Mrs. Baham by her grandmother, the late Mrs. Amy Spellman.

Charlotte S. Baham, New Orleans, LA

Stuffed Peppers

1 large eggplant, cooked
1 cup cooked rice
4 large bell peppers
1 pound ground meat
1 medium onion, chopped

Tops of bell peppers, chopped
1½ teaspoons salt
¾ teaspoon pepper
Italian bread crumbs

Cook eggplant and chop into small cubes. Cook rice. Set eggplant and rice aside. Wash peppers, remove tops and seeds. Boil peppers for 5 minutes. Brown meat with onions and chopped pepper tops. Drain off excess fat. Mix chopped eggplant, seasonings and rice into meat mixture. Stuff boiled peppers with mixture. Top with Italian bread crumbs. Place into a square cake pan. Bake in 350 degree oven for 30 to 45 minutes. Yields 4 servings.
Note: After stuffing peppers, they may be individually wrapped in foil and frozen.

Lynn Compton, Alexandria, LA

Pizza Casserole

3 cups twist macaroni
1½ pounds hamburger meat
1 onion, chopped
Salt and pepper to taste
1 6-ounce can tomato paste
1 small can pizza sauce
1 8-ounce can tomato sauce

½ teaspoon sugar
Dash of garlic salt
Dash of onion salt
Dash of oregano
12 ounces Mozzarella cheese, grated

Cook macaroni in unsalted water as directed on package. Brown hamburger meat and onion. Salt and pepper to taste. Combine macaroni with cooked meat-onion mixture. Add tomato paste, pizza sauce, tomato sauce and sugar. Add other seasonings. Place ½ of mixture in a 2-quart casserole. Add ½ of cheese. Add remaining meat mixture. Top with remaining cheese. Bake in 350 degree oven for 45 minutes. Yields 6 servings.

Alta M. Wineland, Boyce, LA

Sicilian Supper

1 pound ground beef	1 8-ounce package cream
½ cup chopped onion	cheese
1 6-ounce can tomato paste	½ cup grated Parmesan
¾ cup water	cheese
1½ teaspoons salt	½ teaspoon garlic salt
¼ teaspoon pepper	½ cup chopped green pepper
¾ cup milk	2 cups egg noodles, cooked

Brown meat and onion until onion is tender. Add tomato paste, water, salt and pepper. Simmer five minutes. Warm milk and blend in cream cheese until smooth. Stir in ¼ cup Parmesan cheese, garlic salt, green pepper and noodles. In a casserole dish alternate layers of noodle mixture and meat sauce. Bake in 350 degree oven for 20 minutes. Sprinkle remaining Parmesan cheese over top of dish after baking. Yields 6 servings.

Carolyn Puckett, Pineville, LA

Grilled Baby Rack of Lamb

1 baby rack of lamb, trimmed	1 teaspoon freshly ground
(about 6 chops)	pepper
Salt to taste	1 teaspoon tarragon leaves
2 pods garlic	1 teaspoon rosemary

Rub the entire rack with salt. Place a thin slice of garlic between each rib. Season both sides with the pepper, tarragon and rosemary. Place on the grill and cook 8 to 10 minutes on each side. The meat should be pink and juicy. Slice chops and serve immediately. Yields 2 servings.

Ian and Carolyn Zwicker, San Francisco, CA

Gingered Ham Slices

1 center cut ham, fully cooked
½ cup ginger ale
½ cup orange juice
¼ cup brown sugar
1 tablespoon salad oil

1½ teaspoons wine vinegar
1 teaspoon dry mustard
¼ teaspoon ground ginger
⅛ teaspoon ground cloves

Remove excess fat from sides of cooked ham, slicing into 1 to 1¼-inch slices. Place ham in shallow dish. Combine remaining ingredients and pour over ham. Refrigerate overnight with occasional basting. Remove ham from marinade. Grill each side 15 minutes, basting occasionally. Serve with marinade spooned over ham slices. Yields 5 to 6 servings.

Mrs. Jean Sain Wilkirson, Jackson, MS

Pork Chop Supper

4 pork chops, 1-inch thick
Salt and pepper to taste
¼ cup oil
1 can cream of mushroom
  soup
½ cup sour cream

¼ cup water
4 cups thinly sliced Irish
  potatoes
4 carrots, thinly sliced
  diagonally

Salt and pepper pork chops to taste. Brown on both sides in oil. Blend together mushroom soup, sour cream and water. Heat over medium heat until well blended. In a 2-quart casserole, well-greased, alternate layers of sliced potatoes, carrots, salt, pepper and soup mixture. Top with pork chops; cover and bake at 350 degrees for 1½ hours or until pork chops and potatoes are done.

Ola Williams, Farmerville, LA

Pork Chop Surprise

6 thin pork chops	1 bell pepper, chopped
Salt and pepper to taste	8 ounces French dressing
1 small onion, chopped	½ cup water

Preheat oven to 350 degrees. Grease a 9 x 13-inch casserole dish. Place pork chops on bottom of dish. Salt and pepper. Cover with onion and bell pepper. Pour French dressing over the ingredients. Add water. Cover with casserole lid or foil and bake for 45 minutes. Uncover and cook for 10 minutes. Yields 4 to 6 servings.

Elvena Spears, Calhoun, LA

Pork Chops

4 to 5 pork chops, trimmed	1 cup ketchup
1 medium onion	¼ cup Worcestershire sauce
1 large apple	3 tablespoons cider vinegar
6 tablespoons brown sugar	

Preheat oven to 350 degrees. Trim pork chops. Chop onion and apple and place in bottom of baking dish. Lay pork chops on top. Mix remaining ingredients and pour over chops. Cover and bake 1½ hours. Yields 4 servings.

Nancye Zwink, Houston, TX

Pork Tenderloin Casserole

1 medium pork tenderloin	1 cup cream of mushroom
1 cup rice, cooked and	soup
seasoned to taste	½ cup water

Place tenderloin in baking pan and bake until done. Place rice around tenderloin. Mix soup and water in bowl, pour over top of meat and rice. Bake at 325 to 350 degrees until most of the moisture has absorbed into the rice.

Mary Elsie, Houston, MO

Marinated Pork Strips

2 pounds pork tenderloins
1½ cups soy sauce
3 tablespoons sugar
2 tablespoons minced onion

2 cloves garlic, minced
2 teaspoons ground ginger
¼ teaspoon sesame oil
2 tablespoons oil

Trim the fat from the tenderloins. Combine the remaining ingredients, except the oil, in a bowl. Marinate the pork, in the mixture, for three hours in the refrigerator, turning and basting frequently. Drain and reserve the marinade. Preheat oven to moderate (375 degrees) temperature. Transfer the pork to an oiled roasting pan and roast until tender, about forty-five minutes. Simmer the marinade for 10 minutes. Cut the pork into thin slices. Serve with Cantonese Fried Rice and the marinade sauce.
Note: Can also be used as an appetizer.

Alicia Clemente, Alexandria, LA

Pork Chops Madrid

4 pork chops
¼ teaspoon seasoned salt
½ cup chopped green pepper
1 can whole tomatoes,
   undrained
1 can whole kernel corn,
   undrained

½ cup long grain rice,
   uncooked
½ cup water
1 teaspoon Louisiana Red Hot
   sauce
1 can French fried onions

Brown pork chops on both sides. Sprinkle with seasoned salt and set aside. In same skillet combine remaining ingredients except onions and bring to boil. Remove from heat; stir in ½ cup of the onions. Place mixture in baking dish; arrange pork chops on top. Bake in 350 degree oven for 35 minutes, covered. Uncover and top with remaining onions. Bake 10 minutes longer. Yields 4 servings.

Helen Owen, West Monroe, LA

Grilled Pork Tenderloins

2 pork tenderloins
1½ cups Wishbone Italian
  dressing
½ cup oil
½ cup red wine
¼ cup garlic wine vinegar
2 cloves garlic, crushed

2 tablespoons Worcestershire
2 tablespoons soy sauce
Salt to taste (very light)
Pepper, red and black, to taste
Lemon pepper to taste
1 teaspoon celery salt
1 teaspoon garlic powder

Mix all ingredients except tenderloins in foil pan. Place tenderloins in marinade. Marinate at least eight hours, turning often. Pour all of marinade off except 1 cup and reserve. Place foil pan with tenderloins and marinade on grill and cook about 45 minutes or until done, turning often and brushing with reserved marinade. Slice ½-inch thick and serve. Yields 4 servings.

Mrs. L. J. Melder, Natchitoches, LA

Jambalaya

½ pound smoked sausage
½ pound hot sausage
1 onion, chopped
1 bell pepper, chopped
3 or 4 ribs celery, chopped
1 bunch scallions, chopped

⅓ cup parsley flakes
1 8-ounce can tomato sauce
1 cup water
1 cup uncooked rice
Salt and pepper to taste

Slice and fry sausages for 15 minutes. Add onion, bell pepper, celery, scallions and parsley to sausages. Cook for 15 minutes. Add tomato sauce and water. Bring to a boil and cook for 15 minutes. Add rice and season to taste. Simmer for 45 minutes, stirring occasionally. Yields 6 to 8 servings.

Charlotte Baham, New Orleans, LA

Sausage Casserole

1 pound pork sausage
4 green onions, chopped
2 celery ribs, chopped
1 small green pepper, chopped

1 cup uncooked rice
1 envelope chicken noodle
  soup
2 cups boiling water

Preheat oven to 350 degrees. Fry sausage until crispy; drain meat and save drippings. Place meat in casserole dish. Add onions, celery and pepper to meat drippings and cook until glazed. Drain and add to casserole dish. Add rice, chicken noodle soup and 2 cups boiling water. Cover and bake for 45 to 60 minutes. Yields 4 to 6 servings.

Susan Mayeaux, New Orleans, LA

Braised Veal Shanks

6 veal shanks, 1-inch thick,
  bone in
Flour for dredging veal
Salt and pepper to taste
3 tablespoons oil or bacon
  drippings
2 15-ounce cans beef broth

1 15-ounce can tomatoes
1 tablespoon Worcestershire
2 cloves garlic, minced
Italian seasoning to taste
4 medium carrots, sliced
4 medium zucchini squash,
  sliced

Flour, salt and pepper shanks. Heat oil in large skillet. Brown shanks and remove. Make brown gravy with pan drippings, flour and oil, if necessary, adding beef broth. Return shanks to liquid. Add tomatoes, Worcestershire sauce, garlic, Italian seasoning and adjust salt and pepper. Cook meat on low heat covered for 2½ hours or until meat is fork tender and is falling from bone. Add carrots and zucchini about 1 hour before finished. Serve over rice with pan gravy. Yields 4 servings.

Gerard F. Thomas, Natchitoches, LA

Veal Parmesan

2 pounds veal cutlets
1 egg, slightly beaten
Salt to taste
Pepper to taste
½ cup Parmesan cheese
1 cup Progresso Bread
  Crumbs Italian style

Olive oil
1 clove garlic, chopped
2 cups tomato sauce
Mozzarella cheese slices

Preheat oven to 350 degrees. Slice cutlets thin. Dip in beaten egg, salt and pepper. Add small amount of Parmesan cheese to bread crumbs, dip cutlets in bread crumb mixture. Cover the bottom of a baking dish with olive oil and chopped garlic. Place the veal cutlets on top. Bake and turn over when brown. Pour tomato sauce over the meat and top with Mozzarella cheese slices. Add remainder of Parmesan cheese. Bake for about 15 more minutes or until cheese melts. Yields 4 to 6 servings.

Annie Giordano, Alexandria, LA

Veal Scaloppine

2 tablespoons butter
1 pound fresh mushrooms,
  sliced
½ small onion, minced
2 slices prosciutto, sliced
  paper thin and chopped

12 thinly sliced medallions of
  veal, trimmed
Salt and pepper to taste
½ cup cream sherry
½ cup dry vermouth

Melt 1 tablespoon butter in skillet and sauté mushrooms, onions and prosciutto. Set aside. In a separate skillet melt 1 tablespoon butter and brown veal medallions lightly. Add salt and pepper and sherry and cook 2 minutes. Add mushroom mixture to veal, then add vermouth. Simmer for 10 minutes and serve immediately. Serves 4.

Elena Roberts, Dunedin, FL

Veal Scaloppine al Limone

1½ pounds veal scallops
Salt
Freshly ground pepper
Flour
2 tablespoons butter
3 tablespoons oil

½ cup beef stock, fresh or
    canned
¼ cup dry white wine
6 paper-thin lemon slices
2 teaspoons lemon juice
2 tablespoons soft butter

Season the veal scallops with salt and pepper, then dip them in flour and shake off the excess. In a large, heavy skillet, melt 2 tablespoons of butter with the 3 tablespoons of oil over moderate heat. When the foam subsides, add the veal, 4 or 5 scallops at a time, and sauté them for about 2 minutes on each side, or until they are golden brown. With tongs, transfer the veal scallops to a plate. Now pour off almost all the fat from the skillet, leaving a thin film on the bottom. Add ¼ cup beef stock and ¼ cup white wine and boil it briskly for 1 or 2 minutes, stirring constantly and scraping in any browned bits clinging to the bottom and sides of the pan. Return the veal to the skillet and arrange the lemon slices on top. Cover the skillet and simmer over low heat for 10 or 15 minutes, or until the veal is tender when pierced with the tip of a sharp knife. To serve, transfer the veal scallops to a heated platter and surround with the lemon slices. Add the ¼ cup remaining beef stock to the juices in the skillet and boil briskly until the stock is reduced to a syrupy glaze. Add the lemon juice and cook, stirring constantly for 1 minute. Remove the pan from the heat, swirl in 2 tablespoons of soft butter and pour the sauce over the scallops. Yields 4 servings.

Cindy Ward, Dallas, TX

Veal Marsala

1½ pounds of thin veal
    scallops
Salt and pepper to taste
Flour to coat veal

4 tablespoons butter
½ cup Marsala wine
Chopped parsley, for garnish
Lemon slices, for garnish

Flatten thin slices of veal and cut into serving portions. Season the veal and coat with flour. Brown quickly in hot butter, turn and repeat on the other side. Add Marsala wine and simmer for 4 minutes. Serve with parsley and lemon slices. Yields 4 servings.

Bunny Laskowski, Houston, TX

149

THE ORIGINAL SAINT MARY'S TRAINING SCHOOL
FOR RETARDED CHILDREN
Clarks, Louisiana

This two story frame building was the old White Hotel and had been built to serve the sawmill town of Clarks, Louisiana. It had thirty-eight rooms, a large commissary, spacious warehouse, and several smaller buildings. In February, 1954, Bishop Greco purchased the property and buildings in order to establish a school for retarded children. On September 15, 1954, the Feast of Our Lady of Sorrows, Saint Mary's Training School for Retarded Children was opened with seven children and four Sisters. Within three years the number of children had increased to approximately three hundred from thirty-four states. The buildings now served as offices, dormitories, kitchen, dining hall and convent. The school remained at Clarks for more than twenty years, and then was moved to Alexandria, Louisiana.

Vegetables and Rice

The Original
St. Mary's Training School
Clarks, Louisiana

Artichoke Casserole

2 cans artichoke hearts,
  reserve liquid
2 cups Progresso Bread
  Crumbs Italian Style
1 cup oil

¼ cup Parmesan cheese
Salt to taste
Pepper to taste
2 tablespoons lemon juice
¼ teaspoon garlic powder

Quarter the artichoke hearts and combine ingredients as listed in an 8 or 9-inch casserole dish. Moisten with liquid from can of artichoke hearts. Bake in 350 degree oven for 15 minutes. Yields 6 to 8 servings.

Mrs. William Hrapmann, New Orleans, LA

Stuffed Artichokes

6 fresh artichokes
6 ounces Progresso Bread
  Crumbs Italian Style
3 ounces grated Romano
  cheese
1 teaspoon oregano
1 teaspoon sweet basil
1 teaspoon garlic powder

1 teaspoon salt
1 teaspoon pepper
¼ cup water
5 tablespoons olive oil
8 cups water
½ cup dry vermouth
⅛ cup olive oil

Wash and trim artichokes. Prepare stuffing mixture by mixing bread crumbs, cheese, spices, salt and pepper in a large bowl. Add ¼ cup water and olive oil and blend into a paste. Place this stuffing mixture inside each leaf and center of artichoke. Tie artichoke with a string to prevent separating. Place artichokes upright in a large dutch oven that contains 8 cups water, ½ cup dry vermouth and ⅛ cup olive oil. Cover with waxed paper and the dutch oven lid. Steam over low heat for approximately 2 hours, adding more water if needed. Yields 6 servings.

Jerry Acerrano, Richmond, TX

Asparagus Casserole

2 cans cut asparagus
1 can tiny green peas
1 can water chestnuts, sliced
1 large can mushrooms
  (stems and pieces)
1 can cream of mushroom
  soup

2 cups grated Cheddar cheese
Red pepper to taste
Tabasco to taste
Garlic salt to taste
4 slices bread cut into 3 strips
1 stick margarine

Drain asparagus, peas, water chestnuts and mushrooms. Butter casserole dish and layer vegetables. Combine soup, mushrooms and seasonings. Pour over vegetables. Top with cheese. Dip bread in melted margarine. Lay on top. Bake at 350 degrees uncovered until lightly browned, about 30 minutes. Yields 8 servings.

Rosemary Baker, Natchitoches, LA

Baked Beans

1 pound hamburger meat
1 small onion
1 small bell pepper
Salt and pepper to taste
½ cup brown sugar
1 teaspoon mustard

2 tablespoons Worcestershire
  sauce
1 cup barbecue sauce
2 medium cans pork and
  beans

Brown meat and drain. Add onion and bell pepper and simmer. Add salt and pepper to taste. Add sugar, mustard, Worcestershire sauce and barbecue sauce. Let simmer for 20 minutes. Add pork and beans and continue to simmer until ready to serve. Serves 10.

Elvena Spears, Downsville, LA

Delicious Baked Beans

1 can B & M baked beans
1 can red kidney beans
1 can butter beans
½ pound bacon chunks

½ cup ketchup
¼ cup brown sugar or
   molasses

Mix all of the above ingredients. Place in a large casserole dish. Bake in 350 degree oven for 30 minutes.

Nancy Donlin, North Haven, CT

Husband: William Patrick Donlin
Knights of Columbus title: Supreme Advocate

Baked Lima Beans

1 package dried lima beans
½ pound salt pork or bacon
½ cup brown sugar

3 tablespoons molasses
Salt to taste
Pepper to taste

Soak lima beans overnight. Drain beans and boil in fresh water with salt pork or bacon until tender and liquid is reduced. Stir in brown sugar and molasses. Pour into baking dish and bake at 350 degrees until bubbly, about 30 minutes. Yields 8 to 10 servings.

Madeline V. Murphy, Hamden, CT

Husband: Howard E. Murphy
Knights of Columbus title: Former Supreme Secretary and
                              Supreme Director

Dutch Green Beans

12 slices bacon
1 large onion, chopped
½ cup sugar
½ cup vinegar

¼ cup mustard
4 cans whole green beans,
   drained

Fry bacon. Remove from pan, cool, crumble and reserve. Sauté onions in bacon drippings, then add sugar, vinegar, mustard and beans. Stir. Cover and cook on low heat for 2 hours. Top with crumbled bacon. Yields 8 to 10 servings.

Carolyn Stanley, Ruston, LA

Green Bean Casserole

2 packages frozen or
  2 17-ounce cans
  green beans
¼ cup chopped onions
1 stick margarine or butter

1 10-ounce package cream
  cheese
1 can cream of mushroom
  soup
1 roll Ritz crackers, crushed

Cook green beans until tender and drain. Meanwhile, sauté onions in butter until tender. Stir the cream cheese into the warm beans until melted. Stir in soup. Remove onions from butter with slotted spoon and add to bean mixture. Combine the cracker crumbs with the butter. Pour the bean mixture into a greased casserole dish and top with the cracker crumb and butter mixture. Bake at 350 degrees about 30 minutes.

Sandy Thompson, Alton, IL

Layered Bean and Artichoke Heart Casserole

3 cans French style string beans, reserving 1 can juice
2 cans artichoke hearts, drained
1 cup grated Parmesan cheese
1 cup seasoned bread crumbs
¼ to ⅓ cup olive oil

Mash artichoke hearts. Into a 9 x 13-inch pan, layer in order given, ½ of the string beans, artichokes, cheese and bread crumbs. Then place other ½ of beans, artichokes, cheese and top with bread crumbs. Gently pour 1 can of bean juice over mixture. Sprinkle olive oil on top of mixture. Bake in 375 degree oven for 45 minutes. Serves 12.

Judy Bouquet, River Ridge, LA

Chinese Beets

3 cans or 6 cups cooked beets
1 cup sugar
1 cup vinegar
3 tablespoons ketchup
1 teaspoon vanilla
Dash of salt
24 whole cloves
2 tablespoons cornstarch
3 tablespoons cooking oil
1½ cups beet juice

Drain beets and reserve 1½ cups juice. If beets are whole, slice them. Mix all ingredients in a saucepan; add beets. Cook for 3 minutes, or until thickened, over medium heat. Let cool. Refrigerate until serving time.

Mrs. Mallie McLaughlin, Nashville, AR

Broccoli Chestnut Casserole

1 16-ounce package frozen
  broccoli
1 medium onion, chopped
¾ cup chopped celery
1 stick margarine
8 ounces American cheese,
  grated

½ cup canned mushrooms,
  chopped
1 can mushroom soup
1 cup bread crumbs
1 8-ounce package water
  chestnuts, drained and
  sliced

Cook broccoli until tender, approximately 3 to 4 minutes. Drain. Sauté onions and celery in margarine until limp. Add cheese, mushrooms, soup and ⅓ of bread crumbs to sautéed vegetables. Place broccoli in bottom of a greased 9 x 13-inch casserole dish. Sprinkle water chestnuts over broccoli and pour cheese mixture over chestnuts. Top with remaining bread crumbs. Bake in 350 degree oven for 30 minutes. Yields 6 to 8 servings.
Note: Garlic cheese roll or other processed cheese can be substituted.

Bill Hollis, Farmerville, LA

Broccoli Cheese Casserole

2 boxes frozen broccoli
1 medium onion, chopped
½ cup chopped celery
½ cup butter
1 small can evaporated milk

1 8-ounce jar Cheez Whiz
1 can cream of mushroom
  soup
1½ cups cooked rice
1 can fried onion rings

Cook broccoli for 5 minutes. Place in colander and drain. Sauté onion and celery in butter. Mix all ingredients except onion rings. Place in a 2-quart, lightly buttered, casserole dish. Bake in 350 degree oven for 35 to 40 minutes. Then remove from oven. Spread fried onions on the top. Return to oven and bake for 5 minutes or until top has browned.

Mrs. Ursula Jeansonne, Cottonport, LA

Cabbage Casserole I

1 cup rice (uncooked)
3 tablespoons cooking oil
2 pounds ground beef
1 or 2 large onions,
  chopped
3 cloves garlic, minced
1 large bell pepper,
  chopped
1 can mushroom steak sauce

1 can Ro-tel tomatoes,
  chopped
½ cup water
1 large head of cabbage,
  grated
1 can Swiss steak sauce
½ pound yellow cheese,
  grated

On top of stove in a medium skillet, mix rice and cooking oil and brown. Place browned rice in a 2-quart casserole. Brown beef, onions, garlic and bell pepper. Pour off excess oil from browned meat. Add mushroom sauce, Ro-tel tomatoes and water. Cook for 15 to 20 minutes. Pour over rice. Top with cabbage, Swiss steak sauce and cheese. Bake in 350 degree oven for 1 hour. Yields 4 to 6 servings.

Mrs. Frank Prioux, New Iberia, LA

Cabbage Casserole II

1 medium cabbage
1 onion, chopped
¼ cup chopped green onion
2 cloves garlic, minced
1 stick margarine
1 can cream of mushroom
  soup

½ pound Velveeta cheese, cut
  in chunks
Bread crumbs
2 teaspoons seasoned salt

Chop cabbage and boil with small amount of water. Set aside. Sauté onions and garlic in margarine. Add soup and cheese. Heat until cheese is melted. Add drained cabbage and ½ cup bread crumbs. Place in a 9 x 9-inch casserole. Sprinkle bread crumbs on top. Bake in 350 degree oven for 30 minutes. Yields 6 to 8 servings.

Marguerite Robin, Alexandria, LA

Corn Casserole I

¼ cup butter
½ cup flour
¼ cup sugar
2 eggs, beaten
1 small bell pepper, chopped
6 slices bacon, fried

¼ cup chopped pimiento
½ cup grated cheese
Pepper to taste
1 can whole kernel corn, drained
1 can cream style corn

Preheat oven to 350 degrees. Grease bottom of 3-quart casserole dish. In another pan melt butter, slowly stir in flour, sugar and eggs. Add bell pepper, bacon, pimiento, cheese, and pepper to taste. Mix with corn and pour into casserole dish. Bake for 40 to 45 minutes. Yields 6 to 8 servings.

Elvena Spears, Downsville, LA

Corn Casserole II

1 can whole kernel corn
1 can creamed corn
1 8½-ounce box corn muffin
  mix

1 cup melted margarine
1 tablespoon sugar
2 eggs, well beaten
1 cup sour cream

Mix all of the ingredients and pour into a greased casserole pan. Bake for 45 minutes at 350 degrees.

Idabel Swafford, Farmerville, LA

Corn Pudding

3 eggs
1 cup milk
1 14.75-ounce can
  cream-style corn

1 tablespoon sugar
2 tablespoons flour
1 teaspoon salt
2 tablespoons melted butter

Beat eggs and milk together and stir in corn. In a separate bowl combine sugar, flour and salt. Add this mixture to the corn mixture. Stir in the melted butter. Pour into a casserole dish and bake at 350 degrees for 45 minutes to one hour. Serves 4.

Nancy H. Sawyer, Memphis,TN

159

Corn and Bean Casserole

2 cans whole kernel corn,
    drained
1 can French style green
    beans, drained
½ cup chopped onion
¼ cup chopped bell pepper
½ cup chopped celery

1 can cream of celery soup
½ cup sour cream
½ cup grated sharp cheese
½ stick margarine
½ box cheese crackers,
    crushed
Slivered almonds

Combine all vegetables with soup, sour cream and cheese in a greased baking dish. Melt margarine in skillet and add crushed crackers and almonds to coat them. Put cracker mixture on top of vegetables. Bake in a 350 degree oven for 45 minutes. Serves 8 to 10.

Mrs. Joe Pierson, Natchitoches, LA

Southwestern Succotash

¼ pound fresh okra or 1
    10-ounce package
    frozen okra
1 cup zucchini slices
½ cup fresh onion rings
1 tablespoon margarine

1 10-ounce can whole kernel
    corn, drained
1 cup chopped fresh tomatoes
½ pound Kraft Jalapeño
    Pepper Cheese Spread,
    cubed

Sauté okra, zucchini and onion in margarine. Stir in corn and tomatoes. Bring to a boil. Cover, simmer for 10 minutes. Add processed cheese spread. Heat until cheese spread is melted, stirring occasionally. Yields 6 to 8 servings.

Neal and Janis Blackstone, Ennis, TX

Maque Choux
(Mock Shoe)

3 cups fresh corn and milk
6 slices bacon
1 tablespoon vegetable oil
1 large onion, chopped
1 bell pepper, chopped
1 clove garlic, minced
5 tomatoes, peeled and
   chopped

½ cup tomato juice
½ teaspoon salt
½ teaspoon pepper
½ teaspoon Tabasco
3 yellow squash, sliced

To make corn milk, cut corn off cob and scrape cob with knife. In a large, heavy skillet fry bacon until crisp. Drain bacon on paper towel and crumble. Reserve bacon for later use. Pour off all but 3 tablespoons of bacon fat. To this add 1 tablespoon vegetable oil. Sauté onion, bell pepper and garlic in bacon fat. Cook until onion is golden. Do not brown. Add peeled and chopped tomatoes, tomato juice, salt, pepper and Tabasco. Bring to a boil, reduce heat to low and simmer, partially covered, for 30 minutes. Add corn and its milk and a little water, if necessary. Cook for 15 minutes. Add squash and cook 12 to 15 minutes, or until squash is tender. Stir in bacon. Yields 6 to 8 servings.
Note: To make this a main dish, add cooked, chopped chicken or ham to vegetables the last 10 minutes of cooking time.

Venita Scott, Natchitoches, LA

Eggplant Patties

2 medium eggplants
¼ cup chopped bell pepper
¼ cup chopped celery
½ cup chopped onion

1 tablespoon oil
¼ cup flour
½ cup seasoned bread crumbs
Oil for frying

Peel, cube and boil the eggplant in salted water. Drain and set aside. Sauté the bell pepper, celery and onion in 1 tablespoon oil until tender. Add the sautéed vegetables to the eggplant. Mix in ¼ cup flour, and if too soft to form patties, add more flour. Form patties, flatten and roll in seasoned bread crumbs. Deep fry in oil until light brown. Serve hot. Yields 12 patties.

Mattie Louviere, Welsh, LA

Eggplant Soufflé

1 medium eggplant
2 tablespoons butter
1 cup milk
2 tablespoons flour
1 cup grated cheese
1 egg, separated

1 tablespoon grated onion
1 slice bread, toasted and
  crumbled
2 tablespoons ketchup
Salt and pepper to taste
Dash of Tabasco

Peel and cube eggplant. Place in saucepan with unsalted water and boil until tender. Drain. Make a white sauce with butter, milk and flour and cook until thickened. Add eggplant, grated cheese, beaten egg yolk, onion, bread crumbs, ketchup and season to taste. Add all of this to white sauce and mix. Beat egg white until stiff peaks form. Fold into eggplant mixture. Pour into a greased soufflé dish or casserole. Bake in 450 degree oven for 30 minutes or until firm. Serve immediately. Serves 4 to 6.
Note: Even if eggplant is not your favorite vegetable, you will love this dish.
Mrs. John Lamm, Jr., Morse, LA

Eggplant Supreme

1 large eggplant, peeled and
  chopped
1 large onion, chopped
1 small bell pepper, chopped
½ stick butter
2 teaspoons Worcestershire
  sauce

Dash of Tabasco
1 cup grated cheese
1 cup ripe olives, chopped
Salt to taste
½ cup bread crumbs

Peel and chop the eggplant. Steam cook until eggplant is tender. Drain and reserve. Sauté onions and bell pepper in butter. Add eggplant, Worcestershire, Tabasco, cheese and olives. Salt to taste. Pour into a casserole dish and top with bread crumbs. Bake in 375 degree oven for 30 minutes. Yields 6 servings.
Santina Brocato, Alexandria, LA

Mushroom Casserole

1 pound fresh mushrooms
2 tablespoons butter
9 slices buttered, toasted
   white bread
½ cup chopped onions
½ cup chopped bell pepper
½ cup chopped celery
¾ teaspoon salt

¼ teaspoon pepper
½ cup mayonnaise
2 large eggs
½ cup milk
1 10½-ounce can cream of
   mushroom soup
1½ cups grated mild Cheddar
   cheese

Wash and slice mushrooms. Sauté in butter for 3 minutes, set aside. Butter the bread and cut each slice into 9 squares. Place 3 slices (27 pieces) of bread in bottom of an ungreased casserole dish, saving the other bread for layering. Mix the onions, celery, bell pepper, salt, pepper, mayonnaise and cooked mushrooms together. Pour over the bread in the casserole dish. Layer 3 slices (27 pieces) of bread over mushroom mixture. Mix eggs and milk and pour over bread. Layer 3 slices (27 pieces) of bread over the egg mixture. Spread the undiluted soup over top of bread. Bake uncovered in 325 degree oven for 50 minutes. Remove and top with grated cheese. Return to oven and bake 10 minutes more. Yields 6 to 10 servings.

Note: Can be prepared 24 hours ahead of serving by omitting soup and cheese until time to bake.

Emma Maestas, Bernalillo, NM

Husband: Paul G. Maestas
Knights of Columbus title: State Deputy

Quick and Easy Hominy Casserole

2 cans golden yellow hominy
1 12-ounce carton sour cream

1 8-ounce jar jalapeño or
   picanté Cheez Whiz

Mix hominy, sour cream and Cheez Whiz. Heat in casserole dish in 350 degree oven until bubbly and lightly browned on top. Serves 6.

Note: So good! Ideal for covered-dish affairs.

Mathilde Bradford, Alexandria, LA

Cheese Grits

3 cups boiling water
1 cup grits
1 teaspoon salt
1 6-ounce roll garlic cheese,
    chopped

1 stick butter, chopped
3 eggs, beaten
¾ cup milk
¼ cup cream

Cook grits in boiling water with salt, until done. Then add cheese and butter and stir until cheese has melted. Blend eggs, milk and cream together and add to grits, mixing well. Pour into a greased 3-quart long casserole dish and bake in 350 degree oven for 45 minutes. Do not overcook as it will finish cooking and become firm as it cools. Cut into squares and serve hot. Yields 12 to 15 servings.

Gloria Evans, Clarksdale, MS

Postead

1 pound thin spaghetti
9 large eggs

3 cups grated Romano cheese
Pepper to taste

Break spaghetti into 4-inch pieces. Boil, but do not fully cook. (Spaghetti will finish cooking in egg mixture.) Beat eggs and mix cheese and pepper. Combine with spaghetti. Place in a buttered 9 x 13-inch pan. Cover and place in 350 degree oven and cook for 1 hour or until done. Serves 4 to 6.

Isabelle Desiderio, Plymouth, PA

Husband: Basil A. Desiderio
Knights of Columbus title: Supreme Director

Hash Brown Potato Surprise

1 32-ounce package frozen
  hash browns
1 stick margarine, melted
1 pint sour cream
Salt and pepper to taste
1 can cream of mushroom
  soup

1 bunch green onions,
  chopped (including tops)
2 8-ounce packages Cheddar
  cheese, grated

Mix all ingredients with the exception of 1 package of cheese. Pour into 9 x 13-inch baking dish and cover with foil. Bake in 350 degree oven for 1 hour. Remove foil and top with remaining cheese and continue to cook for 30 minutes. Yields 10 to 12 servings.

Gloria Allen, Marshall, TX

Potato Fans

8 small Irish potatoes,
  peeled
2 sticks real butter

2 teaspoons fresh parsley,
  chopped
1 to 2 teaspoons paprika

Slice the potatoes but make sure they are not sliced all the way through. Hold a wooden spoon handle next to the potato and this will keep the knife from slipping. Put potatoes in cold water and refrigerate for three hours. This causes the potatoes to "fan out". Place drained potatoes in a baking dish and top with 1 stick of melted butter and sprinkle with fresh parsley. Bake one hour in 375 degree oven. Pour on an additional stick of melted butter and sprinkle with paprika. Bake an additional ½ hour. Baste with the melted butter occasionally during the baking process. Serves 8.

Ann and Frank Gill, Dallas, TX

Roasted Potato Fans

6 medium potatoes, peeled	**¼ teaspoon basil**
6 tablespoons butter	**¼ teaspoon marjoram**
½ teaspoon salt	**⅛ teaspoon pepper**

Cut potatoes into ¼-inch slices, cutting only ¾ of the way though the potato. Preheat oven to 400 degrees. Place butter in baking dish and place in oven to melt. Arrange potatoes cut-side up in baking dish. Brush with melted butter. Sprinkle with seasonings. Bake for one hour or until slices are fanned out and golden brown. Brush occasionally with butter in baking dish during cooking time.

Mrs. Medard Yutrzenka, Argyle, MN

Husband: Medard Yutrzenka
Knights of Columbus title: Supreme Director Emeritus

Potato Pancakes
(Kartoffel Latkes)

4 potatoes	**⅓ cup all-purpose flour**
1 tablespoon grated onion	**¾ teaspoon salt**
1 large egg	**Fat or oil**

Peel potatoes and grate very finely; there should be about 3 cups. Squeeze out some of the moisture in the grated potatoes. Add onion, egg, flour and salt. Beat until well blended. Put ½ inch of fat in the skillet. Drop batter by heaping tablespoonfuls into hot fat and fry until crisp and brown on both sides. Remove pancakes and drain on absorbent paper. Serve hot with sour cream, hot or cold applesauce, cream cheese, or apricot purée, if desired. Makes 4 servings.

Mrs. Dina Scokin, Dallas, TX

Cheesy Potato Casserole

8 medium sized new potatoes
8 ounces Kraft American
  cheese, grated
8 ounces Kraft Velveeta
  cheese, grated

Salt and pepper to taste
2 tablespoons butter
10 ounces Pet milk

Leaving jackets on, slice and boil the potatoes for 20 minutes or until tender. Spray baking dish with Pam and layer ⅓ of the potatoes on bottom of dish. Salt and pepper and sprinkle with ⅓ of the grated cheeses. Repeat this process two more times being sure to end with the grated cheeses. Dot with butter and pour Pet milk over mixture. Do not pour milk to the top of dish. Bake at 375 degrees about 20 minutes. Serves 10 to 12.

Cindy Ward, Dallas,TX

Stuffed Potatoes

4 large baking potatoes
3 green onions, chopped
1½ cups shredded Cheddar
  cheese

2 tablespoons butter
5 tablespoons sour cream
Salt and pepper to taste

Bake cleaned potatoes in oven or microwave until done. Slice off the top of each potato, saving peel, and scoop out inside of potato. Place potatoes in a bowl and add onions, butter, sour cream, 1 cup Cheddar cheese and salt and pepper to taste. Mash with a fork or spoon until mixture is well blended. Stuff mixture back into potato peels. Add ½ cup cheese to top of potatoes. Place in 350 degree oven or microwave oven and bake until cheese is melted. Serve warm. Yields 4 servings.

Bonnie Mahon, Pineville, LA

Potatoes Romanoff

4 medium russet potatoes
1 cup sour cream
4 green onions
1¼ cups shredded sharp
  Cheddar cheese

1 teaspoon salt
Pepper and paprika to taste

Cook potatoes in jacket until just tender. Peel and grate. Combine potatoes with sour cream, onions, ¾ cup cheese, salt and pepper. Toss gently. Turn mixture into buttered 1½-quart casserole. Sprinkle with remaining cheese and paprika. Bake, uncovered, in a 350 degree oven 30 to 40 minutes. May be assembled ahead and refrigerated until time to bake. Add extra baking time if refrigerated. Serves 6.

Ann Comeaux, Baytown, TX

Hot and Spicy Spinach Casserole

2 10-ounce packages chopped
  spinach
4 tablespoons butter
2 tablespoons flour
2 tablespoons finely chopped
  onion
½ cup milk
½ cup vegetable liquor

½ teaspoon black pepper
  (optional)
¾ teaspoon celery salt
½ teaspoon garlic powder
1 6-ounce roll jalapeño cheese
1 teaspoon Worcestershire
  sauce
½ cup Italian bread crumbs

Cook spinach according to directions on package. Drain and reserve ½ cup vegetable liquor. Melt butter in saucepan over a low heat. Add flour, stirring until blended and smooth, but not brown. Add onions and cook until soft, but not brown. Add liquid ingredients, slowly, to avoid lumps. Cook, stirring constantly, until smooth and thick. Add seasonings and cheese which has been cut into small pieces. Stir until melted. Combine with cooked spinach. Put into casserole. Top with bread crumbs. Bake in 375 degree oven until crumbs are brown. Flavor is improved if mixed ahead of time. May be prepared a day before or frozen before baking. Yields 6 to 8 servings.

Melba Simmons, Bunkie, LA

Spinach Artichoke Casserole

2 packages frozen chopped
  spinach
¼ cup chopped green onions
¼ cup chopped onion
1 stick margarine

1 14-ounce can artichoke
  hearts
½ of an 8-ounce package sour
  cream
½ cup Parmesan cheese

Cook spinach according to package directions. Drain and set aside. Sauté onions in margarine. Add to cooked spinach. Fold in drained artichoke hearts. Add sour cream. Place in a 2-quart casserole. Sprinkle Parmesan cheese over top. Bake in 350 degree oven for 20 to 30 minutes. Yields 6 servings.

Mrs. E. C. Hawthorne, Shreveport, LA

Spinach Casserole

4 packages frozen chopped
  spinach
1 can cream of mushroom
  soup
1 pint sour cream
1 tablespoon chopped fresh
  parsley
1 cup chopped green onions
1 tablespoon Worcestershire
  sauce

1 cup sliced fresh mushrooms
  (¼ pound)
3 tablespoons butter
1 tablespoon fresh lemon
  juice, strained
½ teaspoon black pepper
½ teaspoon garlic powder

Cook spinach according to package directions omitting salt; drain well. Combine the mushroom soup, sour cream, parsley, onions and Worcestershire sauce. Sauté the mushrooms in butter; season with lemon juice, pepper and garlic powder. Stir into sour cream mixture along with spinach. Turn into casserole dish and bake in 400 degree oven for 20 minutes. Yields 8 to 12 servings.

Robbie Watson, Dallas, TX

Apple and Squash Casserole

3 cups cubed, cooked
  butternut squash
1½ cups stewed apples
Salt

¾ cup firmly packed brown
  sugar
6 tablespoons margarine
Ground cinnamon

Place 1 cup squash in a buttered casserole, top with ½ cup apples. Sprinkle lightly with salt and ¼ cup sugar, dot with 2 tablespoons margarine. Repeat layers twice. Sprinkle top with cinnamon. Bake at 350 degrees for 45 minutes or until lightly browned. Yields 6 to 8 servings.

Lorraine Zeringue

Mirliton Casserole

6 medium mirlitons
1 stick butter
1 onion, chopped
1 bell pepper, chopped
1 stalk celery, chopped
½ teaspoon thyme

¼ teaspoon garlic powder
1 bay leaf
1 pound peeled raw shrimp
Bread crumbs
Butter

Peel and core mirlitons, cover with water and bring to a boil. Lower heat and cook for 20 minutes or until tender. Drain. Melt butter in skillet and sauté onion, bell pepper and celery until tender, add seasonings. Add mirliton and shrimp and cook for another 15 to 20 minutes. Pour into a greased casserole and top with bread crumbs and dots of butter. Bake in 350 degree oven for about 15 minutes or until brown. Yields 6 to 8 servings.

Note: Ham may be substituted for shrimp.

Mrs. William Hrapmann, New Orleans, LA

Squash Casserole

12 medium yellow squash
1 bunch green onions,
   chopped
2 tablespoons butter
1 can cream of celery soup
2 whole eggs
⅓ cup bread crumbs

¼ teaspoon garlic powder
Pinch basil
1 teaspoon salt
1 tablespoon Worcestershire
   sauce
1½ cups grated cheese
½ cup bread crumbs
Butter

Slice squash. Steam gently until almost tender. Drain. Sauté onions in butter, and stir in celery soup. Add eggs, ⅓ cup bread crumbs and seasonings. Combine with squash. Put into buttered casserole, sprinkle with grated cheese and bread crumbs. Dot with butter. Cook at 375 degrees for 45 minutes. Serves 8 to 10.

Ann Comeaux, Baytown, TX

Stuffed Zucchini

1 large zucchini
1 medium onion, chopped
½ bell pepper, chopped
4 tablespoons olive oil
½ cup chopped mushrooms
1 cup bread crumbs

Dill to taste
Rosemary to taste
Ginger to taste
Basil to taste
1 cup grated cheese

Blanch the whole zucchini in boiling water for 5 to 7 minutes. Remove, cut lengthwise and scoop out and dice the flesh of the squash, saving the two shells. Sauté onion and bell pepper in olive oil until golden. Add squash and mushrooms. Mix and add bread crumbs. This should be a dry and crumbly mixture. If not, add more bread crumbs. Add herbs and cheese. Stuff into the shells. Place in a baking pan and bake in 350 degree oven for 30 minutes or until very hot and bubbly. Yields 4 servings.

Julia Van Tassell, North Haven, CT
Husband: William J. Van Tassell
Knights of Columbus title: Supreme Treasurer

Zucchini with Cheese

1 onion, chopped
½ cup chopped green onion
1 bell pepper, chopped
1 clove garlic, minced
1 cup chopped celery
3 tablespoons butter

6 medium zucchini, sliced
thin
½ teaspoon oregano
Salt and pepper to taste
2 cups Italian plum tomatoes
1 cup grated Cheddar cheese

Sauté onions, pepper, garlic and celery in butter until lightly crisp. Add zucchini and oregano and cook until most of the liquid has evaporated. Season. Place in greased casserole dish. Cover. Bake in 400 degree oven for 10 minutes. Remove and add tomatoes. Bake, uncovered, for 15 minutes more. Remove and add cheese. Bake until cheese has melted. Serves 6.

Sharon Brown, Ponchatoula, LA

Aunt Janet's Sweet Potatoes

4 cups cooked, mashed
sweet potatoes
1 cup sugar
2 eggs, beaten
⅓ cup milk
½ cup butter

1 teaspoon vanilla
½ teaspoon ginger
½ teaspoon cinnamon
½ teaspoon nutmeg
⅛ teaspoon cloves

Combine above ingredients and spread in a 2-quart casserole dish.

Topping:
⅓ cup flour
1 cup brown sugar

⅓ cup butter
1 cup chopped pecans

Combine topping ingredients and spread over sweet potatoes. Bake uncovered in a 350 degree oven for 30 minutes. Serves 8.

Mrs. Janet Ward, Ennis, TX

Candied Yams

6 medium peeled yams
Pecan halves
½ cup butter

½ pound brown sugar
Boiling water

Boil yams until tender (Do not overcook). Allow to cool. Slice into lengthwise slabs, ½-inch thick. Arrange slices in buttered pan. Place pecan halves on each slice. Dot with butter. Make a syrup of brown sugar that has been dissolved in just enough boiling water to melt it. Pour the syrup over the yams. Bake yams at 350 degrees until the pecans are toasted a nice brown and potatoes are well done.

Sook Suard, New Iberia, LA

Pecan Topped Sweet Potato Soufflé

5 pounds cooked sweet
**   potatoes**
2 teaspoons cinnamon
2 teaspoons salt
4 eggs

1 cup brown sugar
½ cup melted butter
¼ to ½ cup orange juice
2 cups pecans

Peel and cook sweet potatoes. When done, mash and add cinnamon and salt. Beat in eggs one at a time. Add ½ cup of brown sugar and ¼ cup of the butter. Add ¼ cup orange juice and mix. If potatoes seem dry, add more juice slowly. Beat until potatoes are moist and fluffy. Place in a well-greased 3-quart casserole dish. Arrange pecans on top. Sprinkle with brown sugar and drizzle remaining butter over the top. Bake, uncovered, in a 375 degree oven for 20 to 25 minutes. Serves 10 to 12.

Kathy Rutter, New Orleans, LA

Sweet Potatoes with Praline Topping

Casserole:

8 to 10 sweet potatoes, peeled
  and cubed
½ teaspoon butter flavoring
½ cup margarine
2 eggs
½ cup milk

1½ cups sugar
½ teaspoon salt
Nutmeg to taste
1 cup miniature
  marshmallows

Boil and mash sweet potatoes until they are smooth. Add remaining ingredients and whip until fluffy. Pour into a casserole dish. Add topping.

Topping:

⅓ cup self-rising flour
1 cup light brown sugar

⅓ stick butter
1 cup pecans, chopped

Mix the topping ingredients and place on top of sweet potatoes. Bake in 350 degree oven for 35 minutes. Serve warm. Yields 8 to 10 servings.

Guy Recotta, Hammond, LA

Turnip Casserole

12 turnips
½ pound chopped bacon
2 chopped onions
1 chopped bell pepper
1 clove chopped garlic
2 egg yolks

3 ounces milk
¾ cup bread crumbs
2 teaspoons chopped onion
  tops
2 teaspoons chopped parsley
Salt and pepper to taste

Pare and boil turnips. Drain and mash. Sauté chopped bacon in heavy pot. When lightly browned, remove bacon. Add onions, bell pepper and garlic. Cook over low heat until tender. Add turnips and cook one-half hour. Beat egg yolks, mix with milk and bread crumbs. Add to mixture with onion tops and seasonings. Top with bacon and bake in casserole at 350 degrees for 30 minutes. Serves 8 to 10.

Mrs. G. F. Thomas, Jr., Natchitoches, LA

Amazing Rice

1 cup raw rice (not instant)	1 can chicken broth or
1 can chicken gumbo soup	bouillon, undiluted
1 soup can of water	½ stick butter or margarine

Mix rice, soup, water and broth in a casserole dish with a tight fitting lid. Put butter or margarine in the middle of the casserole, do not stir. Cover and bake in a 350 degree oven for 45 minutes. Before serving, fluff rice with a fork or serve as it is. Yields 4 to 6 servings.

Emma Maestas, Bernalillo, NM

Husband: Paul G. Maestas
Knights of Columbus title; State Deputy

Ben's Favorite Rice

1 medium onion, finely chopped	1 can cream of mushroom soup
½ cup finely chopped green pepper	1 can beef consommé
2 cups finely chopped celery	1 soup can of water
1 stick butter (do not substitute)	1 small jar pimiento, undrained
1 cup uncooked rice	Salt and black pepper to taste

Sauté onion, bell pepper and celery in a skillet with butter. Add rice and soup. Stir and cook for 2 minutes. Add consommé and water (make sure this makes 2 cups of liquid). Add pimiento and seasonings. Pour into a casserole that has been sprayed with Pam and bake at 350 degrees for 45 to 60 minutes. Serves 6.

Judy Read, Farmerville, LA

Dirty Rice I

2 cups uncooked rice
½ pound ground pork
1 pound ground beef
Salt and pepper to taste
Tabasco to taste
1 pound chicken livers and
    gizzards, mixed and
    chopped
1 bunch green onions,
    chopped

½ bunch parsley, chopped
1 bell pepper, chopped
2 or 3 onions, chopped
3 cloves garlic, minced
½ cup red table wine
1 bay leaf
¼ teaspoon thyme

Boil rice in water for 10 minutes. Drain and set aside. In a large skillet place ground beef and pork and fry until almost done. Drain off excess fat. Season with salt, pepper and Tabasco. Lower heat and continue to cook. Blend chicken livers and gizzards, green onions, parsley, bell pepper, garlic and onions into ground meat mixture, raising heat and cooking until all ingredients are done. Gradually add rice, wine, bay leaf and thyme. Cover and simmer for 30 minutes or place in a casserole, sprinkling top with extra ½ cup wine, and bake in 350 degree oven for 45 minutes. Yields 8 to 10 servings.

Note: This is time consuming, but well worth the effort! It was a Prize Winning Recipe, St. Bernard Guide in 1978.

Mrs. Mary G. Baham, Chalmette, LA

Dirty Rice II

½ pound smoked sausage
1 small onion, chopped
1 small bell pepper, chopped
1 rib celery, chopped
1 clove garlic, chopped
2 cups cold water
¼ teaspoon Tabasco, more if
    desired

1 cup long grain rice
1 teaspoon salt
1 green onion, chopped
½ pound shrimp, peeled and
    deveined
1 jar oysters, drained

Cut sausage in ¼ inch links. Brown in a heavy skillet over medium heat. Remove sausage but leave sausage grease in skillet. Add onion, bell pepper, celery and garlic to the skillet and sauté. Add water and Tabasco. Bring to a full boil and boil for 2 minutes. Remove from heat. Add raw rice, salt, green onion, shrimp and oysters. Stir thoroughly. Pour into a buttered casserole dish. Cover with tight fitting lid. Bake in 375 degree oven for 30 minutes. Lower heat to 350 degrees and bake an additional 45 minutes. Yields 8 to 10 servings.

Donna Graham, Lyon, MS

Green Rice

1 7-ounce box Minute Rice
    (prepared as directed)
2 eggs
¾ cup Crisco oil
1 small can parsley flakes
1 small jar mushroom slices
2 cans cream of mushroom
    soup

1½ cups grated Cheddar
    cheese
1 onion, chopped
1 small can Pet milk
Salt and pepper to taste

Mix all of the ingredients together and pour into greased casserole. Bake for 1 hour at 350 degrees. Serves 6 to 8.

Judy Read, Farmerville, LA

Green Chilies and Rice Casserole

1 8-ounce carton sour cream
½ of a 4-ounce can green
 chilies, chopped
1 teaspoon oregano
1 teaspoon sweet basil
⅓ cup chopped green onions
1 cup raw rice, cooked

3 ounces Monterey Jack
 cheese, shredded
3 ounces Cheddar cheese,
 shredded
1 tablespoon fresh parsley,
 chopped

Combine sour cream, chilies, oregano, basil and green onions. Put half of the cooked rice in the bottom of a casserole and pour over half of the sour cream mixture. Spread half the shredded cheese over this. Repeat the rice, sour cream mixture and top with the shredded cheeses. Sprinkle with fresh parsley. Warm in a 350 degree oven until cheese is bubbly. Serves 6 to 8.

Laura Schneider, Dallas, TX

Jalapeño Rice Casserole

½ cup chopped celery
½ cup chopped onion
½ cup chopped bell pepper
1 cup sliced fresh mushrooms
2 to 4 tablespoons chopped
 jalapeño peppers

2 sticks margarine
2 teaspoons lemon-pepper
 seasoning
2 7-ounce cans white chicken
4 to 5 cups cooked rice

In a skillet sauté celery, onion, bell pepper, mushrooms and jalapeño peppers in 2 sticks margarine until golden brown. Add lemon-pepper seasoning and chicken to sautéed vegetables. Add cooked rice to mixture and blend well. Pour into a 13 x 9 x 2-inch casserole and heat thoroughly. Yields 8 servings.

Natalie Piccolo, Natchitoches, LA

Parsley Rice

3 eggs, beaten
2 cups cooked rice
2 tablespoons chopped parsley
2 cups milk
8 ounces Cheddar cheese,
   grated

1 clove chopped garlic
1 small onion, chopped
¼ cup oil
Salt and pepper to taste

Thoroughly combine all ingredients and pour into a greased 8 x
10 x 2 baking dish. Bake at 350 degrees for 40 minutes. Serve 6
to 8.

Ella H. Nicolas, Corpus Christi, TX
Husband: Alfred N. Nicholas
Knights of Columbus title: Supreme Director and Supreme Master

Royal Treat Rice

2 cups rice, washed and
   drained
1 4-ounce can mushrooms,
   stems and pieces, drained
1 10½-ounce can beef
   consommé

1 10½-ounce can beef broth
1 medium onion, chopped
1 green pepper, chopped
3 stalks celery, chopped
2 sticks butter or margarine
Salt and pepper to taste

Preheat oven to 350 degrees. Mix all ingredients together then
pour into a buttered casserole. Bake 1 hour. Serve hot. Yields 8 to
10 servings.

Gloria Gomez, New Orleans, LA

Rice Parisian

½ cup uncooked rice
⅓ cup sliced fresh mushrooms
   or 1 4-ounce can, drained

2 tablespoons butter
1 can onion soup
½ soup can of water

Lightly brown rice and mushrooms in butter. Stir in onion soup
and water. Cover and cook over low heat for 25 minutes or until
rice is tender and fluffy.. Yields 4 servings.

Marti Greenberg, Denton, TX

Special Wild Rice

1 stick butter or margarine
½ medium onion, chopped
1 small can or jar sliced
  mushrooms, drained
½ cup Uncle Ben's long grain
  rice
¼ cup wild rice
1 teaspoon paprika

1 teaspoon oregano
1 bay leaf
Salt and pepper to taste
1 can Campbell's beef
  consommé (gelatin added)
½ cup cooking sherry
¾ cup water

Sauté onions and mushrooms in butter. Add regular and wild rice
and spices, including salt and pepper to taste. Reduce heat, cover
and simmer for 20 minutes. Spray a 2-quart casserole with cooking
oil spray. Mix simmered ingredients, beef consommé, cooking
sherry and water into casserole dish. Cover and bake 45 minutes
at 375 degrees. Uncover and bake an additional 15 to 25 minutes
(until rice absorbs all liquids). Serves 4 to 6.

Cindy Ward, Dallas, TX

Egyptian Rice

1 pound ground chuck
1 chopped onion
1 can beef bouillon
1 can beef consommé
1 small can mushrooms

1½ tablespoons soy sauce
1 cup uncooked rice
1½ teaspoons Worcestershire
  sauce

In electric skillet brown ground chuck and onion. Add the remaining ingredients. Cover and simmer for 30 minutes. Serves 4.

Doris Cartier, Austin, TX

Fried Rice

1 cup rice (uncooked)
2 tablespoons olive or
Wesson oil
½ cup chopped onions
½ cup chopped celery

1 envelope Lipton onion soup
2¼ cups water
1 small can oriental vegetables
(optional)
Salt and pepper to taste

Heat oil in large skillet over a medium heat. When oil is warm, add rice and brown lightly. Add onion and celery and sauté lightly. Add onion soup to mixture and stir until well mixed. Add water carefully, as it will steam. Cover and cook over a medium heat for 10 minutes. Add drained oriental vegetables and season to taste. Cover and cook for an additional 10 minutes. Do not overcook rice mixture. Let a little moisture remain in bottom of skillet, remove from heat. Stir mixture. Cover and let set for 5 to 10 minutes. Garnish with parsley. Serve with soy sauce. Yields 4 servings.

Deborah Sanders, Anacoco, LA

Fried Rice Cantonese Style

2 or 3 medium eggs
2 teaspoons salt
½ teaspoon monosodium
glutamate (MSG)
½ teaspoon dry sherry
5 tablespoons cooking oil

2 tablespoons minced onion
4 cups cooked rice
1 teaspoon Chinese brown
gravy syrup or ½ teaspoon
Kitchen Bouquet
1 cup bean sprouts

Beat eggs with salt, MSG and sherry. Pour oil in hot skillet over medium heat. Stir in minced onion, then the egg mixture. Scramble and break into small pieces until quite dry. Add rice, brown gravy and bean sprouts. Stir constantly until the ingredients are well blended and thoroughly heated, about 8 to 10 minutes. Yields 4 to 5 servings.

Note: One half cup chopped chicken may be added if desired.

Marti Greenberg, Denton, TX

CONGREGATION
OF THE
SISTERS OF OUR LADY OF SORROWS

Bishop Greco was responsible for bringing this congregation of nuns to the United States from Remini, Italy, in 1947, to assist him in fulfilling a dream of many years, the establishment of a school for "special children."

During his trip to Rome in 1946, Bishop became aware of the desire of Mother Zita Verni, General Superior of the Congregation of Our Lady of Sorrows, to establish her congregation in the United States. He happily accepted the Sisters of Our Lady of Sorrows, and the following year, a group of thirteen sisters arrived in the Diocese of Alexandria with their Mother Superior. Before their arrival, Bishop Greco had purchased a large house in Moreauville, Louisiana, and turned it into a convent. The sisters came on a temporary three-month visa, and a distressing dilemma developed as the sisters overstayed their visitors' visa by fifteen months. Immigration authorities were sympathetic, but helpless to extend the time limits under the existing immigration laws. Once again, Bishop Greco was able to meet the challenge. He traveled to Washington and succeeded in having a special bill passed through Congress which made it possible for the sisters to remain in this country. One of the men who helped in this important matter was a young senator by the name of John F. Kennedy!

Sauces and Accompaniments

St. Anne Chapel
Clarks, Louisiana

A & A Barbecue Sauce

1 stick butter
½ cup water
2 tablespoons Worcestershire
½ cup white vinegar
1 teaspoon sugar
⅛ teaspoon garlic powder
3 teaspoons black pepper

1 teaspoon dry mustard
1¼ teaspoons paprika
1 teaspoon salt
¼ teaspoon red pepper
Dash Tabasco
½ lemon

Combine all ingredients in a saucepan and bring to a boil. Simmer for 20 minutes.
Note: This is wonderful for barbequed chicken.

A & A Kitchens, Marshall, TX

Barbecue Sauce I

4 tablespoons margarine
2 onions, chopped
2 pods garlic, minced
1 cup celery, chopped
½ cup chopped bell pepper
½ cup chopped shallots
2 cups ketchup
4 tablespoons vinegar

4 tablespoons lemon juice
4 tablespoons brown sugar
2 teaspoons dry mustard
2 teaspoons salt
½ teaspoon red pepper
1 20-ounce can tomato juice
4 tablespoons Worcestershire
  sauce

Melt butter and sauté onions, garlic, celery and bell peppers until tender. Add other ingredients and simmer for 30 minutes. Yields 1 quart.

Mrs. Thomas J. Foret, III, Lutcher, LA
Husband: Thomas J. Foret, III
Knights of Columbus title: Gramercy 1817

Barbecue Sauce II

⅓ cup margarine, melted
3 cloves garlic, pressed
1 large onion, chopped
½ bottle prepared barbecue
　sauce
1 bottle chili sauce
¼ can Hunts tomato sauce

½ bottle red cocktail sauce
1 small bottle ketchup
1 tablespoon grated lemon
　rind
1 teaspoon black pepper (to
　taste)
Louisiana Hot Sauce
　(to taste)

Combine all ingredients and mix thoroughly. Yields about 2 quarts.
Excell King, Dallas, TX

Bearnaise Sauce

2 tablespoons white wine
1 tablespoon dry minced
　onion
1 tablespoon dry parsley
1 teaspoon tarragon leaves
½ teaspoon chervil leaves
Dash of garlic powder
3 egg yolks at room
　temperature

1 tablespoon fresh lemon
　juice, strained
¼ teaspoon salt
⅛ teaspoon cayenne or
　white pepper
⅔ cup butter, bubbling hot

Allow dry seasonings (onion, parsley, tarragon, chervil and garlic powder) to sit in the wine for several minutes. Strain and reserve wine. Set seasonings aside. Place egg yolks, lemon juice, salt, pepper and wine in blender and mix on medium speed. Reduce the speed to low and slowly dribble in the bubbling hot butter. Gently fold in the wine-soaked seasonings. Delicious on meats, chicken, and fish. Yields about 1 cup.

Cindy Ward, Dallas, TX

Hollandaise Sauce

3 egg yolks at room
  temperature
1 tablespoon fresh lemon
  juice, strained

¼ teaspoon salt
Dash of cayenne or
  white pepper
⅔ cup butter, bubbling hot

Place egg yolks, lemon juice, salt and pepper in blender and mix on medium speed. Reduce the speed to low and slowly dribble in the bubbling hot butter. Yields 1 cup.

Cindy Ward, Dallas, TX

Mandarin Orange Sauce

1 cup sugar
½ cup butter
½ cup frozen orange juice,
  concentrated
3 tablespoons fresh lemon
  juice

Grated rind of one orange
1 tablespoon Galliano liqueur
1 11-ounce can mandarin
  oranges, drained

Combine sugar, butter and orange juice in a saucepan and bring to a boil. Add remaining ingredients and heat thoroughly before serving.
Note: Excellent with duck, pheasant, or other game birds. Keeps well in refrigerator.

Lynn A. Fulbright, Marshall, TX

Mornay Sauce

2 tablespoons butter
2 tablespoons flour
1½ cups milk

½ cup grated cheese
  (½ Parmesan, ½ Gruyere)

In a saucepan over low heat melt butter, stirring in flour a little at a time. Slowly add milk and cheeses stirring until well blended. Serve hot over vegetables.

Betty Bellamy, Marshall, TX

Remoulade Sauce

2 hard-boiled eggs, chopped
  or grated
2 stalks celery, finely chopped
1 tablespoon Worcestershire
8 tablespoons creole mustard

2 to 3 tablespoons dry mustard
1 teaspoon salt
1 teaspoon sugar
1 pint mayonnaise
1 garlic clove, minced

Mix all ingredients and refrigerate. Serve on chopped lettuce with shrimp. Garnish with tomatoes, hard-boiled eggs, green olives, etc. Serve with crackers.

Gloria Evans, Clarksdale, MS

Shrimp Remoulade Sauce

10 ounces olive oil
5 ounces vinegar
7½ ounces Dijon mustard or
  creole mustard
5 ounces tomato ketchup
5 tablespoons fresh
  horseradish

2 cloves garlic, crushed
1 teaspoon Tabasco sauce
Tony's Creole Seasoning to
  taste or salt and pepper
  to taste

Blend ingredients as listed. Serve over boiled shrimp mixed with shredded lettuce and finely diced celery. Yields 10 servings.

Mrs. William Hrapmann, New Orleans, LA

Sour Cream Sauce

1½ cups sour cream
½ cup whipping cream
½ cup chicken broth
½ cup chopped chives
¼ cup butter

1 cup fresh mushrooms,
  thinly chopped
3 tablespoons flour
Salt and pepper to taste
2 tablespoons dry white wine

Combine creams, broth and chives. Simmer, over low heat, but do not boil. Separately sauté mushrooms in butter; blend in flour, salt and pepper. Add wine to sautéed mushrooms; blend into creams. Serve with Chicken Kiev. (See Index)

Bunny Laskowski, Houston, TX

Teriyaki Marinade

1½ cups water
1 cup sugar
1 cup soy sauce

½ teaspoon ginger
1 clove garlic, minced

Make a syrup by boiling ½ cup water and sugar together until syrupy. Add remaining ingredients to syrup. Refrigerate until needed. Yields 1½ cups marinade.
Note: Marinade can be used to marinate chicken, shrimp or beef.

Mary West

Krispy Luncheon Pickles

18 to 20 medium cucumbers
   (4 quarts sliced)
2 large white onions
2 large bell peppers
½ cup pickling salt

5 cups white vinegar
5 cups sugar
2 tablespoons mustard seed
1 teaspoon turmeric
½ teaspoon whole cloves

Wash cucumbers and slice as thinly as possible. Slice onions thin and chop bell pepper. Combine cucumbers, onions, bell pepper and salt. Cover with cold water and let set 3 hours. Drain well. In a 6-quart kettle or cooker, combine vinegar, sugar and spices. Bring to a boil. Add cucumbers, onions and bell pepper. Heat thoroughly, but do not boil. Pack while hot into sterilized, hot jars and seal at once. Let stand three weeks before opening. Chill before serving. Yields 14 to 16 cups.

Melba Simmons, Bunkie, LA

Simple Sweet Pickles

1 gallon whole sour or dill
   pickles, drained
5 pounds sugar

Tabasco as needed
5 garlic cloves, chopped

Drain pickles completely. Slice pickles to desired thickness. Return pickles to original jar in five layers in the following order: pickles, sugar, Tabasco (sprinkle a few drops on each layer), chopped garlic. Pack firmly into original jar and close lid tightly. Let stand at room temperature for 6 days, turning the jar once a day. (Alternate, turning rightside up to upside down.) To store, transfer pickles to glass containers of desired size and store in refrigerator.

Mary Lancaster, Marshall, TX

Clarebelle's Pickled Okra

½ bushel okra
2 tablespoons alum
Dill weed, 1 teaspoon per jar
Garlic, 1 to 2 cloves per jar,
   or to taste

10 to 12 fresh hot chili
   peppers
12 cups water
1½ cups salt
4 cups vinegar

Wash okra and sprinkle with alum. Add enough water to cover. Let stand overnight. Next morning, drain, wash and pack in quart sterilized jars. Add to each jar: dill, garlic and chili peppers. Bring to boil: water, salt and vinegar. Pour in jars. Seal.

Lucille Schaider, La Porte, TX

Dill Pickled Okra

1 pint white vinegar
½ cup salt
1 quart water
3 pounds young okra, whole
1 teaspoon celery leaves per
  pint jar

1 garlic clove per pint jar
1 pod red hot pepper per
  pint jar
1 teaspoon dill weed per
  pint jar

Combine vinegar, salt and water and bring to a boil. Wash okra and place in hot jars. Add to each pint jar celery leaves, garlic, pepper and dill weed. Pour boiling mixture into each jar, covering okra. Seal lids. Let stand a few weeks before using.

Donna Ward, Farmerville, LA

Lakeside Green Tomato Pickles

16 cups diced, green tomatoes
4 cups onions (cut in wedges)
¼ cup pickling salt
9 cups water
1½ teaspoons alum

1 tablespoon whole, mixed
  pickling spices
1 tablespoon celery seed
3 cups cider vinegar
4 cups sugar

Sprinkle tomatoes with salt and let stand overnight. Mix alum into 8 cups of water and bring to a boil. Pour over tomato and onion mixture and let stand 20 minutes. Drain well and rinse with fresh cold water. Drain again. Combine spices and tie in a cheesecloth bag. In saucepan, combine vinegar, remaining 1 cup water, sugar and spice bag and bring to a boil. Pour mixture over tomatoes and onions and let stand for 24 hours. After 24 hours drain the liquid into a saucepan and bring to a boil. Pour the liquid over tomatoes and onions and let set for another 24 hours. The next day bring entire mixture to a boil. Pack into hot sterilized jars and seal immediately. Makes 4 quarts or 8 pints of delicious pickled tomatoes and onions.

Note: Sliced jalapeño peppers may be added if you prefer them hot.

Edgar Allen, Marshall, TX

Chow Chow

8 cups chopped cabbage
4 cups chopped green
 tomatoes
6 large onions, chopped
3 red bell peppers, chopped
Salt to taste
2 pounds sugar
4 tablespoons dry mustard

3 tablespoons white mustard
 seed
1½ tablespoons celery seed
½ tablespoon ginger
8 cups vinegar (or enough
 to cover)
1 tablespoon ground cloves

Place each vegetable into individual bowl and sprinkle lightly with salt. Let stand 4 hours. Drain and squeeze as much juice from vegetables as possible. In a 6 to 8-quart saucepan mix dry ingredients and add a small amount of vinegar to make a paste. Add remaining vinegar and bring to a boil. Place vegetables in boiling vinegar mixture; lower heat and cook slowly for 20 minutes. Pack into sterilized pint jars and seal. Place jars in deep kettle covering with water, and simmer for 15 minutes. Yields 5 to 6 pints.

Mary Francis, Boston, MA

Cranberry-Peach Relish

1 pound cranberries
1 large can sliced peaches
2 cinnamon sticks

4 tablespoons whole cloves
2 cups sugar
⅓ cup cider vinegar

Wash cranberries and set in colander to drain. Drain peaches and reserve syrup. Cut peaches into 1-inch pieces. Put cinnamon, cloves and sugar in large pan with cider vinegar and all of the peach syrup. Heat to rolling boil and continue to boil until liquid is reduced to half of original volume. Strain to remove spices. Return syrup to pan and add cranberries and peaches. Bring to a boil, cover and cook for 5 minutes or until cranberries pop open. Remove and pour into jars. Chill. May be served as soon as it has chilled. Yields 2 quarts.

Note: This is good served with turkey or ham. Makes excellent gifts.

Mrs. Patricia Farnsworth Bowser, Washington, DC

Pear Relish

6 pounds or 20 hard pears,
  peeled, cored, and
  quartered
1 pound of onions, peeled and
  quartered
2 green peppers, seeded and
  quartered

2½ cups white vinegar
½ teaspoon ground cinnamon
2 cups sugar
1 tablespoon salt
1 tablespoon whole pickling
  spice
1 tablespoon turmeric

Grind the pears, onions and peppers in food grinder or processor. Drain off all liquid. In a 6-quart saucepan combine vinegar, cinnamon, sugar, salt, pickling spice and turmeric. Boil vinegar mixture for 10 minutes. Add pears, onions, and peppers. Return to boil, continue boiling for 15 minutes. Place mixture in hot sterile jars and seal immediately. Yields 4 to 5 pints.

Amanda A. Greene, Marshall, TX

Hot Pepper Jelly

1 cup finely chopped jalapeño
  peppers
1 cup finely chopped green
  peppers
1½ cups cider vinegar

5½ cups sugar
1 6-ounce bottle liquid pectin
  or Certo
Green food coloring

Wash peppers and soak in ice water until cold. Chop in food processor. Simmer peppers, vinegar, and sugar 10 minutes or until tender. Add pectin and boil 1 minute. Reduce heat and cook 15 minutes. Add green food coloring drops to mixture. Pour into sterilized jars and seal. Delicious served with cheese and crackers or spread on cream cheese.

Gloria Evans, Clarksdale, MS

Old-Fashioned Fig Preserves

7 cups sugar
¼ cup lemon juice
1½ quarts hot water

2 quarts peeled, firmly ripe
figs
2 lemons, thinly sliced

Add sugar and lemon juice to hot water. Cook until sugar dissolves. Add figs and cook rapidly 10 minutes. Stir occasionally to prevent sticking. Add sliced lemons and continue cooking rapidly until figs are clear, about 10 to 15 minutes. If syrup becomes too thick before figs become clear, add boiling water ¼ cup at a time. Cover and let stand in cool place for 12 to 24 hours. Pack into hot canning jars, leaving ¼ inch head space. Adjust caps. Process half pints and pints 30 minutes at 180 to 185 degrees in hot water bath. Makes 10 half pints.

Lucille Schaider, La Porte, TX

Strawberry Fig Preserves

3 cups chopped figs
6 ounces strawberry Jello

3 cups sugar

Thoroughly mix figs, Jello and sugar in a large pot. Place over medium heat and bring to a boil. Boil for 3 minutes, stirring often. Pour into sterilized jars and seal. Makes 3 pints.
Variation: Fig stems may be removed but do not peel figs. Combine figs and sugar and cook until figs are tender. Add Jello and continue cooking for 2 to 3 minutes longer.

Mrs. Marianna Eggers

HOLY ANGELS SCHOOL

"Prayer is never offered in vain," Bishop Greco said. "To try our faith and love, or to protect us from our own wills, God, in His goodness, often refuses to hear our requests, but then grants us another and often greater gift."

Many prayers, years of work, disappointment and frustration preceded the granting of that "greater gift" that gave Bishop Greco the opportunity to develop his dream of bigger and better things for "God's Special Children". After St. Mary's Training School in Clarks, Louisiana, was established, Bishop Greco shared his thoughts and dreams with a close friend, Monsignor Bordelon. In March, 1963, Monsignor Bordelon was having lunch with Mr. and Mrs. W. J. O'Brien, Jr., and discussed finding property to establish a residential training school in Shreveport. Definite interest was shown and soon resulted in the donation of forty acres of land for the construction of Holy Angels School.

Bishop Greco secured the services of an architect and consultants to design the new school, which was to include administration buildings, quarters for the sisters, two dormitories, cafeteria, vocational building and rooms for academic studies. On August 2, 1964, ground was broken, and exactly one year later, ceremonies were held turning the first buildings over to the Bishop. In August, 1965, Mother Zita Verni came from Italy to assist Sister Zita, the directress, in organizing the operations of the new school.

Nineteen sixty-six proved to be an exciting year. A formal open house was held on the third of April, and construction of an activities building and roads encircling the facility began. June saw the beginning of the Nursery School, and November the completion of the chapel.

Holy Angels School continued to grow, with a major construction program begun in 1974. A million-dollar facility to house children who had reached the age of maturity at St. Mary's and Holy Angels and to provide all the needs of young adults was begun and finished in 1976. A recreation building soon followed.

The school is located among beautiful pine trees on rolling hills on Ellerbe Road in Shreveport, Louisiana. Today, a welcome smile and a warm heart greet the 180 contented residents, under the care of the present directress, Sister Concetta Scipioine, seven other sisters, and a capable professional staff.

Breads and Breakfast

Chapel
Holy Angels School
Shreveport, Louisiana

Jalapeño Corn Bread

1½ cups white corn meal
1 tablespoon flour (heaping)
3 teaspoons salt
½ teaspoon baking soda
1 cup buttermilk
4 green onions, chopped
⅔ cup cooking oil

2 eggs, beaten
1 small can cream style corn
3 to 5 jalapeño peppers,
   chopped and seeded
½ bell pepper, chopped
1½ cups grated Cheddar
   cheese

Mix dry ingredients. Add other ingredients, except cheese. Mix well. Pour half of mixture into a greased iron skillet and top with half of the grated cheese. Pour other half of mixture over cheese and top with other half of cheese. Bake in 375 degree oven for 45 minutes or until golden brown.

Mrs. Barbara Thompson, Natchitoches, LA

Jalapeño Hush Puppies

2 cups yellow corn meal
1 cup all-purpose flour
2 eggs, beaten
3 teaspoons baking powder
1 small can cream style corn

4 jalapeño peppers, chopped
½ bell pepper, chopped
6 green onions, chopped
1 cup buttermilk
½ teaspoon baking soda

Mix all ingredients. Should be consistency of a drop batter. Drop by spoonfuls into medium hot cooking oil. Fry until brown.
Note: If hush puppies are heavy, add more baking powder. If greasy and crumbly, add more flour. Should be light and fluffy.

Venita Scott, Natchitoches, LA

Basic Corn Bread

1 cup flour
¾ cup corn meal
3 tablespoons baking powder
1 teaspoon salt

¼ cup oil
1 cup milk
2 eggs, slightly beaten

Combine all dry ingredients in mixing bowl. In separate bowl combine milk, oil and eggs and mix well. Pour liquid mixture into dry mixture and mix well. Add enough oil to a 9-inch pan to coat bottom and sides and pour in batter. Bake in a preheated 400 degree oven for 20 minutes.

Gloria Allen, Marshall, TX

Yellow Devils

¾ cup self-rising corn meal
¼ cup flour
½ teaspoon salt
½ teaspoon baking powder
1 egg

½ cup buttermilk
1 cup cooked, puréed yellow
   squash
4 green onions, chopped

Combine dry ingredients then stir in remaining ingredients. Drop by teaspoonfuls into 375 degree oil, frying until golden. Do not substitute any other squash for yellow. Yields 12 to 18.

Dixie Harlan, Paris, TX

Greek Bread

1 loaf French bread
2 cups grated Mozzarella
  cheese
½ cup mayonnaise
½ cup margarine, softened

6 green onions, chopped
1 small can chopped black
  olives
½ teaspoon garlic powder

Slice bread lengthwise. Combine remaining ingredients and blend by hand until well mixed. Spread on bread and bake at 350 degrees for 15 minutes or until hot and bubbly. Slice and serve hot.
Note: Very good with smoked or charcoaled meats.

Judy Read, Farmerville, LA

Whole Wheat Bread

3 packages dry yeast
½ cup lukewarm water
1 cup sugar
1 tablespoon salt
1 cup butter-flavored Crisco

2 cups boiling water
2 cups buttermilk
6 cups whole wheat flour
6 cups unbleached flour
½ cup melted butter

Dissolve yeast in ½ cup warm water. Combine sugar, salt, Crisco and boiling water stirring until Crisco is melted. Stir in the buttermilk and the yeast mixture. Sift together the whole wheat and the unbleached flour. Add 6 cups of the flour mixture to the other combined ingredients and mix well. Cover with wet tea towel and let rise until dough is doubled in bulk. Push dough down and put out on floured board and work in remaining flour. Put in well greased bowl turning to coat all sides and cover with towel and let rise again until doubled in bulk. Divide into 4 equal portions and shape into loaves. Put in four 9 x 5-inch loaf pans that have been well greased. Spread tops of each loaf with melted butter. Allow to rise again. Bake in 350 degree oven for 30 to 40 minutes. Turn out on wire racks and cool. Yields 4 loaves.

Sue Tebow, Shreveport, LA

Irish Bread

4 cups flour, sifted
½ cup sugar
5 teaspoons baking powder
1 teaspoon salt
2 tablespoons butter

2 cups raisins (dark or white)
3 tablespoons caraway seed
1 egg, beaten
1 cup milk

Sift flour and mix with sugar, baking powder and salt. Work butter into this mixture until it is absorbed. Stir in raisins and caraway seed. Add beaten egg and milk. Mix and knead on a floured board. Bake in a greased loaf pan in a 350 degree oven for 50 to 60 minutes. Cool before slicing. Yields 1 loaf of Irish bread.

Kathleen Maloney, Hamden, CT

Husband: Edward J. Maloney
Knights of Columbus title: Administrative Assistant to
Supreme Knight

Angel Wings

½ teaspoon salt
4 egg yolks
2 eggs
½ cup powdered sugar

¼ cup butter
1 jigger rum
2 cups sifted flour

Add salt to egg yolks. Then beat egg yolks and eggs until thick and lemon colored. Add sugar, butter and rum. Beat until well mixed. Fold in flour and knead until the dough blisters. Transfer to a well floured board. Cut in half. Roll each half until it is very thin. Cut into 4-inch long by 2-inch wide strips. Slit each strip in the center and pull one end through the slit. Drop into hot oil and fry until lightly browned. Drain on absorbent paper and sprinkle with powdered sugar.

Stella Dunaway, Kensington, CT

Butter Horn Rolls

4 cups flour	½ cup warm water
1 cup shortening	½ cup sugar
1 cup milk, scalded	½ teaspoon salt
1 yeast cake	2 eggs, beaten

Mix flour and shortening with fork like pie crust. Add scalded milk. Dissolve yeast in warm water and add to dry ingredients. Add eggs and blend. Set in warm place and let rise 2 hours. Divide into 5 parts. Roll out like pie crust and cut each into 8 triangles, then roll each triangle from wide end up. Place on greased cookie sheet. Let rise 1 hour, then bake in 350 degree oven for 15 to 20 minutes. Yields 40 rolls.

Note: To scald milk, heat but do not boil.

Audrey Morehouse, Alexandria, LA

Easy Yeast Rolls

1 package active dry yeast	½ teaspoon salt
¾ cup warm water (105 to 115 degrees)	1 egg
2 tablespoons sugar	2½ to 2¾ cups flour
2 tablespoons vegetable oil	Soft butter or margarine

Dissolve yeast in water in 2½-quart bowl. Add sugar, oil, salt and egg. Stir to dissolve sugar and salt. Stir in 1 cup of the flour until smooth. Cover with a cloth and place on rack over bowl of hot water; let rise 15 minutes. Grease a square pan, 9 x 9 x 2-inches. Stir down batter and add 1½ cups flour. Stir until mixed and turn onto floured, cloth-covered board. Knead three minutes. If sticky, knead in ¼ cup flour. Divide dough into 16 pieces and shape quickly into balls; arrange in pan and brush tops with butter. Cover with cloth and place on rack over bowl of hot water; let rise 25 minutes. Bake in a 425 degree oven for 12 to 15 minutes or until light brown. Remove from pan to wire rack. Brush tops with soft butter. Yields 16 rolls.

Betty Loyd, Natchitoches, LA

French Bread Rolls

2½ cups warm water
1½ packages dry yeast
2 tablespoons sugar

2 teaspoons salt
7 cups flour, sifted
3 egg whites, beaten (mixer)

In a large bowl dissolve yeast in warm water. Add salt and sugar and stir to dissolve. Gradually add flour and mix with spoon until *well* blended. Place plate over bowl and place in warm place until dough doubles in size. Punch down and knead on floured surface. Roll into large finger rolls and place far apart on well-greased cookie sheets. This may take 3 large cookie sheets. Slash each roll with a knife and cover with beaten egg whites. Let rise again until doubled in size. Bake 15 minutes in 450 degree oven or 30 minutes in 350 degree oven until lightly brown. May freeze in Ziploc bags and rewarm in foil as needed. Dough may also be divided into 4 loaves and baked in greased loaf pans. Slash top of each loaf and brush on egg whites. Rolls will be hard on the outside. Delicious served hot with *real* butter. Yields 20 to 24 rolls or 4 loaves of bread.

Gloria Evans, Clarksdale, MS

Angel Flake Biscuits

5 cups flour
1 teaspoon salt
1 teaspoon soda
3 tablespoons baking powder
3 tablespoons sugar

1 cup shortening
1 package yeast dissolved in
 2 tablespoons warm water
2 cups buttermilk

Sift dry ingredients into bowl. Cut in shortening with fork until mixture looks like peas. Then add liquid all at once and stir until well mixed. Roll dough out to ½ to ¾-inch thickness. Cut with floured cutter. Bake on greased sheet in 450 degree oven for 10 minutes. Dough may be stored in a tightly closed container in refrigerator. Will keep in refrigerator for 1 week. *Do not let rise at any time.* If frozen, bake at 400 degrees for 15 minutes.

Lucille Schaider, La Porte, TX

Drop Biscuits

2½ cups self-rising flour
1 teaspoon salt
1 teaspoon baking powder
¼ cup shortening
1¼ cups milk
¼ cup cooking oil

Sift together flour, salt and baking powder; cut in shortening. Add milk, mix well. Using a tablespoon, drop small portions into skillet. After you have dropped the dough, dip fingers in oil and flatten dough shaping and smoothing the top. Bake at 450 degrees for 10 to 12 minutes.
Note: Pour oil into iron skillet or baking pan before dropping biscuits.
Norma Kay Angell, Tioga, LA

Quick Biscuits

6 tablespoons shortening
3 cups self-rising flour
1 cup milk

Preheat oven to 450 degrees. Cut shortening into flour with pastry cutter (or by hand). Add milk and mix until dough will form a ball. Knead gently to smooth dough. Put dough on a floured surface. Cut with a floured biscuit cutter. Place on a well-greased 11½ x 8½-inch pan, turning to grease both sides of biscuits. Place in oven and bake for 10 to 12 minutes. Yields 18 biscuits.
Becky Hebert, Natchitoches, LA

All-Bran Muffins

¼ teaspoon salt
1 teaspoon baking powder
1 cup flour
¾ cup sugar
1 cup All-Bran
½ teaspoon baking soda
1 cup buttermilk
1 egg, beaten
6 tablespoons cooking oil

Add salt and baking powder to flour and sift. Add sugar and All-Bran. Dissolve soda in buttermilk. Stir buttermilk into all dry ingredients. Add egg and stir in cooking oil. Fill greased and floured muffin pan cups ¾ full of batter. Bake in 350 degree oven for 30 to 40 minutes or until brown. Yields 12 to 18 muffins.
Mrs. Mary Ann Madeley Metcalf, Conroe, TX

Six-week Bran Muffins

5 cups flour
3 cups sugar
5 teaspoons baking soda
2 teaspoons salt
1 tablespoon cinnamon
1 teaspoon allspice
15-ounce box Raisin Bran
  cereal

1 cup vegetable oil
4 eggs, beaten
1 quart buttermilk
1 cup chopped pecans
  (optional)

Sift flour, sugar, soda, salt and spices together. Add cereal and mix. Combine oil, eggs and buttermilk and mix with dry ingredients. Bake in greased muffin tins at 400 degrees for 15 to 20 minutes. *Note: This batter can be stored in the refrigerator in an airtight container and used as desired up to 6 weeks.*

Jane R. Parnell, Newport, AR

Carrot Muffins

½ cup sugar
2 cups flour
1½ teaspoons baking powder
½ teaspoon baking soda
½ teaspoon salt
1 teaspoon cinnamon
¼ teaspoon cloves

½ cup maple flavored syrup
½ cup cooking oil
2 eggs
1 7½-ounce jar baby food
  carrots
1 teaspoon vanilla

Preheat oven to 350 degrees. Blend sugar, flour, baking powder, soda, salt and spices. Set aside. Mix syrup, oil, eggs, carrots and vanilla. Stir in flour mixture. Grease and flour muffin tin. Fill each muffin cup half full of batter. Bake for 20 minutes or until done. Yields 18 muffins.

Kim Boystel, Suffolk, England

Best Ever Banana Bread

1¾ cups flour
1½ cups sugar
½ teaspoon salt
1 teaspoon baking soda
¼ cup plus 1 tablespoon
   buttermilk

½ cup vegetable oil
2 eggs, beaten
1 teaspoon vanilla
2 ripe bananas, mashed
1 cup walnuts, coarsely
   chopped

Grease and flour 9 x 5-inch loaf pan. Combine flour, sugar and salt. Add baking soda to buttermilk. Stir in buttermilk, oil, eggs and vanilla. Mix this well. Fold in mashed bananas and walnuts. Pour mixture into greased and floured loaf pan. Bake at 325 degrees for 1 hour and 20 minutes or until top is golden brown and bread splits.

Kathie Erickson, Dallas,TX

Cinnamon Bread

Layer 1:
½ cup margarine
1 cup sugar
2 eggs, beaten
½ teaspoon Watkins vanilla
1 cup sour cream

¼ cup milk
2 cups flour
1½ teaspoons baking powder
1 teaspoon baking soda
½ teaspoon Watkins cinnamon

Cream margarine and sugar and add remaining ingredients. Pour into prepared 9-inch bread pan.

Layer 2:
1 tablespoon margarine,
   melted

1 tablespoon brown sugar
1 teaspoon Watkins cinnamon

Combine ingredients and spread over the batter in the bread pan. Bake at 350 degrees for 1 hour.

Glaze:
1 cup powdered sugar
½ cup milk

1 teaspoon Watkins vanilla

Combine ingredients and pour over bread while warm.
Note: This is a good bazaar item.

Nell Oliver, Farmerville, LA

Date Nut Bread

1½ cups boiling water
1½ cups chopped dates
1 cup walnuts
2 teaspoons soda
1½ cups sugar

2 tablespoons melted butter
2 eggs, beaten
2½ cups flour
1 teaspoon vanilla

Pour water over chopped dates, walnuts and soda. Mix well. In separate bowl combine the sugar, butter and eggs. Add date mixture to this and stir in flour and vanilla. Pour into 2 prepared loaf pans and bake in 350 degree oven until brown. Makes 2 loaves.

Audrey Morehouse, Alexandria, LA

Gingerbread

1 cup butter
1 cup brown sugar, firmly
  packed
1 cup white sugar
4 tablespoons molasses
2 teaspoons ginger
2 teaspoons cinnamon

1 teaspoon ground cloves
1 teaspoon nutmeg
⅛ teaspoon salt
2 teaspoons baking soda
2 cups buttermilk
2 eggs, well beaten
3 cups flour, sifted

Melt the butter and add the sugar, molasses, ginger, cinnamon, cloves, nutmeg and salt. Stir this mixture well. Dissolve the soda in the buttermilk and combine with other mixture. Add beaten eggs and stir in flour. Pour into a greased 9 x 12-inch baking pan. Bake at 350 degrees for 35 to 40 minutes. Serve hot with butter or favorite topping.

Ann Pelton, Dallas, TX

Pumpkin Bread

1½ cups sugar
½ cup Crisco oil
2 eggs
1 cup cooked pumpkin,
  mashed
1¾ cups flour
1 teaspoon baking soda

½ teaspoon salt
½ teaspoon baking powder
½ teaspoon cloves
½ teaspoon cinnamon
½ teaspoon allspice
⅓ cup water
1 cup raisins

Cream sugar, oil and eggs. Add remaining ingredients. Mix well and place in a greased loaf pan. Bake in 350 degree oven for 1 hour. *Note: Excellent as muffins.*

Bunny Laskowski, Houston, TX

Strawberry Bread

1 cup butter
1½ cups sugar
1 teaspoon vanilla
¼ teaspoon lemon extract
4 eggs
2½ cups flour

1 teaspoon salt
1 teaspoon cream of tartar
½ teaspoon baking soda
1 cup strawberry preserves
½ cup sour cream
1 cup pecans, chopped

Cream butter and sugar. Add vanilla and lemon extract. Beat until fluffy. Add eggs, one at a time. Sift dry ingredients. Combine preserves and sour cream. Add dry ingredients and preserves, alternately beginning and ending with flour mixture. Stir in nuts. Grease and flour 5 small loaf pans or 3 coffee cans. Pour into pans and bake at 350 degrees for 50 to 55 minutes. Makes nice, sweet gifts.

Mary Anne Hawkins, Dallas, TX

Pull-Apart Cinnamon Cake

3 cans biscuits
Cinnamon and sugar mixture
1 stick margarine, melted

1 cup powdered sugar
Milk

Preheat oven to 350 degrees. Cut biscuits into fourths. Roll in cinnamon and sugar. Drop into bundt pan in layers. Sprinkle extra cinnamon and sugar over each layer. Pour melted margarine over all. Bake for 25 minutes or until done. Make glaze with one cup powdered sugar and enough milk to make it the right consistency to pour but not too thin to stay on the cake. Pour part of glaze over cake while still in pan. Let soak into cake for a few minutes. Then turn out onto plate and pour remaining glaze over cake. Serves 10.

Lynda Thiels, Alexandria, LA

Sour Cream Coffee Cake

1 cup margarine
1 cup sugar
3 eggs
1 cup sour cream
2 teaspoons vanilla

2½ cups flour
1 teaspoon soda
1 teaspoon baking powder
¼ teaspoon salt

Filling:
¾ cup sugar
1 teaspoon cinnamon

1 cup nuts, chopped
1 cup raisins (optional)

Cream margarine and sugar. Add eggs. Beat well. Add sour cream and vanilla to sugar mixture. Beat well. Add flour, soda, baking powder and salt. Mix well. Pour ½ of cake batter into a greased tube pan. Combine the sugar, cinnamon, nuts and raisins to make the filling. Sprinkle ½ of filling over the batter. Add remaining batter to tube pan and then sprinkle remaining filling over top. Bake in 350 degree oven for 1 hour or until cake tests done. Cool in pan for 10 minutes before removing cake.

Nancy M. Donlin, North Haven, CT
Husband: W. Patrick Donlin
Knights of Columbus title: Supreme Advocate

Cake Mix Cinnamon Rolls

2 packages dry yeast
2½ cups lukewarm water
1 tablespoon sugar
Pinch of salt

5 cups flour, sifted
1 package yellow cake mix
  (with pudding or without)

In large bowl, dissolve yeast in lukewarm water. Add remaining ingredients and stir well. Knead for several minutes. Let dough rise in warm place, free from draft, for 2 to 3 hours, or until dough doubles in size. After dough rises, divide into 3 portions. Roll each portion into a rectangular shape, ¾-inch thick. Yields 36.

Filling:
¼ to ½ cup soft butter
1 cup sugar

3 teaspoons cinnamon

Combine above ingredients for filling. Spread on rolled out dough. Roll into a log shape and slice each portion into a dozen rolls, 3 dozen in all. Place in two 9 x 13-inch well-greased pans. Let rise for 2 to 3 hours. Bake in 350 degree oven for 20 minutes.

Glaze:
1 tablespoon margarine
1 cup confectioners' sugar

Few teaspoons milk

Mix the above ingredients. Place on hot cinnamon rolls.
Note: For sticky rolls some margarine melted with brown sugar and Karo syrup may be put in baking pan before rolls are placed there.

                                               Dixie Harlan, Paris, TX

Spanish Coffee Cake

2½ cups flour
1 cup sugar
1 cup brown sugar
⅔ cup oil
1 teaspoon cinnamon
½ teaspoon salt

1 cup chopped pecans
1 well-beaten egg
1 cup buttermilk
1 teaspoon baking soda
1 teaspoon baking powder

Grease and flour an 8 x 12-inch pan. Mix flour, sugar, brown sugar, oil, cinnamon and salt. Set aside ¾ cup of this mixture and add chopped pecans to it. Add to remainder of first mixture, egg, buttermilk, soda and baking powder. Pour in baking pan, spread reserved pecan mixture on top. Bake at 350 degrees for about 40 minutes. Serves 6 to 8.

Ida Harris, Waco, TX

Fluffy Pancakes

2 cups flour
½ teaspoon salt
2 tablespoons sugar
2 tablespoons baking powder
2 eggs

2 cups milk
5 tablespoons sour cream
4 tablespoons melted
   margarine

Mix dry ingredients in large bowl. Combine eggs, milk and sour cream. Pour gradually into dry ingredients beating with a whisk to prevent lumping. Add margarine and beat until smooth. Cook on prepared griddle. One-half cup batter makes large pancakes. Serves 4 to 5 people. Left over batter may be kept in refrigerator for a couple of days.

Bill Hollis, Farmerville, LA

Green Chilies Omelet

½ cup flour
1 cup milk
1 cup half and half
¼ cup butter
5 eggs
½ teaspoon salt

Tabasco to taste
4 ounces Monterey Jack
  cheese, grated
1 4-ounce can green chilies,
  with juice

Mix flour and half of milk in a saucepan. Stir in rest of milk and the half and half. Heat, stirring, until sauce thickens. Add butter. Remove from heat. Beat in eggs, salt, Tabasco and cheese. Add green chilies. Turn into a buttered 9-inch square pan. Bake in 400 degree oven for 25 to 30 minutes. Cut into squares to serve. Serves 6.

Bernadine C. Laborde

Crawfish Omelet

1½ cups crawfish tails
Salt and pepper to taste
Red pepper to taste
½ cup fresh mushrooms,
  sliced

½ cup chopped green onions
6 eggs, well beaten

Season crawfish with salt, black and red pepper, to taste. Set aside. In a skillet melt margarine and sauté mushrooms until soft. Add green onions and cook for 3 to 5 minutes. Add seasoned crawfish tails and cook until crawfish are done (approximately 3 to 5 minutes). Add well beaten eggs. Cover and cook slowly until eggs are done. Serve immediately. Yields 2 to 3 servings.

Thelma R. Foret, Lutcher, LA

Husband: Thomas J. Foret, III
Knights of Columbus title: Gramercy 1817

Eggs-Cheese-Ham Casserole

Butter
3 cups diced cooked ham
8 slices white bread
½ pound sharp Cheddar
  cheese, grated
6 to 8 eggs

2 cups milk
Salt and pepper to taste
2 teaspoons Worcestershire
  sauce
1 teaspoon dry mustard
½ teaspoon paprika

Preheat oven to 350 degrees. Butter a 3-quart casserole dish. Layer in order given, ham, bread and cheese in casserole. Repeat layers with ham, bread and cheese. Beat eggs and milk. Add seasoning. Pour over layered ingredients in casserole. Bake at 350 degrees for 1 hour. Serves 4 to 6.

Diane Smith, New Orleans, LA

Sausage Egg Strata

8 slices bread, crust removed
1 to 2 sticks butter
½ to 1 pound sausage, fried
  and crumbled
5 eggs

1 teaspoon salt
1 teaspoon dry mustard
2½ cups milk
½ pound American or
  Cheddar cheese, grated

Lightly butter bread (crust removed) and cut into quarters. In a 3-quart greased casserole place a layer of bread quarters and then a layer of sausage. Mix eggs, seasoning and milk. Pour ½ of egg mixture over sausage. Add another layer of sausage and bread. Pour remaining egg mixture over. Top with cheese. Cover casserole with foil and refrigerate overnight. Remove from refrigerator 1 hour before cooking. Bake in 350 degree oven in a pan of hot water for 1 hour. Yields 7 to 8 servings.

Note: Delicious for a brunch or an easy Sunday night supper. Ham may be substituted for sausage.

Gloria Evans, Clarksdale, MS

211

Brie Bake

8 slices Pepperidge Farm
  bread, cut in half
6 to 8 ounces Brie cheese,
  sliced ¼-inch thick
2 cups milk

3 eggs
¼ teaspoon salt
⅛ teaspoon pepper
½ teaspoon paprika

In a shallow casserole dish place 8 pieces of bread. Layer with half the cheese slices. Top with remaining bread and layer with remaining cheese. Beat milk, eggs, salt, pepper and paprika until frothy. Pour over bread and cheese. Let stand one hour. Bake in moderate 350 degree oven about one hour or until puffed and golden brown. Serve at once! (Any desired cheese may be substituted for Brie.)

Carol C. Morgan, Dallas, TX

Quiche

1 unbaked pie crust
½ large onion, sliced
¼ stick margarine
½ pound smoked bacon or
  ham
1½ cups grated Swiss cheese

1 tablespoon flour
3 eggs, beaten
½ cup half and half cream
Dash of nutmeg and cayenne
  pepper
½ teaspoon salt

Bake prepared pie crust until done but still very light in color. Break sliced onion into rings and sauté in margarine until tender. Drain and place on bottom of pie crust. Fry bacon or ham until crisp; drain and crumble over top of onion rings. Mix cheese and flour and sprinkle over bacon or ham. Mix eggs, cream and seasonings. Pour into pie shell. Bake in 450 degree oven for 15 minutes. Reduce heat to 350 degrees and bake for 15 minutes more. Allow to cool for 10 to 15 minutes before slicing. Yields 4 to 6 servings.

Mary West

Breakfast Soufflé

12 slices frozen white bread
¼ cup butter
8 ounces Cheddar cheese,
   grated

6 eggs, well beaten
1 quart milk
3 strips crisp bacon

Trim crust from bread; butter and cut into cubes. Layer bread and grated cheese in greased 9 x 13-inch baking dish. Beat together eggs and milk and pour over bread and cheese. Cover and leave in refrigerator overnight. Bake at 325 degrees for one hour. Top with crumbled bacon. Serves 8.

Linda McQueen, Dallas, TX

Duck Hunter's Delight
(Eggs Benedict)

1 can Cheddar cheese soup
1 can of milk
½ can white wine
Butter and garlic to taste

3 to 4 English muffins
6 to 8 eggs
6 to 8 slices Canadian Bacon
Paprika (optional)

In saucepan combine Cheddar cheese soup, milk and wine; stirring with a whisk until smooth and hot. Slice muffins in half. Spread butter and garlic on muffins and toast to light brown. Lightly fry Canadian Bacon. Remove from skillet and drain on a paper towel. Poach eggs to desired degree of doneness. Place muffin on plate and top with Canadian Bacon, poached egg and sauce. Sprinkle with paprika if desired.

Haywood Moseley, Marshall, TX

SAINT MARY'S TRAINING SCHOOL
FOR
RETARDED CHILDREN
Alexandria, Louisiana

The new Saint Mary's Training School was formally dedicated May 5th, 1974. There were feelings of happiness and sadness when leaving Clarks and the White Hotel which had been home for some twenty years. After months of planning and hard work, the children were moved sixty miles from Clarks to the new facility located on Highway 1 North, approximately five miles from Alexandria.

The arrival at the new modern facilities in Alexandria was a gala and impressive occasion. The complex consisted of twelve buildings on forty acres of land. Today, several new buildings have been added and additions made to most of the original structures. The modern buildings are planned and designed to offer the utmost in the training and care of retarded children. The school is operated by the Sisters of Our Lady of Sorrows with Sister M. Antoinette Baroncini as administrator. They employ a capable staff of professionals, consultants and direct care personnel. The present capacity is one hundred and fifty-two children.

Sweets

Ave Maria Chapel
St. Mary's Training School
Alexandria, Louisiana

Easy Banana Pudding

6 to 8 bananas
¾ box vanilla wafers
2 cups cold milk
1 large box instant vanilla
 pudding mix

1 can sweetened condensed
 milk
1 8-ounce carton frozen
 whipped topping

Slice the bananas. Crumble vanilla wafers. Layer bananas and wafers in a large bowl. Blend milk and pudding mix, stirring until thick. Fold in can of condensed milk and whipped topping. Pour over banana and wafer mixture. Refrigerate until serving. Yields 6 to 8 servings.
Note: This is delicious, easy to prepare and no cooking.
Barbara Thompson, Natchitoches, LA

Bread Pudding with Whiskey Sauce

3½ cups half and half
½ cup bourbon
3 tablespoons butter
2 cups sugar
3 eggs (beaten)

1 loaf French bread (very
 hard and stale)
2 teaspoons vanilla
1 cup raisins

In a 3-quart casserole combine half and half, bourbon, butter, sugar, and eggs. Crumble bread into mixture and refrigerate for several hours, stirring occasionally. Fold in vanilla and raisins. Bake at 350 degrees for about 1 hour or until top of pudding becomes very crusty. Serve with Whiskey Sauce. Yields 8 to 12 servings.

Whiskey Sauce:
1 stick butter
1 cup sugar

1 egg, beaten
2 tablespoons bourbon

In a saucepan melt butter and sugar until sugar is dissolved. Add beaten egg quickly and stir in bourbon.
Note: This recipe was served at Commander's Palace in New Orleans, Louisiana many years ago!

Carol C. Morgan, Dallas, TX

Baked Chocolate Pudding

1 cup flour
¾ cup sugar
2 teaspoons baking powder
½ teaspoon salt
4½ teaspoons cocoa
2 tablespoons melted butter
1 teaspoon vanilla

½ cup milk
½ cup chopped pecans or
   walnuts (optional)
½ cup sugar
½ cup brown sugar
4 tablespoons cocoa
1 cup water

Sift together three (3) times the flour, sugar, baking powder, salt and cocoa. In a separate bowl combine the melted butter, vanilla and milk. Blend the liquid mixture with the dry mixture and add the nuts. Pour into a square, greased baking dish. To make the topping combine the sugar, brown sugar and cocoa and spread on the pudding mixture. Carefully pour the 1 cup of water over the entire pudding and topping that has been placed in the pan. Bake at 350 degrees for 40 minutes. The pudding can be served at room temperature or warm topped with whipped cream. Very rich and delicious.

Reba Todd, Magnolia, AR

English Trifle

1 fresh pound cake
1 12-ounce jar raspberry
   preserves
1 16-ounce can peaches,
   drained
1 16-ounce can pears, drained

1 cup Amontillado sherry
2 envelopes of Bird's Dessert
   Mix
3½ cups milk
1 pint whipping cream

Cut the pound cake into two layers and spread the raspberry preserves between the layers. Assemble the cake again and cut into pieces two inches by one inch. Slice the fruit into one-inch cubes. Arrange cake strips in the bottom of a large serving dish and intersperse with the fruit. Pour sherry over cake. Prepare the custard according to instructions but use only 3½ cups of milk. Allow to cool and pour evenly over cake. When the custard is cold, beat the whipping cream until thick and dollop over the custard.

Andrea Rucker, Dallas, TX

Banana Split Cake (No Bake)

1 stick margarine (melted)
2 cups graham cracker crumbs
2 sticks margarine (softened)
2 eggs
2 cups powdered sugar
3 to 4 sliced bananas
1 20-ounce can crushed
   pineapple (well drained)
1 16-ounce carton of
   Cool Whip
¾ cup finely chopped
   pecans
½ cup chopped maraschino
   cherries

Mix together melted margarine and graham cracker crumbs. Pat into 9 x 13 x 2-inch pan. (Do not bake.) Beat the 2 sticks softened margarine, eggs and powdered sugar for no less than 15 minutes. Spread this mixture over the graham cracker crust. Cover mixture with bananas and crushed pineapple. Cover with Cool Whip. Sprinkle with pecans and cherries. Refrigerate overnight. Cut into squares to serve. Makes 18 squares.

Donna Ward, Farmerville, LA

Boiled Custard

1 14-ounce can Eagle Brand
   sweetened condensed milk
1 quart milk
4 eggs
½ teaspoon vanilla

Combine the milks and heat in the top of a double boiler. In a separate pan beat eggs well and pour a little of the milk over the eggs slowly, stirring constantly. Add the remaining milk. Return to heat and cook for 5 to 10 minutes or until thickened. Stir in vanilla. Chill.

Note: This can be served in a stemmed glass or custard cup topped with whipped cream.

Mary Anne Hawkins, Dallas, TX

Chocolate Ice Box Dessert

1 cup crushed vanilla wafers
2 1-ounce squares
   unsweetened chocolate
⅔ cup butter
2 cups powdered sugar, sifted
1 cup chopped pecans

1 teaspoon vanilla
2 tablespoons water
2 egg whites, beaten stiffly
½ gallon butter pecan ice
   cream

Spread wafers on the bottom of a buttered 9 x 13-inch pan. Melt the chocolate and butter together. Cool and stir in sugar, pecans, vanilla and water. Fold in egg whites. Spread mixture over crumbs. Freeze 2 hours. Soften ice cream completely and spread on top. Sprinkle top with additional cookie crumbs. Freeze again. When ready to serve, remove from freezer and thaw 15 to 20 minutes. Cut into squares. Serves 12.

Gloria Evans, Clarksdale, MS

Butter Pecan Ice Cream

1½ cups toasted pecans
¼ cup butter or margarine
5 eggs, beaten
1 box dark brown sugar

½ cup white sugar
½ pint half and half cream
½ pint whipping cream
Milk

Toast pecans in melted butter in oven. Remove. Beat together eggs and sugar until thick and fluffy. Add pecans, half and half and whipping cream. Finish filling 1-gallon freezer to fill line with milk. Freeze.

Note: Pecans may be broken into pieces or coarsely chopped.

Donna Ward, Farmerville, LA

Chris' Chocolate Dream

First Layer:
1 cup flour
1 stick butter or margarine,
  melted

2 tablespoons sugar
Dash salt

Combine all ingredients and press thinly into a 9 x 13-inch baking dish. Bake 15 to 20 minutes. Cool completely.

Second Layer:
1 8-ounce package cream
  cheese, softened

1 cup powdered sugar
1 9-ounce carton Cool Whip

Mix cream cheese, sugar and 2 cups Cool Whip and pour over crust.

Third Layer:
3 cups milk

2 3¾-ounce boxes of instant
  chocolate pudding

Beat milk into pudding mix for three minutes and pour over second layer.

Fourth Layer:
Remaining Cool Whip from
  9-ounce carton

½ cup chopped pecans
  (optional)

Top with Cool Whip and pecans. Refrigerate several hours.
Chris Byerly, Athens, TX

Vanilla Ice Cream

4 eggs
2½ cups sugar
½ teaspoon salt

2 tablespoons vanilla
2 pints half and half cream
5 cups milk

Beat eggs until foamy. Add sugar gradually, mixing well. Add other ingredients. Mix well and pour into 1-gallon ice cream freezer.
Dr. Doug Ezell, Ruston, LA

Buttermint Freeze

Crust:
2 tablespoons butter, melted

14 chocolate Oreo cookies, finely crushed

Mix melted butter and crushed Oreo cookies until cookie crumbs are coated with butter. Press into a 9 x 14 x 2-inch pyrex dish and bake in 400 degree oven for 5 minutes. Remove and cool.

Filling:
1 20-ounce can and
1 8-ounce can crushed pineapple, undrained
3½ cups miniature marshmallows
1 cup Kraft Buttermints

1 3-ounce package lime Jello
1 9-ounce carton frozen dessert topping
6 chocolate Oreo cookies, crushed or Baker's German sweet chocolate, grated

In a large bowl, combine undrained pineapple, marshmallows, buttermints and Jello (no water added to Jello). Cover and let set until marshmallows are softened and begin to melt. May heat to hasten melting of marshmallows. Fold in frozen dessert topping. Pour into cooled cookie crust and sprinkle with more cookie crumbs. Cover with Saran Wrap and freeze overnight or longer. Remove from freezer 15 to 20 minutes before serving. Garnish with whipped cream and crushed Oreos or grated Baker's German sweet chocolate. Serve with sprig of mint. Yields 12 servings.

Mrs. Louis Reno, Natchitoches, LA

Banana Nut Ice Cream

5 eggs
1½ cups sugar
1 can Eagle Brand milk
1 13-ounce can Pet milk

Pinch of salt
1 teaspoon vanilla
5 bananas, mashed
Milk (about ½ gallon)

Beat eggs and sugar together. Add Eagle Brand milk, Pet milk, salt and vanilla. Fold in mashed bananas. Pour into freezer can and add milk to "fill line". Freeze as directed. Yields about 1 gallon.

Linda Mitchell, Bossier City, LA

221

Bill's Favorite Ice Cream

7 large eggs	1 tablespoon vanilla
2 cups sugar	2 large cans Pet milk
¼ to ½ teaspoon salt	9 cups whole milk

Beat eggs one at a time alternating with sugar. Add salt, vanilla and Pet milk. Stir in 9 cups whole milk and pour into freezer can. Allow mixture to chill about two hours before freezing ice cream. Serve with favorite topping of fruit. Yields about 3 quarts.

Cindy Ward, Dallas, TX

Apple Crunch

Crust:

1 cup flour	½ cup margarine
¼ cup sugar	1 teaspoon vanilla
1 egg yolk	

Mix together and pat into a 9 x 13-inch pan. Bake 15 minutes at 350 degrees.

Filling:

2 cups unsweetened applesauce	½ teaspoon nutmeg
	1 cup light brown sugar
6 cups chopped apples	½ teaspoon cinnamon

Mix all ingredients together and spread over crust.

Topping:

½ cup oatmeal	¼ cup margarine
½ cup flour	½ cup light brown sugar

Mix all ingredients until blended. Sprinkle over filling. Bake 45 minutes at 350 degrees until apples are bubbling through topping. Serve warm with whipped cream and nuts or ice cream. Yields 18 pieces.

Julia Van Tassell, North Haven, CT

Husband: William J. Van Tassell
Knights of Columbus title: Supreme Treasurer

Cherry Crunch Cake

Crust:
2 sticks margarine
2 cups self-rising flour, sifted   1 cup chopped pecans

Mix margarine, flour and pecans. Press into a 15 x 10-inch pan. Bake in 400 degree oven for 20 minutes. Cool.

Filling:
1 box powdered sugar, sifted   2 packages of Dream Whip
1 8-ounce package cream   1 16-ounce can cherry pie
  cheese   filling

Mix powdered sugar and cream cheese. Prepare Dream Whip according to package instructions. Fold Dream Whip into sugar and creamed cheese mixture. Spoon onto cooled crust. Cover with cherry pie filling. Chill before serving. Serves 8 to 10.

Mrs. Mallie McLauglin, Nashville, AR

Fruit Crisp

6 cups sliced fresh apples,   ½ cup honey
  pears or peaches or 2 20-   ½ cup flour
  ounce cans of canned fruit,   ¼ teaspoon cinnamon
  drained   ¼ cup margarine
1 tablespoon lemon juice   ¾ cup chopped pecans
½ cup brown sugar, divided

Butter a 9 x 9 x 2-inch baking dish. Preheat oven to 375 degrees. Pare and slice fresh fruits or drain canned fruit and add lemon juice, ¼ cup brown sugar and honey. Pour into baking dish. Combine flour, ¼ cup brown sugar and cinnamon. Cut margarine into flour mixture. Stir in chopped pecans. Sprinkle on fruit mixture. Bake for 30 to 40 minutes if using canned fruit and 50 minutes or longer if using fresh fruit. Yields 6 to 8 servings.

Edna Polker

Butter Pecan Dessert

Crust:

1½ cups flour	1½ sticks butter
¾ cup chopped pecans	

Mix above ingredients and press into 9 x 13 x 2-inch pan. Bake at 350 degrees for approximately 20 minutes or until lightly brown. Cool.

Filling:

1 8-ounce package cream cheese, softened	1 8-ounce carton Cool Whip
	1 cup powdered sugar

Combine ingredients and spread gently on cooled crust.

Topping:

3 boxes 3⅝-ounce size butter pecan instant pudding	4 cups milk

Mix pudding and milk until mixture begins to thicken. Spread over top of filling. Refrigerate.

Optional: Sprinkle a few chopped pecans on top. Any flavor pudding can be used. May be topped with Cool Whip.

Anne Riesbeck, Hamden, CT

Husband: Charles P. Riesbeck, Jr.

Knights of Columbus title: Supreme Secretary

Aunt Mary's Chocolate Sauce

2 squares unsweetened chocolate	⅔ cup sugar
2 tablespoons butter	1 cup half and half cream
	½ teaspoon vanilla

Melt the chocolate in butter. Slowly add sugar and stir until dissolved. Add cream. Cook slowly until smooth and thick. Remove from heat and add vanilla.

Mrs. Billie McDougall, Paris, TX

Hot Fudge Sauce I

2 tablespoons butter
2 12-ounce bags sweet
   chocolate chips

1 can sweetened condensed
   milk
¼ to ½ cup liqueur

Place butter and chocolate in a saucepan and heat until chocolate has melted. Add sweetened condensed milk and heat, while stirring, for 1 to 2 minutes or until thoroughly heated. Add liqueur and mix well. Pour into 2 pint jars and refrigerate until using.
Note: Grand Marnier, Amaretto, creme de menthe, coffee or cherry liqueurs can be used.

Maryann Ingersall, New Orleans, LA

Hot Fudge Sauce II

1 stick butter
6 squares Baker's chocolate,
   unsweetened

2 cups sugar
1 large can evaporated milk
2 teaspoons vanilla

Melt butter and chocolate over hot water and stir until smooth. Alternately, add sugar and milk, stirring constantly. Add 2 teaspoons vanilla. Cool until thickened. Refrigerate in jar and use as needed.

Dr. Doug Ezell, Ruston, LA

Variation: Same recipe as above but using 4 squares unsweetened chocolate, 3 cups sugar and omitting vanilla. Stir just sugar into chocolate mixture a little at a time making sure sugar is completely moistened after each addition. *Slowly* stir milk, a little at a time, into the sugar and chocolate mixture (that has become very thick and dry). Stir constantly until smooth and satiny looking. Serve hot. Can be refrigerated and reheated as needed. Makes about 1 quart.

Judy Read, Farmerville, LA

Blueberry Torte

Crust:

16 graham crackers,   ½ cup sugar
  crumbled   ½ cup butter, softened

Mix the graham cracker crumbs with sugar and softened butter. Stir until well mixed. Press into bottom of a 9 x 13-inch baking dish.

Filling:

8 ounces cream cheese   ½ cup sugar
2 eggs   1 can blueberry pie filling
½ teaspoon vanilla   Cool Whip or whipping cream

Cream the cheese and add eggs, vanilla and sugar. Mix. Place over the graham cracker crust. Bake in 350 degree oven for 20 minutes. Remove and cool. Top with blueberry pie filling. Top with Cool Whip or sweetened whipped cream. Yields 6 to 8 servings.

Audrey Morehouse, Alexandria, LA

Strawberries Romanoff

2 pints ripe strawberries   1 orange
⅓ cup plus 2 tablespoons   ¾ cup heavy cream
  sugar
⅓ cup Grand Marnier or
  Cointreau

Remove the stems from the strawberries. Rinse well and drain. Pat dry with paper towel. Place the strawberries in a bowl and add ⅓ cup of the sugar and the Grand Marnier. Using a swivel-bladed potato peeler, cut around the orange to produce a very thin spiral of peel. Do not cut into the white pulp. Cut the peel into wafer-thin shreds. Add to the strawberries and fold together gently. (Use the orange in another dish.) Cover the bowl and refrigerate until ready to serve. Whip the cream and flavor it with the remaining 2 tablespoons of sugar. Serve the cream with the strawberries. Yields 8 servings.

Alicia Clemente, Alexandria, LA

Fresh Fruit Torte

Crust:
2 cups flour   ½ cup brown sugar
1 cup butter

Mix all ingredients together and spread in a 9 x 13-inch pan. Bake in 400 degree oven for 15 minutes. Do not overcook.

Filling:
1 large Cool Whip   1½ cups powdered sugar
8-ounce package cream cheese   1 pint fresh strawberries

Mix first 3 ingredients and spread on top of cooled crust. Wash and slice strawberries. Layer on top of filling.

Glaze:
1 cup sugar   3 tablespoons cornstarch
1 cup water   2 tablespoons strawberry Jello

Mix and cook glaze ingredients until thick. Cool. Pour over fresh strawberries. Keep refrigerated. Yields 8 servings.

Pam Kilpatrick, Ruston, LA

Homemade Ice Cream

3 pints half and half cream   1 ounce vanilla flavoring
1½ pints whipping cream   1 cup sugar
6 large eggs   Whole milk

Mix half and half with whipping cream. Beat eggs and blend into cream mixture. Add vanilla flavoring and sugar to mixture and mix well. Pour the mixture into freezer can and fill to "fill line" with whole milk.

Note: To make peach, strawberry or other fruit ice cream with above recipe, use 8 peaches, mashed into pulp, and 1 cup sugar or 3 cups strawberries and 1 cup sugar. Add fruit to cream mixture before pouring into freezer.

Van Parkman, Columbia, MS

Meringue Torte

6 egg whites
2 teaspoons vanilla
½ teaspoon cream of tartar

Dash of salt
2 cups sugar

Bring egg whites to room temperature. Beat with an electric mixer until soft peaks form. Add vanilla, cream of tartar and dash of salt. Gradually add sugar and continue beating until stiff peaks form. Cover 2 cookie sheets with ungreased paper. (I use a paper sack.) Using a plate, draw a 9-inch circle on each paper. Spread meringue evenly over both circles. Bake in 275 degree oven for 1 hour. Turn off heat; keep door closed, and let dry for at least 2 hours. Fill and frost meringue with the following topping recipe. Makes 2 9-inch tortes.

Topping:
6¾-ounce chocolate coated
    English toffee (Heath) bars,
    chilled and crushed

2 cups whipping cream,
    whipped
Dash of salt

Mix ¾ of the crushed toffee bars with the whipped cream. Add dash of salt. Spread ⅓ of the mixture between the meringue layers. Frost top and sides. Garnish with remaining candy. Refrigerate and chill overnight. Keep refrigerated. Yields 16 servings.

Gloria Evans, Clarksdale, MS

Chantilly Creme

1 cup whipping cream
½ teaspoon vanilla
2 to 3 tablespoons sifted
    confectioners' sugar

1 heaping tablespoon sour
    cream

Whip cream until stiff and fluffy; stir in vanilla. Fold in sugar and sour cream. Serve with any fresh fruit or as a topping for pies and cakes. Chantilly Creme is especially delicious on all kinds of berries. Yields just over a cup.

Cindy Ward, Dallas, TX

Fruit Pizza

1 20-ounce roll sugar cookie
  dough
1 8-ounce package cream
  cheese
½ teaspoon vanilla
⅓ cup sugar

Fruit of choice
2 tablespoons cornstarch
¼ teaspoon salt
⅔ cup sugar
1 cup orange juice (diluted)

Press cookie dough completely over bottom of jellyroll pan and bake for 12 minutes at 350 degrees. Remove from oven and let cool. Beat cream cheese, vanilla and sugar. Spread over cooled cookie dough. Arrange fruit over cream cheese mixture. (Use your imagination in your creation of a design.) Mix cornstarch, salt, sugar and orange juice in saucepan and boil for 1 minute. Pour over fruit. Allow to cool completely in refrigerator before serving.
Note: If a lot of fruit is used, double the sauce that is made to pour over the fruit.
Fourth of July: Use blueberries, strawberries and bananas and arrange in a flag design.

Judy Read, Farmerville, LA

Fruit Torte

1 10¾-ounce frozen pound
  cake, thawed
1 large banana, thinly sliced
  (or sliced peaches)

Lemon juice
1½ cups fresh strawberries
1½ cups Cool Whip

Cut pound cake horizontally in three layers. Set aside. Dip banana slices in lemon juice. Arrange one-half of bananas or peaches over bottom layer of cake. Spread one-third of the Cool Whip over bottom layer. Top Cool Whip with a layer of strawberries. Add middle layer of cake. Spread with second one-third of the Cool Whip and a layer of berries. Top with the last layer of the cake. Frost top of cake with remaining one-third of Cool Whip. Garnish with bananas (or peaches) and berries. Cut into slices to serve. Yields 6 servings.
Lorine Kordsmeier, Morrilton, AR
Husband: William Kordsmeier
Knights of Columbus title: State Membership

Lemon Mousse

4 eggs, separated
2 envelopes unflavored gelatin
1½ cups granulated sugar
⅓ cup grated lemon peel (use
  less if using dried peel)

1½ cups whipping cream,
  whipped
¼ cup confectioners' sugar

Separate the eggs and allow the whites to warm to room temperature. In a microwave bowl, combine gelatin and ½ cup sugar. In
a separate bowl beat egg yolks until thick and lemon colored (approximately 3 minutes). Gradually add ½ cup granulated sugar a
few tablespoons at a time. Beat until very thick. Slowly add lemon
juice and mix. Stir into gelatin mixture and blend well. On lowest
heat of microwave, cook this mixture until it has thickened. Stir in
lemon peel. Set in bowl of ice cubes to cool and thicken, about 15
minutes. (Do not let it get too thick. It should mound when
dropped from spoon.) In a large bowl beat egg whites at high speed
until soft peaks form. Beat in remaining ½ cup granulated sugar,
a tablespoonful at a time. Beat until stiff peaks form when beaters
are raised. Gently fold gelatin mixture into egg whites. Beat 1½
cups whipping cream with confectioners' sugar until stiff. Gently
fold into gelatin mixture. Pour into 1-quart soufflé dish that has
had a waxed paper collar placed around the top. To serve, remove
collar. Whip ½ cup whipping cream and put through pastry bag in
decorative way. Garnish with lemon peel. Yields 8 servings.

Dixie Harlan, Paris, TX

Lemon Sauce

2 tablespoons butter
2 tablespoons flour
1½ cups hot water
⅓ cup sugar

1 egg, well beaten
1 tablespoon lemon juice
2 tablespoons grated lemon
  peel

Combine butter, flour, water and sugar. Add well beaten egg. Cook
until thick, stirring constantly. Add lemon juice and lemon peel.
Stir. Let cool and pour over fresh fruit salad.

Eckie Rutherford, Jefferson, TX

Caramel Sauce

⅓ cup brown sugar
1 cup water
2 tablespoons butter

1 tablespoon flour
½ cup toasted pecans
1 teaspoon vanilla

In small saucepan mix sugar and water; stir in butter and flour and cook until thickened. Remove from heat and add chopped toasted pecans and vanilla. Goes great over ice cream or poached fruit, but try it on fruit bread, hot or cold.

Eckie Rutherford, Jefferson, TX

Crisp Popcorn with Nuts

3 tablespoons corn oil
⅓ cup popcorn
1 cup light or dark corn syrup
1 cup sugar
⅛ teaspoon salt

¼ cup water
4 tablespoons margarine
¾ cup cashew nuts, unsalted
1 teaspoon soda
2 teaspoons hot water

Heat corn oil in a 3-quart kettle over medium heat for 3 minutes. Add popcorn. Cover, leaving small air space at edge of cover. Shake frequently over medium heat until popping stops. Spread on greased flat pan. Place corn syrup, sugar, salt, water and margarine in a medium saucepan. Stir over low heat until sugar is dissolved; then increase heat and cook to the hard crack stage (300 degrees) stirring occasionally, or until a small amount separates into threads which are hard and brittle when tested in very cold water. Stir in nuts, remove from heat. Combine soda and hot water; stir into hot mixture. Pour mixture over popped corn in flat pan and mix quickly. It is necessary to work fast. Leave in pan to cool turning at least once. When cool and hard, break into small pieces.

Alice Williamson, Palmyra, NY

Blackberry Jam Cake

½ pound margarine
1½ cups sugar
3 eggs
10 ounces blackberry jam
2½ cups flour
¼ teaspoon allspice

⅛ teaspoon salt
¼ teaspoon nutmeg
1 teaspoon baking soda
½ teaspoon cinnamon
1 cup buttermilk
1 cup chopped nuts

Preheat oven to 350 degrees. Cream margarine and sugar, add eggs and jam, beating well. Sift all dry ingredients together and add alternately with buttermilk to creamed mixture. Fold in nuts. Pour into three 9-inch greased and floured cake pans. Bake for 27 minutes. Frost with Coconut Pecan Frosting. (See Index)

Peggy Melton, Conroe, TX

Butternut Cake

1 cup shortening, margarine
   or butter
2 cups sugar
4 eggs
Dash of salt

1 cup plain flour
1½ cups self-rising flour
1 cup sweet milk
1 tablespoon butternut
   flavoring

Cream together for 10 minutes the shortening, sugar and eggs. Add salt and plain flour. Beat to blend well. Add the self-rising flour, milk and flavoring. Bake in 3 or 4 layers at 350 degrees for approximately 35 minutes or until tests done. Cool completely and frost with Butternut Frosting.

Butternut Frosting:
1 8-ounce package cream
   cheese
1 stick margarine
1 box confectioners' sugar

1 tablespoon butternut
   flavoring
1 cup pecans

Mix all ingredients together thoroughly. Add enough milk for spreading consistency, if necessary.

JoAnn Gilmore, Ruston, LA

Spicy Carrot Cake

2 cups sugar
2 cups flour
2 teaspoons soda
2 teaspoons cinnamon
1 teaspoon allspice

½ teaspoon black pepper
1 teaspoon salt
4 eggs
1½ cups oil
3 cups grated carrots

Combine dry ingredients and mix well. Add eggs and oil. Mix well. Add carrots and beat on medium speed 2 minutes. Grease and flour three 8 or 9-inch cake pans. Pour batter into pans. Bake in 350 degree preheated oven for 25 to 35 minutes. When done cool cake in pans 10 minutes. Remove and place on rack to completely cool before icing.

Icing:
1 8-ounce package cream
  cheese, softened
1 stick margarine, softened

1 box confectioners' sugar
1 teaspoon vanilla
1 cup finely chopped pecans

Cream cheese and margarine until light and fluffy. Add sugar gradually and mix well. Add vanilla and pecans. Mix well. Ice between layers and top (not sides). Chill. Store in refrigerator.
Note: Black pepper makes spices taste tangier. Do not omit.

Melba Simmons, Bunkie, LA

Cherry Pineapple Delight

1 stick butter or margarine
1 box yellow cake mix
1 cup chopped nuts
  (your choice)

1 21-ounce can cherry pie
  filling
1 20-ounce can crushed
  pineapple, undrained

With pastry blender, blend butter and cake mix into coarse crumbs. Add nuts to mixture. Pour ½ of cake mixture into a 9 x 14-inch pyrex dish which has been sprayed with Pam. Pour cherry pie filling over cake mix; then pineapple and juice. Top with other ½ of cake mix. Bake at 350 degrees for 25 minutes. Top with Cool Whip to serve. Yields 12 servings.

Mrs. Louis Reno, Natchitoches, LA

Holiday Coconut Cake

⅓ cup shortening
⅓ cup butter, softened
1¾ cups sugar
3 cups flour
3½ teaspoons baking powder
¾ teaspoon salt
1⅓ cups milk

2 teaspoons vanilla extract
4 egg whites
1 recipe Lemon Filling
  (below)
1 recipe 7 Minute Frosting
  (see index)
Freshly grated coconut

Cream shortening, butter and sugar until light and fluffy. Sift flour, baking powder and salt together. Add to creamed butter mixture alternately with milk. Beat after each addition of dry ingredients and milk. Stir in vanilla. Beat egg whites until stiff, fold into batter. Pour batter into 3 greased and floured 9-inch cake pans. Bake in 350 degree oven for 25 minutes or until a wooden toothpick inserted into center of cake comes out clean. Cool in pans for 10 minutes before removing. Remove from pan and cool on rack. Spread Lemon Filling between each layer. Frost top and sides with 7 Minute Frosting. (See Index) Sprinkle coconut over frosting. Yields 1 3-layer cake.

Lemon Filling:
1 cup plus 2 tablespoons sugar
¼ cup cornstarch
1 cup plus 2 tablespoons water
2 egg yolks, slightly beaten

2 tablespoons butter
3 tablespoons lemon juice
1 tablespoon grated lemon
  rind

Combine sugar and cornstarch in a saucepan. Gradually stir in water. Cook over medium heat, stirring constantly, until mixture thickens and comes to a boil. Boil for 1 minute. Slowly stir about ¼ of the hot mixture into the egg yolks. Add the remaining hot mixture. Add butter, lemon juice and grated lemon rind to mixture. Mix. Spread between layers.

Elizabeth Ardoin, Alexandria, LA

7 Minute Frosting

1½ cups sugar   ½ cup water
3 egg whites   1 teaspoon vanilla
½ cup Karo syrup (light)

Place sugar, egg whites, Karo and water in top of a double boiler. Cook with constant beating for 7 minutes. Remove from heat and place cooked mixture into a bowl. Beat with mixer until stiff peak forms. Add vanilla. Beat for a second. Frost top and sides of cake. Sprinkle coconut over frosting.

Elizabeth Ardoin, Alexandria, LA

Four-Day Coconut Cake

The frosting is to be made the first day.

Frosting:
3 packages frozen coconut   2 cups sugar
1 8-ounce carton sour cream

Mix coconut, sour cream and sugar. Refrigerate overnight.

The cake is to be made the second day.

Cake:
2 cups self-rising flour   4 eggs
2 cups sugar   1 pint whipping cream
1 teaspoon vanilla

Mix flour and sugar. Stir in vanilla, eggs and cream. Divide batter between 3 9-inch cake pans. Bake in preheated 300 degree oven 40 minutes. Remove from cake pans and cool. Frost between layers and on top, but not sides. Refrigerate for 3 days before cutting. Great for holidays.

Jane R. Parnell, Newport, AR

Italian Cream Cake

1 teaspoon soda
1 cup buttermilk
1 stick margarine
½ cup shortening
2 cups sugar

1 teaspoon vanilla
5 eggs (separated)
2 cups flour
1 cup pecans
1 cup coconut

Preheat oven to 350 degrees. Add soda to buttermilk. Cream margarine and shortening. Add sugar gradually, then vanilla and egg yolks. Mix well and add buttermilk and flour alternately, beginning and ending with flour. Add pecans and coconut. Fold in stiffly beaten egg whites. Bake in 3 greased and floured cake pans for 25 minutes.

Icing:
1 stick margarine
1 box powdered sugar
1 8-ounce package cream
  cheese

1 teaspoon vanilla
Pecans, finely chopped

Cream margarine, powdered sugar, cream cheese and vanilla until well blended. Ice cake when it has cooled. Sprinkle with finely chopped pecans.

Marlene Roussel, Baton Rouge, LA

Cotton Pickin Cake

1 box Duncan Hines Golden
  Butter cake mix
½ cup Crisco oil

4 eggs
1 11-ounce can mandarin
  oranges with juice

Mix all ingredients with electric mixer. Divide into 3 9-inch greased and floured layer pans. Bake at 325 degrees for 20 minutes. Cool completely.

236

Icing:
1 small package instant vanilla
  pudding
1 large can crushed pineapple,
  with juice

1 13½-ounce carton Cool
  Whip

Mix ingredients with electric mixer. Spread between layers and on top and sides. Keep covered in refrigerator. (Better if made the night before.)

Brenda Ingram, Natchitoches, LA

Hummingbird Cake

3 cups all-purpose flour
2 cups sugar
1 teaspoon salt
1 teaspoon soda
1 teaspoon ground cinnamon
3 eggs, beaten
1½ cups vegetable oil

1½ teaspoons vanilla extract
1 8-ounce can crushed
  pineapple, undrained
2 cups chopped pecans,
  divided
2 cups chopped bananas

Combine dry ingredients in a large mixing bowl; add eggs and oil, stirring until dry ingredients are moistened. Do not beat. Stir in vanilla, pineapple, 1 cup chopped pecans, and bananas. Spoon batter into 3 well-greased and floured 9-inch cake pans. Bake at 350 degrees for 25 to 30 minutes or until cake tests done. Cool in pans 10 minutes; remove from pans, and cool completely. Spread frosting between layers and on top and sides of cake. Sprinkle with remaining pecans.

Cream Cheese Frosting:
1 8-ounce package cream
  cheese, softened
½ cup butter or margarine,
  softened

1 16-ounce package powdered
  sugar
1 teaspoon vanilla extract

Combine cream cheese and butter; cream until smooth. Add powdered sugar, beating until light and fluffy. Stir in vanilla. Yields enough for a 3 layer cake.

Elizabeth Ardoin, Alexandria, LA

Pineapple Cake I

1 pineapple cake mix	4 eggs
1 box pineapple instant pudding	¾ cup oil
	1 10-ounce 7-Up

Grease and flour two 9-inch cake pans or three 8-inch cake pans. Preheat oven to 350 degrees. Mix the first two ingredients. Add eggs and oil. Mix together. Add 7-Up and mix. Pour into pans and bake for 30 to 45 minutes or until top springs back to touch. Cool before topping with Pineapple Cake Icing.

Pineapple Cake Icing:

1 16-ounce can crushed pineapple	3 tablespoons cornstarch
1½ cups sugar	Dash of salt
2 egg yolks	½ stick margarine

Mix all ingredients except margarine in a medium saucepan. Place on medium heat and cook until ingredients thicken. Add margarine. Stir until margarine is dissolved. Ice between layers and on top.

Janet Morgan, Pineville, LA

Raisin Apple Cake

3 cups unsifted flour	½ teaspoon ground nutmeg
2 cups sugar	½ teaspoon salt
1 cup mayonnaise	¼ teaspoon ground cloves
2 eggs	3 cups chopped, peeled apples
⅓ cup milk	1 cup raisins
2 teaspoons baking soda	½ cup chopped walnuts or
1½ teaspoons cinnamon	pecans

Grease and flour 2 9-inch round baking pans. In a mixing bowl place first 10 ingredients and mix with electric mixer on low speed for 2 minutes, scraping bowl frequently to completely mix. Stir in apples, raisins and nuts. Pour into prepared pans. Bake in 350 degree oven for 45 minutes. Remove and cool before frosting. Frost with whipped cream or Cool Whip.

Donna Graham, Lyon, MS

New Haven Date Cake

Step 1:

1 cup chopped dates   1½ cups boiling water
1 teaspoon soda

Mix dates and soda. Pour boiling water over. Set aside to cool.

Step 2:

2 eggs   ¾ teaspoon soda
1 cup sugar   Pinch of salt
½ cup butter
1½ cups plus 3 teaspoons
   flour

Beat eggs and add sugar and butter. Add date mixture. Blend in flour, soda and salt. Pour into a greased and floured 9 x 13-inch pan. Set aside.

Step 3:

12 ounces chocolate chips   ½ cup sugar
½ cup chopped nuts

Mix these three ingredients. Pour over cake batter. Place in pre-heated 350 degree oven and bake for 30 to 40 minutes or until done.

Nancy M. Donlin, North Haven, CT
Husband: W. Patrick Donlin
Knights of Columbus title: Supreme Advocate

239

Miss Martha's Apple Nut Cake

½ cup butter
2 cups sugar
2 eggs
2 cups sifted all-purpose flour
1 teaspoon baking powder
¾ teaspoon baking soda
½ teaspoon salt

½ teaspoon nutmeg
½ teaspoon cinnamon
3 Washington delicious apples
   pared, cored and chopped
1½ cups chopped nuts
Sauce and/or whipped cream,
   optional

Preheat oven to 325 degrees. Cream butter, gradually adding sugar and beat until light and fluffy. Beat in eggs, one at a time. Sift together flour, baking powder, baking soda, salt, nutmeg and cinnamon. Gradually add to egg mixture. Dough will be fairly stiff. Stir in apples and nuts. Turn into a buttered 9 x 12-inch pan. Bake for 55 to 70 minutes.

Rum Sauce:
1 cup sugar
½ cup butter

½ cup half and half cream
3 teaspoons rum extract

Combine sugar, butter and cream. Warm over low heat. Stir occasionally until hot. Stir in rum extract. Serve over cake and top with whipped cream if desired. Yields 12 to 15 servings. Very rich and special.

Martha Shoffner, Little Rock, AR

Decorator's Icing

½ cup Crisco shortening
1 pound confectioners' sugar,
   sifted
4½ tablespoons water

1 teaspoon flavoring of your
   choice
½ teaspoon salt
Food coloring, optional

Cream Crisco and gradually add sifted sugar. Add water, flavoring and salt. Beat until completely smooth. If using a lot of food coloring, use less water. This will frost one 8-inch layer cake. If you want to use a lot of piped decorations on the cake, double the recipe.
Note: Keep icing covered while not using to prevent a film from forming on top.

Judy Read, Farmerville, LA

Fig Cake

1½ pints fig preserves
1 cup sugar
1 cup shortening
1 cup lukewarm water
1 teaspoon baking soda
½ teaspoon salt

3 cups sifted all-purpose flour
2 teaspoons cinnamon
1 teaspoon ginger
1 teaspoon nutmeg
1 cup chopped pecans

Preheat oven to 350 degrees. Mix together figs, sugar, shortening and water in large bowl. Mix the dry ingredients together. Add dry ingredients to fig mixture gradually. Mix well. Pour into a well greased and floured 9 x 13 pan. Bake for 50 to 55 minutes. Yields 18 servings.

Myrtle Girouard, Loreauville, LA

Pecan Pie Cake

Crust:
1 box Duncan Hines Butter
  Recipe Golden cake mix
  (reserve ¾ cup)

1 egg
1 stick margarine, softened

Into a bowl place cake mix, less ¾ cup, egg and margarine. Mix well. Press into the bottom of a greased and floured 9 x 13-inch pan. Bake at 350 degrees for 15 minutes.

Filling:
¾ cup reserved cake mix
½ cup brown sugar
½ cup dark Karo syrup

1 teaspoon vanilla
3 eggs
2 cups chopped pecans

Mix ¾ cup of cake mix from crust recipe with brown sugar, Karo, vanilla, eggs and chopped pecans. Mix well. Pour over crust. Bake at 350 degrees for 30 to 35 minutes. Serves 12.

Mrs. Angela Gonsoulin, Loreauville, LA

Cajun Cake

2 cups self-rising flour
1½ cups sugar
1½ teaspoons baking soda

2 eggs
1 pinch of salt
1 large can crushed pineapple.

Add all ingredients together and beat for 3 minutes. Pour into a greased and floured oblong pan. Bake in 350 degree oven for 30 minutes. Remove from oven and cover with the following icing.

Icing:
1 stick margarine
1 small can Pet milk
1 cup sugar

1 cup chopped pecans
1 cup coconut

Mix margarine, milk and sugar in a saucepan. Place on stove and bring to a boil and continue cooking for 4 to 5 minutes. Remove from heat and add pecans and coconut. Ice cake while still warm.

Lena Mae Rizzo, Alexandria, LA

Pineapple Cake II

2 cups flour
2 cups sugar
2 teaspoons soda
1 teaspoon salt
¼ cup oil

2 eggs
1 large can sweetened crushed
  pineapple, undrained
1 cup chopped nuts

Preheat oven to 350 degrees. Grease and flour a 9 x 12-inch pan. Sift flour, sugar, soda and salt together in a mixing bowl. Add oil, eggs and pineapple with juice to flour mixture. Mix until well blended. Add nuts. Pour into prepared pan. Bake for 45 minutes.

Icing:
1 stick butter
1 box powdered sugar
1 8-ounce package cream
  cheese

2 teaspoons vanilla

Melt butter and add sugar, cream cheese and vanilla. Mix until creamy and spreadable. Pour over cake while it is still warm.

Linda Cannon, Freeport, TX

Surprise Cake

5 tablespoons butter
1 package coconut almond
   frosting mix
1 cup uncooked oats
1 cup sour cream

4 eggs
1½ cups ripe bananas,
   thinly sliced
1 package yellow cake mix

Preheat oven to 350 degrees. Grease and flour 10-inch tube pan. In a saucepan melt butter, stir in frosting mix and rolled oats until crumbly. Set aside. In a large bowl blend sour cream, eggs and bananas until smooth. Blend in cake mix. Beat 2 minutes at medium speed. Pour 2 cups of the batter into tube pan. Sprinkle with 1 cup of the crumb mixture. Repeat twice with batter and crumbs, ending with crumb mixture. Bake for 50 to 60 minutes. Cool upright in pan 15 minutes. Remove from pan and turn cake so crumb mixture is on top.

Martha Meador, Clinton, MS

Mississippi Mud Cake

1 cup butter
½ cup cocoa
2 cups sugar
1½ cups flour
1 cup pecans

1 cup coconut
4 eggs
1 package miniature
   marshmallows

Melt butter, cool. Add other ingredients, mix well and pour into a greased 10 x 15-inch pan. Bake at 350 degrees for 30 minutes or until center springs back at touch. While hot, add marshmallows on top. Add icing while cake is hot.

Icing:
1 stick butter
½ cup cocoa
1 box powdered sugar

½ can evaporated milk
½ teaspoon vanilla

Melt butter, add other ingredients. Heat and pour hot icing over marshmallows. Serves 12 to 15.

Lucille Schaider, La Porte, TX

Chocolate Ice Box Cake

8 ounces German sweet
chocolate
4 eggs
2 cups heavy cream, whipped
Pinch of salt

1 teaspoon vanilla
12 to 24 ladyfingers (sponge
cakes)
½ pint whipping cream,
whipped

Line a springform pan with waxed paper. Melt chocolate in a double boiler. Separate eggs and add yolks to chocolate, one at a time mixing after each addition. Cool. Whip the 2 cups of heavy cream and gently fold into chocolate mixture. Add salt and vanilla. Mix gently. Beat egg whites until stiff peaks form. Gently fold egg whites into chocolate mixture. Split the ladyfingers in half, lengthwise, and line sides and bottom of springform pan with ladyfingers. Spoon half of the chocolate mixture into pan. Top with ladyfingers. Add remaining chocolate. Top with ladyfingers. Refrigerate overnight. Next day, unmold cake and carefully remove waxed paper. Serve topped with whipped cream. Cherries or slivered chocolate will make an excellent garnish.

Gloria Evans, Clarksdale, MS

Mahogany Cake

1 cup shortening
2 cups sugar
4 eggs
2½ cups cake flour
1 cup buttermilk

4 tablespoons cold coffee
4 tablespoons cocoa
1 teaspoon soda
Pinch of salt
1 teaspoon vanilla

Grease and flour 3 cake pans. Cream shortening and sugar until fluffy. Add eggs and beat well. Add flour, buttermilk, coffee, cocoa, soda, salt and vanilla. Mix well. Pour into prepared cake pans. Bake in 325 degree oven for 20 minutes. Remove and cool.

Icing:

1 stick margarine	1 box powdered sugar
4 tablespoons cocoa	4 tablespoons cold coffee
2 teaspoons vanilla	

Soften and cream margarine. Add cocoa, vanilla, sugar and coffee to creamed margarine. Beat until creamy. Spread between cake layers and then frost top and sides with icing.

Helen Owen, West Monroe, LA

Red Velvet Cake

½ cup shortening	1 tablespoon vanilla
1½ cups sugar	1 cup buttermilk
2 eggs	2 ounces red food coloring
2½ cups flour, well-sifted	1 teaspoon soda
1 teaspoon cocoa	1 teaspoon vinegar
½ teaspoon salt	

Grease and flour 2 9-inch or 3 8-inch pans. Cream shortening, sugar and eggs. Add flour, cocoa, salt, vanilla and buttermilk. Mix together red coloring, soda and vinegar and fold into creamed mixture. Bake at 350 degrees for 30 to 35 minutes.

Icing:

1 cup milk	1 stick margarine
¼ cup flour	1 cup sugar
Dash of salt	1 teaspoon vanilla
½ cup shortening	

Cook milk, flour and salt over low heat to pudding stage. Cream other ingredients thoroughly and add to pudding mixture. Beat until smooth and spread on cake, when cooled.

Marie Vail Chandler, Arcadia, LA

Peter Paul Mound Cake

2 cups sugar	1 teaspoon baking soda
2 cups sifted flour	½ teaspoon cinnamon
1 cup margarine	1 teaspoon vanilla
4 tablespoons cocoa	3 eggs
1 cup water	½ cup milk
1 teaspoon vinegar	

Blend sugar and flour, set aside. Combine margarine, cocoa and water in a saucepan. Bring to a boil. Pour over sugar and flour mixture and blend. Mix remaining ingredients together and stir into first mixture. Blend well. Pour into 2 greased and floured 9-inch cake pans. Bake in 325 degree oven for 20 to 30 minutes or until cake tests done. Cool completely.

Filling:

1 cup sugar	20 large marshmallows
1 cup evaporated milk	1 can coconut
1 stick margarine	

Mix sugar, milk and margarine in a saucepan. Boil for four minutes while stirring constantly. Take off of burner and add marshmallows. Stir until marshmallows are melted. Add can of coconut, stir well. Cool. When cooled spread between layers of cake.

Icing:

3 cups powdered sugar	6 tablespoons margarine
½ cup cocoa	⅓ cup evaporated milk

Mix powdered sugar, cocoa, margarine and milk. Mix well. Ice sides and top of cake.

Mrs. Mallie McLaughlin, Nashville, AR

Chocolate Glaze

2 1-ounce squares
  unsweetened chocolate
2 teaspoons butter

4 tablespoons boiling water
2 cups confectioners' sugar

Melt the chocolate and butter in top of a double boiler. Add boiling water and sugar. Beat until smooth to make a thin glaze.

Judy Read, Farmerville, LA

German Sweet Chocolate Cake

1 4-ounce package Baker's
  German Sweet Chocolate
½ cup boiling water
1 cup butter
2 cups sugar
4 egg yolks
1 teaspoon vanilla

2¼ cups sifted all-purpose
  flour
1 teaspoon baking soda
½ teaspoon salt
1 cup buttermilk
4 egg whites, stiffly beaten

Melt chocolate in boiling water. Cool. Cream butter and sugar until fluffy. Add yolks, one at a time, beating well after each. Blend in vanilla and chocolate. Sift flour, soda and salt; add alternately with buttermilk to chocolate mixture, beating after each addition until smooth. Fold in beaten egg whites. Pour into 3 greased and well-floured 9-inch layer pans. Bake at 350 degrees for 30 to 35 minutes. Cool. Frost tops only.

Frosting:
1 cup evaporated milk
1 cup sugar
3 egg yolks, slightly beaten
½ cup butter

1 teaspoon vanilla
1⅓ cups coconut
1 cup chopped pecans

Combine first 5 frosting ingredients. Cook and stir over medium heat until thickened; about 12 minutes. Add coconut and pecans. Cool until thick enough to spread, beating occasionally. Makes about 2½ cups. Frost between layers and top of cake.

Ola Williams, Farmerville, LA

247

Chocolate Eclair Cake

2 3½-ounce boxes French
  instant vanilla pudding mix
3½ cups milk
8 ounces Cool Whip

1 box graham crackers,
  crushed and divided into
  3 portions

Mix pudding with milk and beat for 2 minutes. Let set until thickened (5 minutes). Gently stir in Cool Whip. Set aside. Butter a 9 x 13-inch pan and sprinkle ⅓ of crushed graham crackers on bottom, spreading evenly. Add ½ of pudding and top with ⅓ of graham cracker mixture. Add remaining pudding and top with ⅓ graham crackers. Refrigerate 4 hours and add frosting.

Frosting:
6 tablespoons margarine
3 cups confectioners' sugar
12 tablespoons cocoa

4 tablespoons cooking oil
4 teaspoons white corn syrup
6 tablespoons milk

Place all frosting ingredients together in a bowl and mix until smooth. Frost cooled cake. Refrigerate overnight before serving. When serving cut into squares. Yields 20 squares.

Irene Crichton, Westtown, PA

Turtle Cake

1 box German chocolate cake
  mix
14-ounce bag vanilla caramels
¾ cup butter

½ cup evaporated milk
1 cup chocolate chips
1 cup chopped pecans

Preheat oven to 350 degrees. Mix cake according to package directions. Grease and flour a 9 x 13-inch pan. Pour half of the cake batter into pan and bake for 15 minutes. In a saucepan melt caramels, butter and milk over low heat until caramels are melted. Pour caramel mixture over the baked cake. Top with chocolate chips and pecans. Pour the remaining cake batter over this mixture and return to 350 degree oven and bake 20 minutes. Cool completely before cutting.

Polly Taylor, Farmerville, LA

Fudge Cake

2 cups sugar
2 cups flour
1 stick butter
4 tablespoons cocoa
½ cup Wesson oil
1 cup water

1 teaspoon baking soda
½ cup buttermilk
1 teaspoon vanilla
1 teaspoon cinnamon
2 eggs, beaten

Preheat oven to 350 degrees. Grease and lightly flour an 11 x 16-inch pan. Sift together 2 cups sugar and 2 cups flour. Into a saucepan place butter, cocoa, oil and water. Heat until butter has melted and then bring to a boil. Pour over sifted sugar and flour mixture. Beat well using an electric mixer or by hand. Add soda to buttermilk. Mix and add vanilla and cinnamon. Pour into flour mixture and add beaten eggs. Mix until well blended. Pour into prepared cake pan. Bake for 20 minutes or until done. Remove from oven and ice while cake is hot.

Icing:
4 tablespoons cocoa
1 stick butter
6 tablespoons milk

1 box powdered sugar
1 teaspoon vanilla
1 cup chopped pecans

Place cocoa, butter and milk in a saucepan. Heat until butter is melted and then bring to boil. Remove from heat and add powdered sugar, vanilla and pecans. Blend. Ice cake while hot and still in cake pan. Cool and cut into squares to serve. This cake can be frozen.

Susan Cartier Willis, Austin, TX

Chocolate Icing

½ cup margarine
½ cup evaporated milk
1 cup sugar

6 ounces semi-sweet chocolate
  chips
1 teaspoon vanilla

Combine margarine, milk, and sugar; bring to a boil and boil 2 minutes. Remove from heat and add chocolate and vanilla. Stir until chocolate is melted. Spread on cake layers.
Note: May be varied by using half butterscotch or peanut butter chips.

Helen Owen, West Monroe, LA

249

Aunt Lola's Angel Food Cake

1¼ cups Swans Down cake
  flour
1¾ cups sugar (divided)
1½ cups egg whites

¼ teaspoon salt
1½ teaspoons cream of tartar
1½ teaspoons vanilla
½ teaspoon almond flavoring

Sift flour and ¾ cup sugar together 4 times. Set aside. Beat egg whites until foamy; add salt and beat until soft peaks form; add cream of tartar and beat until stiff peaks form. Beat in 1 cup of sugar. Carefully fold in the flour-sugar mixture, turning the bowl as you fold. Add vanilla and almond flavoring. Pour into ungreased angel food cake pan and cut through batter with a knife. Bake at 325 degrees for 45 minutes. Invert pan over bottle to cool. When completely cooled, cut around sides with a knife and remove from pan.
Note: 12 to 15 egg whites equal 1½ cups egg whites.

Lola Thompson, Cotton Valley, LA

Cheesecake

Crust:
2 cups graham wafers,
  crushed
½ teaspoon cinnamon

¼ cup sugar
3 tablespoons melted butter

Mix above ingredients and press into bottom of a 9 x 12-inch pan.

Filling:
4 8-ounce packages cream
  cheese
4 large eggs, beaten
¼ cup flour

1 tablespoon lemon juice
1 tablespoon vanilla
1½ cups sugar
½ cup whipping cream

Soften cheese and add beaten eggs, flour, lemon juice, vanilla and sugar. Blend together into a creamy mixture. Add whipping cream. Mix. Pour into graham wafer crumb crust. Bake in 350 degree oven for 50 minutes. Turn off heat, leaving in oven, with oven door ajar, to cool for 1 hour. Remove from oven. Yields 16 to 20 servings.

Irene Potoczniak, Houston, TX

Coconut Angel Food Cake

1 cup sifted cake flour	¼ teaspoon salt
¾ cup sugar	1½ teaspoons vanilla
1½ cups (12) egg whites	¾ cup sugar
1½ teaspoons cream of tartar	1 cup coconut

Sift flour with ¾ cup sugar, twice; set aside. Beat egg whites with cream of tartar, salt and vanilla until stiff enough to form soft peaks, but still moist and glossy. Add remaining ¾ cup sugar, 2 tablespoons at a time, continuing to beat the egg whites until stiff peaks form. Sift ½ of the flour mixture over egg whites; fold in. Repeat process using a fourth of the flour at a time, until all flour has been folded in. Fold in coconut, ½ cup at a time. Pour in ungreased 10-inch tube pan. Bake in 375 degree oven for 35 to 40 minutes or until done. Invert cake in pan until cool. Frost with your favorite frosting.

Jane Jackson, Alexandria, LA

Peach Cheesecake

¾ cup flour	3 tablespoons butter, softened
1 teaspoon baking powder	3 large cans sliced peaches,
½ teaspoon salt	drained reserving 3
1 3-ounce package vanilla	tablespoons juice
pudding (not instant)	8 ounces cream cheese
1 egg	½ cup plus 1 tablespoon sugar
½ cup milk	½ teaspoon cinnamon

Combine ¾ cup flour, baking powder, salt, pudding, egg, milk and butter. Beat with electric mixer on medium speed for 2 minutes. Pour into a greased 9-inch deep dish. Set aside. Layer peaches over batter. Set aside. Combine cream cheese, ½ cup sugar and peach juice. Beat with mixer for 2 minutes. Pour over batter and peaches. Mix 1 tablespoon sugar and ½ teaspoon cinnamon. Sprinkle over cheese mixture. Place in 350 degree oven and bake for 30 to 35 minutes.

Anne Riesbeck, Hamden, CT
Husband: Charles P. Riesbeck, Jr.
Knights of Columbus title: Supreme Secretary

Strawberry Glazed Cream Cheesecake

Crust:
¾ cup coarsely ground
walnuts
¾ cup finely crushed graham
crackers

3 tablespoons melted unsalted
butter

Filling:
4 8-ounce packages cream
cheese, room temperature
4 eggs

1¼ cups sugar
1 tablespoon fresh lemon juice
2 teaspoons vanilla

Topping:
2 cups sour cream
¼ cup sugar

1 teaspoon vanilla

Strawberry Glaze:
2 pints fresh strawberries
1 cup sugar
1 tablespoon cornstarch

1 cup water
1 package strawberry Jello

Position rack in center of oven and preheat to 350 degrees. Lightly butter a 9 or 10-inch springform pan.

For Crust:
Combine walnuts, graham cracker crumbs and butter. Press compactly onto bottom of pan.

For Filling:
Beat cream cheese in large bowl of food processor until smooth. Add eggs, sugar, lemon juice and vanilla and beat thoroughly. Spoon over crust. Set pan on baking sheet to catch any batter that may drip out. Bake 10-inch cake 40 to 45 minutes or 9-inch cake 50 to 55 minutes. (Cake may rise slightly and crack in several areas; it will settle again, cracks will minimize and topping will cover.) Remove from oven and let stand at room temperature 15 minutes.

For Topping:
Combine sour cream, sugar and vanilla and blend well. Spoon topping over the cake, starting at center and extending to the edge. Refrigerate cheesecake for approximately 24 hours.

For Glaze:
Several hours before serving, wash and hull berries and let dry completely on paper towels. Combine sugar and cornstarch in saucepan and mix well. Add water and cook over medium heat, stirring frequently, until thickened and clear, about 5 minutes. Remove from heat and stir in the package of Jello. Place the strawberries on top of cheesecake, in circular design, then pour glaze mixture over all the berries. Return to the refrigerator for several hours until glaze is set. Using knife, loosen cake from pan, and remove springform. The cake is ready to slice and serve. Also may be served with whipped cream around the sides of the cake. Yields 10 to 12 servings.

Note: In June 1986 Jean Futch entered this cheesecake in a cooking contest sponsored by KTVE Television Station on their Midday Program in El Dorado, Arkansas. She made the cake on the television program, which was a month long contest with winners each week. The Strawberry Glazed Cream Cheesecake was the final winner and the Grand Prize was a top of the line Litton Microwave Oven.

Jean Futch, Farmerville, LA

Minature Cheesecakes

2 8-ounce packages cream
  cheese, softened
2 eggs, beaten
¾ cup sugar
1 teaspoon vanilla

16 to 18 vanilla wafers
16 to 18 paper cupcake
  holders
1 can cherry pie filling or fruit
  filling of your choice

Beat cream cheese, eggs, sugar and vanilla until smooth. Place one vanilla wafer in each paper cupcake holder. Place 1 tablespoon cream cheese mixture on top of each wafer. Bake in 325 degree oven for 12 to 15 minutes. Cool. Place a spoonful of pie filling on top of each cupcake. Refrigerate several hours before serving. Yields 16 to 18 servings.

Faith Matthews, Farmerville, LA

Oreo Cheesecake

Crust:

6 tablespoons butter, melted

1½ cups chocolate wafer crumbs (approximately 20 Oreos)

To make crust, melt butter and set aside. If using Oreos, separate cookies, remove and discard filling, and crush (may use processor) to produce 1½ cups chocolate crumbs. Combine crumbs with butter and press into a 9-inch springform pan. Wrap foil around pan and place on a cookie sheet.

Filling:

2 cups sour cream
1½ pounds cream cheese
3 eggs

1 cup sugar
2 teaspoons vanilla
10 Oreo cookies

Preheat oven to 300 degrees. All filling ingredients should be at room temperature. Using a food processor or mixer, mix sour cream, cream cheese, eggs, sugar and vanilla. Blend until smooth. Quarter Oreos (OK if they crumble) and fold into mixture. Pour into springform pan. Place springform pan in a larger pan of hot, not boiling, water and put on a cookie sheet. Place in the middle rack of oven. The aluminum foil will prevent water from getting into cheesecake. Bake in oven for 70 minutes. Do not open oven door. Turn oven off. Let cake remain in oven for 2 hours. The cake will firm as it cools. When it comes to room temperature it is ready for the refrigerator. Remove from refrigerator 20 minutes before serving. Yields 10 to 12 servings.

Donna Graham, Lyon, MS

Daffodil Cake

Layer 1:

6 egg whites	**½ cup sifted flour**
½ teaspoon cream of tartar	**¼ teaspoon vanilla flavoring**
Pinch of salt	**¼ teaspoon almond flavoring**
¾ cup sugar	

Beat egg whites until stiff. Beat in cream of tartar and salt. Mix sugar and flour together and sift four times. Then add to egg white mixture. Add vanilla and almond; blend well. Pour into a large ungreased tube pan.

Layer 2:

6 egg yolks	**1 teaspoon baking powder**
¾ cup sugar	**¼ cup boiling water**
Pinch of salt	**¼ teaspoon vanilla flavoring**
¾ cup flour	**¼ teaspoon lemon flavoring**

Beat egg yolks until thick. Gradually add sugar and salt. Mix flour and baking powder together and sift four times. Combine water and flavorings together and add alternately with flour mixture to egg yolk mixture. Pour in tube pan on top of egg white mixture. Bake for 55 to 65 minutes in a 325 degree oven.

Madeline Murphy, Hamden, CT

Husband: Howard E. Murphy
Knights of Columbus title: Supreme Director

Coconut Pecan Frosting

1⅓ cups evaporated milk	**1½ teaspoons vanilla**
1⅓ cups sugar	**1½ cups coconut**
4 egg yolks	**1½ cups chopped pecans**
1⅓ sticks margarine	

Blend together milk, sugar, egg yolks, margarine and vanilla. Cook over medium heat until thickened. Add coconut and finely chopped pecans. Beat until cool enough to spread. Fill between layers and frost top.

Peggy Melton, Conroe, TX

Banana Cake

2 cups flour
1 teaspoon soda
½ teaspoon salt
1½ cups sugar

1 cup sour cream
2 eggs
1 cup mashed bananas (3 or 4)
1 cup nuts, chopped (optional)

Sift flour, soda and salt together. Cream sugar, sour cream, eggs and bananas together. Gradually add flour mixture until all is blended. Add nuts if desired. Pour into a greased and floured loaf pan. Bake in 350 degree oven for 40 minutes. You may prefer to eat cake plain or to frost with your favorite frosting recipe.

Ann Dechant, Hamden, CT

Husband: Virgil Dechant
Knights of Columbus title: Supreme Knight

Apricot Nectar Cake

1 package Lemon Supreme
  cake mix (Duncan Hines)
1 cup apricot nectar
⅔ cup Crisco oil

½ cup sugar
2 tablespoons flour
5 eggs

Mix all ingredients. Beat well. Bake in greased and floured tube pan in 350 degree oven for 1 hour. Cool about 10 minutes and remove from pan. Pour glaze over warm cake.

Glaze:
1½ cups powdered sugar

½ cup unsweetened orange
  juice

Mix by hand or electric mixer until smooth.

Audrey Morehouse, Alexandria, LA

Amaretto Cake

2 eggs, separated	1 package butter cake mix
½ cup brown sugar, firmly	with pudding in the mix
packed	1 cup sour cream
1 cup coconut	½ cup Amaretto
½ cup ground pecans or	½ cup water
other nuts	2 eggs

Heat oven to 350 degrees. Using 2 tablespoons shortening, generously grease a 10-inch tube pan. In small bowl, beat 2 egg whites until foamy. Gradually add brown sugar, beat until stiff peaks form, about 3 minutes. Fold in coconut and nuts. Spread meringue on bottom and sides of pan to within 1-inch of top of pan. In large bowl, blend cake mix, sour cream, Amaretto, water, eggs and 2 egg yolks at low speed until moistened; beat 2 minutes at highest speed. Pour batter evenly into prepared pan. Bake at 350 degrees 55 to 65 minutes or until toothpick inserted in center comes out clean. Cool upright in pan 10 minutes; loosen sides and invert onto serving plate. Cool completely.

Glaze:

1 cup confectioners' sugar,	1 tablespoon corn syrup
sifted	2 to 4 teaspoons water
2 tablespoons cocoa	2 teaspoons ground pecans or
2 tablespoons Amaretto	nuts
1 tablespoon butter, softened	6 maraschino cherries

In small bowl, blend confectioners' sugar, cocoa, Amaretto, butter, corn syrup and water until smooth. Spoon over top of cake, allowing some to run down sides. Sprinkle with ground pecans; garnish with cherries. Yields 16 servings.

Lucille Schaider, La Porte, TX

Bishop Cake

2 cups sugar	**2 teaspoons vanilla**
½ pound butter	**5 eggs**
2 cups flour	

Take all ingredients from refrigerator at least 1 hour before preparing cake. Preheat oven to 325 degrees. Cream sugar and butter. Add flour and vanilla. Add eggs one at a time, beating with mixer after each addition. Butter tube pan generously with soft butter. Bake one hour. When cool, drizzle glaze over cake.

Glaze:

1 cup powdered sugar	**1 to 2 tablespoons lemon juice**

Combine powdered sugar and enough lemon juice to make drizzling consistency. Glaze cooled cake.

Marti Greenberg, Denton, TX

Brown Sugar Pound Cake

1 cup butter	**½ teaspoon baking powder**
½ cup shortening	**3 cups flour**
1 16-ounce package brown sugar	**1 cup milk**
	2 tablespoons vanilla
½ cup sugar	**1 cup chopped pecans**
5 large eggs	

Cream butter and shortening. Gradually add sugars, beating well. Add eggs, one at a time, beating well after each egg. Combine baking powder and flour. Add flour mixture alternately with milk. Stir in vanilla and pecans. Bake in greased and floured tube pan for 1½ hours in preheated 325 degree oven. Invert on wire rack and cool completely. Frost with Cream Cheese Frosting, if desired. (See Index.)

Sylvia Burenake

Buttermilk Pound Cake with Glaze

1 cup buttermilk
5 eggs, separated
1 cup butter or margarine
3 cups sugar, separate ½ cup
1 teaspoon lemon flavoring

1 teaspoon almond flavoring
⅓ teaspoon soda
1 tablespoon warm water
3 cups flour

Have buttermilk, eggs and butter at room temperature. Separate eggs. Beat egg whites until stiff. Gradually add ½ cup sugar while beating. Set aside. Cream butter and 2½ cups sugar until fluffy. Add egg yolks and flavorings to butter and mix. Dissolve soda in warm water and add buttermilk. Alternately, add flour and butter-milk mixture to eggs and butter. Mix well. Fold in egg whites. Pour into a greased and floured tube pan. Bake in 350 degree oven for 1 hour and 15 minutes. Cool in pan. Cover with glaze.

Glaze:
Grated rind of 1 orange and
 1 lemon

½ pound powdered sugar
Juice of orange and lemon

Mix grated rind, powdered sugar and enough juice to make glaze pourable. Ice pound cake.

Mrs. Jack F. Dietle

Fresh Apple Cake

2 cups sugar
1¼ cups Wesson oil
2 eggs
3 cups flour
1 teaspoon salt
1½ teaspoons soda

½ teaspoon nutmeg
½ teaspoon cinnamon
3 Jonathan apples, peeled and
 chopped fine
1 cup pecans, chopped fine
2 teaspoons vanilla

Mix and beat sugar, oil and eggs. Sift together flour, salt, soda, nut-meg and cinnamon and add to liquid mixture. Add apples, pecans and vanilla to batter. Pour into greased and floured angel food pan. Bake in 325 degree oven for 1 hour.

Rhea Jenkins, Marshall, TX

Flourless Chocolate Cake

12 egg yolks
½ cup sugar, divided
18 ounces semi-sweet
   chocolate chips

½ cup soft butter
5 egg whites

Grease a 10-inch springform pan and set aside. Beat together egg yolks and ¼ cup sugar for about 5 minutes, or until smooth and thickened. Melt chocolate chips in top of double boiler over hot (not boiling) water or in microwave (about 1 to 2 minutes on high). Cool slightly and combine with very soft butter. Combine chocolate mixture with egg yolks; set aside. Beat the egg whites until frothy. Continue beating at high speed, gradually adding ¼ cup sugar, until egg whites form soft peaks. Gently fold egg whites into chocolate mixture combining thoroughly. Pile batter into greased pan, softly smoothing the top. Bake at 300 degrees 45 to 50 minutes. Cake will be "set". (It may not appear done, but it is!) Let cool slightly, then remove sides of pan. I suggest "frosting" the cake with Chantilly Creme (See Index) or whipped cream and decorating with fresh raspberries or strawberries and kiwi. This is definitely a chocolate lover's dream!

Cindy Ward, Dallas, TX

Chocolate Hershey Cake

½ teaspoon soda
1 cup buttermilk
2½ cups sifted flour
1 teaspoon baking powder
½ teaspoon salt
8 regular size plain Hershey
   bars

½ pound butter
2 cups sugar
4 eggs
2 teaspoons vanilla
1 cup chopped pecans

Dissolve soda in buttermilk. Sift dry ingredients together. Melt Hesheys over warm water. Cream butter and sugar until light. Add 1 egg at a time beating well after each. Beat in melted Hersheys. Alternate dry ingredients and buttermilk beginning and ending with dry ingredients. Add vanilla and nuts. Pour the batter in a large tube pan. Bake in a 350 degree oven for 1½ to 2 hours.

Gloria Allen, Marshall, TX

Orange Cake Loaf

1 small box lemon Jello	¾ cup cooking oil
¼ cup hot water	4 eggs
1 package yellow cake mix	1 teaspoon vanilla
½ cup orange juice	

Dissolve Jello in hot water. Mix with cake mix, alternating orange juice and oil. Beat well. Add eggs, one at a time, beating well after each egg. Add remaining orange juice and vanilla. Mix. Pour in a well-greased tube or bundt pan. Bake in 350 degree oven for 55 minutes. Frost with topping while hot.

Topping:

2 cups powdered sugar	1 cup chopped nuts
½ cup orange juice	

Mix sifted powdered sugar with orange juice. Place on hot cake. Sprinkle with nuts, if desired.

Mrs. Charlotte Baham, New Orleans, LA

Plum Spice Cake

2 cups self-rising flour	1 cup nuts, chopped
2 cups sugar	1 teaspoon vanilla
3 eggs	1 teaspoon cinnamon
1 cup Wesson oil	
2 small jars plum baby food (any flavor will do)	

Combine all the above ingredients. Mix well. Pour into a lightly greased and floured tube or bundt cake pan. Bake in 350 degree oven for 1 hour.

Eileen Duke, Haughton, LA

Golden Butter Rum Cake

1 package Duncan Hines
  Butter Recipe Golden
  cake mix
½ cup Crisco oil
1 8-ounce carton sour cream

½ cup sugar
1 tablespoon rum
4 eggs
Pecan pieces

Mix cake mix, oil, sour cream, sugar, and rum together. Add eggs, one at a time and beat. Grease and flour bundt pan. Put pecan pieces in bottom of pan. Pour batter in pan and bake at 300 degrees for 15 minutes then 325 degrees for 30 minutes or until done.

Glaze:
½ cup sugar
¼ cup buttermilk
1 tablespoon margarine

¼ teaspoon soda
¼ teaspoon salt
1 tablespoon rum

Mix glaze ingredients together and boil for three minutes. Pour over warm cake.

Pam Kilpatrick, Ruston, LA

Strawberry Pound Cake

1 box of strawberry cake mix
1 3½-ounce package instant
  pineapple pudding mix
⅓ cup Crisco oil

1 cup water
4 eggs
1 3-ounce package
  strawberry Jello

Preheat oven to 325 degrees. Mix all ingredients and beat for 2 minutes at medium mixer speed. Pour into a greased and floured tube pan. Bake for about 55 minutes. Cake is done when toothpick comes out clean when inserted into center. Cool for 25 minutes before removing cake from pan.

Jannette Liner, Farmerville, LA

7-Up Pound Cake

½ cup shortening
2 sticks butter or margarine
3 cups sugar
5 eggs
1½ teaspoons vanilla

3 cups flour
1 10-ounce 7-Up (use 8½-
ounces for cake and reserve
1½-ounces for icing)

Cream together shortening, butter and sugar. Add eggs one at a time mixing well. Add vanilla. Alternately add flour and 7-Up to this mixture. Pour into greased bundt pan and bake at 350 degrees for 1 hour.

Icing:
1 cup powdered sugar   1½-ounces 7-Up

Mix together powdered sugar and remaining 7-Up and drizzle over cooled cake.

Betty Martinez, San Angelo, TX

Sour Cream Pound Cake

2 sticks butter
3 cups sugar
1 cup sour cream
1 tablespoon vanilla
2 tablespoons light rum

1 teaspoon almond extract
6 eggs
½ teaspoon baking soda
3 cups flour
1 teaspoon cinnamon

Cream the butter and sugar until blended well. Add sour cream, vanilla, rum and almond extract. Stir in one egg at a time, alternating with the soda and flour. Pour half the batter in a large oiled and floured bundt pan. Sprinkle 1 teaspoon of cinnamon on top and thread through the batter with a knife. Add remaining batter. Bake for 1 hour at 325 degrees.

Ruth Lynn Huskey, Baton Rouge, LA

Pumpkin Cake

2 cups flour
2 cups sugar
1 teaspoon salt
2 teaspoons baking soda
3 teaspoons cinnamon

4 eggs
1½ cups canned pumpkin
1½ cups Wesson oil
1 teaspoon vanilla

Mix flour, sugar, salt, baking soda and cinnamon. Drop in eggs one at a time and mix well. Add pumpkin, Wesson oil and vanilla. Bake in greased and floured bundt pan at 350 degrees for 1 hour. Cool in pan.

Icing:
1 box powdered sugar
1 stick margarine, melted
   and hot
1 3-ounce package cream
   cheese
2 teaspoons vanilla

1 teaspoon strong coffee
   (use instant made with
   hot water)
Pinch of salt
½ cup chopped pecans
   (optional)

Mix all ingredients until smooth and creamy and ice cooled cake.

Cindy Ward, Dallas, TX

Rum Pound Cake

2 sticks margarine
3 cups sugar
6 eggs
1 teaspoon vanilla

¾ cup light rum
3 cups flour
¼ teaspoon soda
1 cup sour cream

Preheat oven to 325 degrees. Cream margarine and sugar, add eggs one at a time, beating one minute after each addition. Stir in vanilla. Add rum and mix well. Add dry ingredients alternately with sour cream. Pour into a greased and floured bundt pan. Bake for 30 minutes at 325 degrees, then reduce heat to 300 degrees for 45 minutes or until done.

Note: ½ cup dark rum may be substituted for light rum.

Susan Cartier Willis, Austin, TX

Old-Fashioned Pound Cake

1 pound butter	4 cups flour
4 cups sugar	1 tablespoon Watkins vanilla
12 eggs	

Cream butter and sugar together. Add one egg at a time. Then add flour a little at a time. Add vanilla and pour into greased and floured tube pan. Bake at 325 degrees for 2 hours.

Nell Oliver, Farmerville, LA

Aunt Vickie's Fruitcake

1½-pounds candied cherries	1 cup shortening
1½-pounds candied pineapple	2 cups brown sugar
2 pounds dates	4 eggs
½ pound Brazil nuts	1 cup dark corn syrup
½ pound dark raisins	1 teaspoon soda
¼ pound candied lemon peel	1 teaspoon allspice
¼ pound candied orange peel	2 teaspoons cinnamon
½ pound pecans	2 teaspoons cloves
½ pound golden raisins	1 teaspoon nutmeg
¼ pound candied citron	4 cups flour
½ pound walnuts	Sweet wine as needed
½ pound almonds	

Dice all fruits and nuts except those to be saved to decorate the top of the cakes. Mix shortening and sugar, add eggs, and syrup in which soda has been mixed. Add all spices, nuts, fruits and mix well with hands. Add flour; batter must be thick. If it is not, add more flour. Place mixture in floured loaf or tube pans lined with foil. Use whole fruit and nuts to decorate the tops of the cakes. Bake at 200 degrees until a straw can be inserted in the cakes and will come out clean. Baking time is usually 7 to 9 hours. After cakes cool, remove from the pans and baste with sweet wine. Basting with wine may be done periodically if cake appears dry.

Note: It is best to buy candied fruit that has not been pre-cut.

Dorothy Staskey, Flagstaff, AZ

Husband: Paul J. Staskey
Knights of Columbus title: Supreme Warden

No-Bake Fruitcake

¾ cup milk
1 pound marshmallows
2 teaspoons rum flavoring
  (optional)
1 pound graham crackers,
  crushed
1 pound raisins (white
  preferred)

2 pounds candied fruit
  (not peels)
4 cups walnuts or pecans
1 small package blanched
  almonds (optional)
Candied cherries

Put milk in a large pan and scald. Add marshmallows and stir until smooth. Remove from heat. Add rum. Mix together graham cracker crumbs, raisins, candied fruit and nuts. Mix well with marshmallow mixture. Line any mold with waxed paper. Press mixture down into mold. Decorate with almonds and cherries. Store, tightly covered, for at least a month. September or early October are best months to make as age improves taste.
Note: This is my mother's recipe and is very delicious. If you don't usually like fruitcake, you will love this one.

Christine Hisel Meade, New Orleans, LA

Father: Robert Hisel
Knights of Columbus title: Supreme Director

Caramel Frosting

2 cups brown sugar (packed)
¼ cup margarine
¾ cup milk
2 tablespoons Karo

¼ teaspoon salt
¼ cup butter
1 teaspoon vanilla

Place all the above ingredients, except vanilla, in a large saucepan. Slowly, bring to a boil and let boil for 2 minutes. Cool to lukewarm and add vanilla. Beat until the mixture loses its gloss. Spread between cake layers and on top of cake.

Delzie Courtney, Ruston, LA

Christmas Nut Cake

1 pound candied pineapple
1 pound candied cherries
4 cups pecans (whole or
  chopped)
4 cups flour
¾ pound soft butter

2 cups sifted powdered sugar
6 eggs
1 cup bourbon
2 teaspoons baking powder
1 teaspoon nutmeg

Preheat oven to 300 degrees. In a large bowl, dust fruit and nuts lightly with part of the flour listed, reserve the remaining flour. In a separate large bowl, cream the butter and sugar. Add eggs one at a time. Add bourbon to creamed mixture. Sift reserved flour, baking powder and nutmeg. Add flour, floured nuts and fruit to the creamed mixture. Blend well. Pour into greased and floured large tube pan or 2 loaf pans. Bake for 1 hour and 20 minutes. Remove and sprinkle bourbon over top of cake and wrap in a cloth that has been soaked in bourbon. Refrigerate or freeze. This cake will keep indefinitely in the refrigerator or freezer.

Mary Frances Bowling, Jackson, MS

Candy Fruitcake

8 ounces candied red cherries,
  cut in quarters
8 ounces candied pineapple,
  coarsely chopped
8 ounces chopped dates
1 tablespoon all-purpose flour

2½ cups coarsely chopped
  pecans
2½ cups coarsley chopped
  walnuts
1 can sweetened condensed
  milk (14-ounce can)

Preheat oven to 250 degrees. Grease and flour 9 x 3-inch tube pan with removable bottom. In large bowl combine cherries, pineapple, dates and sprinkle with flour. Toss well. Add pecans and walnuts and toss well. Add sweetened condensed milk; stir and mix well. Spoon mixture into prepared pan and smooth top. Bake in oven at 250 degrees for 1½ hours. Do not overcook. Cool and remove from pan. Wrap tightly in foil. Refrigerate for at least 4 days. When ready to slice use serrated knife. Cuts best when cold.

Larry Guillory, Hessmer, LA

Date Loaf

1 cup Pet milk
3 cups sugar
⅓ stick margarine

1 8-ounce box dates, chopped
1 teaspoon vanilla
1 cup chopped pecans

Cook milk, sugar, margarine and dates over medium heat to soft ball stage, 236 to 238 degrees. Remove from heat and add vanilla and pecans. Beat until sugary. Pour on a damp cloth and roll into a long rectangular log. Refrigerate until completely cold. Slice and serve. Yields 2½ to 3 dozen.
Note: An electric knife makes slicing easier.

Donna Aguillard, Loreauville, LA

Divinity I

1 cup boiling water
1 cup light Karo syrup
4 cups sugar

4 egg whites, stiffly beaten
2 teaspoons vanilla
2 cups chopped pecans

Cook water, Karo and sugar on moderate heat to the hard ball stage (250 degrees on candy thermometer), stirring occasionally. Slowly pour the hot syrup mixture over the stiffly beaten egg whites until they are thoroughly mixed. Beat the mixture on highest speed of electric mixer until the gloss changes to a dull shine. Stop beating and fold the vanilla and pecans into mixture with a wooden spoon. When thoroughly mixed, drop by teaspoonfuls onto waxed paper. If mixture becomes too hard too fast, mix a *little* boiling water in and continue dropping.
Note: Egg whites reach their fullest volume if beaten in a copper bowl.

Judy Read, Farmerville, LA

Divinity II

Step I:
1 cup sugar   **2 egg whites, beaten stiff**
½ cup water

Boil sugar and water until it threads (248 degrees). Whip syrup mixture into the egg whites and let stand.

Step II:
3 cups sugar   **1 teaspoon vanilla**
½ cup water   **1 cup chopped nuts (walnuts)**
1 cup light Karo syrup

Cook sugar, water and syrup until it threads (248 degrees), firm ball stage. Pour this mixture slowly into the first mixture and beat until it is quite stiff. Add vanilla and nuts. It should hold its shape, but test it several times. Drop by teaspoonfuls onto waxed paper. Yields 3½ pounds.

Helen M. Fischer, Bismarck, ND

Husband: Clarence J. Fischer,
Knights of Columbus title: State Deputy

Whiskey Balls

3 cups ground vanilla wafers   **3 tablespoons light Karo syrup**
1 cup ground nuts   **½ tablespoon cocoa (optional)**
1 cup powdered sugar   **½ cup whiskey**

Grind wafers and nuts finely in food processor or blender. Mix thoroughly with sugar, Karo, cocoa and whiskey. Form into balls the size of cherries. Roll in powdered sugar and store in airtight container.

Maude Thompson, Litchfield, IL

Creamy Pralines

2 cups sugar
¼ teaspoon soda
½ cup light corn syrup
½ cup milk

1 teaspoon vanilla
2 tablespoons butter
2 cups pecans

Mix sugar, soda, corn syrup and milk in large heavy boiler. Cook to soft ball stage. Add vanilla, butter and pecans. Beat until creamy, just until it beings to lose shine. Drop by teaspoonfuls onto waxed paper. This will harden fast. Do not overbeat and work quickly to spoon out of boiler. Yields 3 dozen.
Note: These are very creamy pralines.

Melba Simmons, Bunkie, LA

Easter Nest

1 6-ounce package
  butterscotch chips
1 6-ounce package milk
  chocolate chips
2 3-ounce cans Chow Mein
  Noodles

Flaked coconut
Green food coloring
Jelly Beans

Melt butterscotch and chocolate chips over hot (not boiling) water. Mix chow mein noodles until thoroughly coated. Drop by teaspoon onto waxed paper. Press coconut (which has been tinted with food coloring) down on top of candy to make it look like a nest, then put 2 or 3 jelly beans on top of coconut. You have perfect little bird nests for your bunny's Easter Party.

Carolyn Stanley, Ruston, LA

270

Chocolate Fudge

3 cups sugar
3 tablespoons cocoa
2 tablespoons light Karo syrup
2 tablespoons butter

1 13-ounce can Carnation
  evaporated milk
1 teaspoon vanilla extract
Pinch of salt

Cook all ingredients in heavy iron skillet over low heat, stirring constantly. Let come to a boil; cook 10 minutes. Let cool to luke-warm, whip until creamy. Pour in a buttered dish and allow to cool before cutting into squares.

Shellie Futch, Farmerville, LA

Peanut Butter Fudge

2 cups sugar
2 tablespoons light corn syrup
⅔ cup milk
¼ teaspoon salt

½ cup peanut butter (crunchy
  or creamy)
1 teaspoon vanilla

Combine sugar, syrup, milk and salt. Cook over medium heat until soft ball forms when dropped into cold water. Remove from heat. Do not stir, cool for 5 minutes. Add peanut butter and vanilla. Beat until mixture is creamy and begins to thicken. Pour into a buttered pan or platter. When cool cut into squares.

Elvena Spears, Downsville, LA

Quickie Fudge

1 pound powdered sugar
½ cup cocoa
¼ cup milk

¼ pound butter, melted
1 tablespoon vanilla
½ cup chopped nuts

In an oven proof bowl mix sugar and cocoa. Place milk and butter over sugar mixture. Do not mix. Cook in microwave oven for 2 minutes. Remove and stir just enough to mix. Add vanilla and nuts and stir until blended. Pour into a greased dish and place in freezer for 20 minutes or refrigerate for 1 hour. Cut and serve.

Mrs. E. C. Hawthorne, Shreveport, LA

Chocolate Apple Candies

1 12-ounce package Nestle's
  chocolate chips
1 cup applesauce
1 teaspoon almond extract
5 cups powdered sugar

⅔ cup chopped maraschino
  cherries
1 cup chopped walnuts
1 3½-ounce can flaked
  coconut

Combine chocolate chips, applesauce and almond extract in a saucepan. Heat and stir until chocolate chips are melted. Blend in sugar, cherries and nuts. Chill until firm (approximately 1 hour). Shape into small balls and roll in coconut.

Bunny Laskowski, Houston, TX

Chocolate Roll

12 ounces semi-sweet
  chocolate
¼ pound butter
½ pound chopped walnuts

12 ounces miniature
  marshmallows
Shredded coconut

Using a double boiler, melt chocolate and butter together. Let cool. Mix walnuts and marshmallows together and then add chocolate mixture. Mix. Spread coconut on a sheet of aluminum foil then pour chocolate mixture over coconut. Form into a long roll and tighten aluminum foil around the chocolate. Place in freezer to harden. Slice and serve.

Irene Potoczniak, Houston, TX

Peanut Butter Crunchies

1 cup sugar
1 cup white Karo syrup

2 cups peanut butter
4 cups Rice Krispies

Mix sugar and syrup and bring to a rolling boil. Remove from stove. Stir in remaining ingredients. Drop by teaspoonfuls onto waxed paper. Let set for a few minutes to harden.

Ann Comeaux, Baytown, TX

Pecan Millionaires

1 14-ounce package Kraft
  Vanilla Caramels
4 tablespoons Pet milk

2 cups chopped pecans
10 regular size Hershey bars
¼ block paraffin

Melt caramels and milk in the top of a double boiler. Remove from heat and stir in pecans. Drop by small spoonfuls onto waxed paper or a buttered board. Let harden. Melt Hershey bars and paraffin in the top of a double boiler until completely dissolved. Gently scoop candy balls up from paper or board and drop into chocolate mixture. When completely coated with chocolate, remove using a teaspoon and drop back on paper to cool. Buttered board works best.

Judy Read, Farmerville, LA

Texas Millionaires

4½ cups sugar
1 tall can Pet milk
1 stick margarine
1 jar marshmallow creme
  (small)

1 quart chopped pecans
1 12-ounce package chocolate
  chips
12 small Hershey bars (plain)
2 teaspoons vanilla

Combine sugar, milk and margarine in a large boiler. Stir over medium heat until mixture reaches a full boil. Then lower heat and boil slowly for 5 minutes, stirring constantly. Remove from heat and add marshmallow creme, pecans, chocolate chips, Hershey bars and vanilla. Stir until chips are melted and beat until candy holds its shape when dropped by teaspoonful onto waxed paper.

Ola Williams, Farmerville, LA

K. C. Bars

1 cup light corn syrup
1 cup sugar
1½ cups crunchy peanut
  butter

6 cups Special K cereal
1 cup chocolate chips
1 cup butterscotch chips

Mix corn syrup and sugar in a saucepan. Place on heat and bring mixture to a boil. Boil to a soft ball stage (about 1 minute). Remove from heat and add peanut butter, mixing until well blended. Pour over cereal and stir until well coated. Spread in a greased 9 x 13-inch cake pan. Melt chocolate chips and butterscotch chips together and spread on top. Cool and cut into squares.

Mrs. Al Lentz, Huron, SD

Husband: Al F. Lentz
Knights of Columbus title: State Deputy

Buckeyes

1 pound plus ½ cup
  confectioners' sugar
  (more if needed)

¾ cup butter, melted
10 ounces crunchy peanut
  butter

Mix the above ingredients together with your hands. Form into small balls (approximately 1-inch); place on cookie sheet and refrigerate until hardened.

Chocolate Coating:
6 ounces semi-sweet chocolate
  chips

6 ounces milk chocolate chips
½ block paraffin wax

Combine ingredients in double boiler; melt and mix well. Dip ready-prepared balls half way into chocolate mixture. (Use a nut picker or toothpick to dip the balls into chocolate.) Set balls back on cookie sheet and allow time to set. Refrigerate again.

Isabell Desiderio, Plymouth, PA

Husband: Basil A. Desiderio
Knights of Columbus title: Supreme Director

Potato Chip Cookies

1 pound butter or margarine   3½ cups flour
1 cup sugar   1 cup crushed potato chips
2 teaspoons vanilla

Preheat oven to 350 degrees. Cream butter and sugar, add vanilla and flour. Mix in potato chips. Drop batter off teaspoon onto ungreased cookie sheet. Bake for 15 minutes. Yields 6 dozen.
Note: Cookies may be colored pink or green with food coloring for holidays.
Isabelle Desiderio, Plymouth, PA
Husband: Basil A. Desiderio
Knights of Columbus title: Supreme Director

Billy Goats

1 cup margarine or butter   ¼ teaspoon cloves
1½ cups sugar   ⅛ teaspoon salt
3 egg yolks   1 tablespoon buttermilk
1 teaspoon vanilla   4 cups coarsely chopped
2½ cups flour   walnuts
1 teaspoon baking soda   1 pound chopped dates
1 teaspoon cinnamon

Cream the margarine or butter and sugar. Add egg yolks and vanilla. Beat well. Sift together the flour, soda, cinnamon, cloves and salt and gradually add to first mixture with buttermilk. Fold in nuts and dates, blending thoroughly. Drop by teaspoonful onto cookie sheet. Bake in 325 degree oven for 20 minutes. Yields 2 dozen.
Note: A bit of vinegar added to milk will substitute for buttermilk.
Elsie Bullard, Rockledge, FL

Lafleur's Cookies

1 box yellow cake mix
½ cup margarine
3 eggs
6 ounces chocolate chips

1 cup chopped pecans
1 cup flaked coconut
16 ounces confectioners' sugar
8 ounces cream cheese

Preheat oven to 350 degrees. Mix cake mix, margarine and 2 eggs together and pat into the bottom of a lightly-greased 9 x 13-inch baking pan. Spread a layer of chocolate chips over the dough. Next a layer of pecans and then a layer of coconut. Press down gently with a spoon. Mix confectioners' sugar, cream cheese, and one egg together until smooth. Pour mixture over other ingredients. Bake for 30 to 40 minutes. Remove from oven, let cool a few minutes and cut into squares. Yields 2 to 3 dozen.

Glenda Lafleur, Ville Platte, LA

Peanut Butter Blossoms

1⅓ cups flour
1 teaspoon soda
½ teaspoon salt
½ cup shortening
½ cup peanut butter
½ cup brown sugar

1 unbeaten egg
2 tablespoons milk
1 teaspoon vanilla
½ cup sugar
1 package chocolate kisses

Sift together flour, soda and salt. Cream together shortening and peanut butter. Gradually add sugars and cream well. Add egg, milk and vanilla and beat well. Blend in the dry ingredients gradually and mix thoroughly. Shape by rounded teaspoonfuls into balls. Roll in sugar and place on ungreased cookie sheet. Bake at 375 degrees for 8 minutes; remove from oven and place a solid chocolate candy kiss on top of each cookie. Press down so that cookie cracks around the edge. Return to oven and bake 2 to 5 minutes longer.

Audrey Morehouse, Alexandria, LA

Crispy Date Bars

Crust:

1 cup all-purpose flour
½ cup firmly packed brown
  sugar

½ cup margarine or butter,
  softened
½ cup ground nuts

Heat oven to 375 degrees. Combine the crust ingredients; mix until crumbly. Press into ungreased 11 x 7 or 9-inch square pan. Bake for 10 to 12 minutes or until golden brown.

Filling:

1 cup chopped dates
½ cup sugar
½ cup margarine or butter
1 egg, well beaten

2 cups Rice Krispies
1 cup chopped nuts
1 teaspoon vanilla

In a medium saucepan, combine dates, sugar and margarine. Cook over medium heat until mixture boils, stirring constantly; simmer 3 minutes. Blend about ¼ cup hot mixture into beaten egg; return egg mixture to saucepan. Cook just until mixture bubbles, stirring constantly. Remove from heat; stir in Rice Krispies, nuts and vanilla. Spread over baked crust; cool completely.

Frosting:

2 cups powdered sugar
2 to 3 teaspoons milk
½ teaspoon vanilla

3 ounces cream cheese,
  softened

Combine frosting ingredients; beat at low speed until smooth. Spread over filling. Refrigerate. Yields 2 dozen bars.

Judy Read, Farmerville, LA

Fruit Drop Cookies

1 cup soft shortening	1½ cups broken pecans
2 cups brown sugar, packed	2 cups cut up candied cherries
2 eggs	1 cup chopped dates
½ cup buttermilk	1 cup white raisins
3½ cups sifted flour	Pecan half for each cookie
1 teaspoon salt	(optional)

Cream shortening, sugar and eggs. Stir in buttermilk. Sift flour and salt together and then add to mixture. Stir in pecans and fruits. Chill at least one hour. Preheat oven to 400 degrees. Drop by rounded teaspoonfuls about 2½ inches apart onto a lightly greased baking sheet. Place a pecan half on each cookie if desired. Bake 8 to 10 minutes, until almost no imprint remains when lightly touched with finger. Makes about 8 dozen cookies.

Delzie Courtney, Ruston, LA

Chocolate Drop Cookies

1 12-ounce package semi-sweet chocolate chips	1 stick butter
4 tablespoons sugar	1 cup flour
1 can sweetened condensed milk	1 cup chopped nuts
	1 teaspoon Watkins Vanilla

Melt chocolate chips and sugar in the top of a double boiler until melted. Add condensed milk and butter and stir until butter is completely melted. Remove from fire and pour over flour. Mix well and add nuts and vanilla. Blend well by hand. Put in refrigerator for about an hour before baking. (Overnight would be better.) Drop by teaspoonfuls onto an ungreased cookie sheet and bake at 350 degrees for 8 to 10 minutes. Take up immediately.

Nell Oliver, Farmerville, LA

Texas Gold Bars

Crust:
1 stick margarine
1 box yellow cake mix
  (without pudding)

2 eggs, slightly beaten
½ cup chopped pecans

Preheat oven to 300 degrees. Melt margarine in saucepan. Add cake mix, eggs, and nuts and blend well. Press mixture onto bottom of 9 x 13-inch pyrex dish.

Filling:
1 8-ounce package cream
  cheese, softened
1 box powdered sugar

2 eggs, beaten
1 teaspoon vanilla

Mix above ingredients and pour over crust. Bake at 300 degrees for 50 minutes. Cool before cutting.

Ruth Guillory, Hessmer, LA

Chocolate Chip Blitz Bars

1 8-ounce package cream
  cheese, softened
½ cup margarine
½ cup packed brown sugar
¼ cup granulated sugar
1 egg
1 teaspoon vanilla
1 cup old-fashioned or quick
  oats, uncooked

⅔ cup flour
½ teaspoon baking powder
¼ teaspoon salt
1 6-ounce package semi-sweet
  chocolate pieces
¼ cup chopped nuts

Combine cream cheese, margarine and sugars, mixing until well blended. Blend in egg and vanilla. Add combined dry ingredients; mix well. Stir in chocolate pieces and nuts. Spread into greased 13 x 9-inch baking pan. Bake at 350 degrees for 30 minutes. Cool and cut into bars. Makes approximately 2 dozen.

Lorraine Zeringue

Toffee Bars

Graham crackers (whole, not crushed)
½ cup margarine
1 cup butter
1½ cups brown sugar

1 cup chopped walnuts or pecans
1 12-ounce package milk chocolate chips

Fill a jellyroll pan with a single layer of graham crackers, placed as close together as possible. Fill all spaces. Melt margarine and butter in medium saucepan. Add brown sugar, stir to dissolve and boil for 3 minutes. Stir frequently. Mix nuts in hot mixture and pour over top of graham crackers, covering well. Put in 350 degree oven and bake for 10 minutes. Remove. Pour chocolate chips over hot bars and allow to set for a few minutes until they begin to melt. Spread over top of mixture as well as possible. Cool and cut into bars. Makes about 3 dozen bars.

Judy Read, Farmerville, LA

Chocolate Chip Cookies

1½ cups Crisco shortening
1½ cups brown sugar
1½ cups white sugar
3 eggs
1½ teaspoons soda
1½ teaspoons salt

3 teaspoons vanilla
3 cups flour
1 cup chopped walnuts
1 12-ounce package chocolate chips

Preheat oven to 350 degrees. Cream Crisco shortening and sugars. Add vanilla and eggs. Combine dry ingredients and add to mixture. Add nuts and chocolate chips and mix well. Drop by teaspoonfuls on cookie sheet. Bake for 8 to 12 minutes. Yields 6 to 7 dozen.

Helen M. Fischer, Bismarck, ND

Husband: Clarence J. Fischer
Knights of Columbus title: State Deputy

Wil's Favorite Chocolate Chip Cookies

2¼ cups all-purpose flour
1 teaspoon baking soda
1 teaspoon salt
1 cup butter, softened
¾ cup sugar
¾ cup brown sugar, firmly
  packed

1 teaspoon vanilla
2 eggs
1 12-ounce Nestle semi-sweet
  morsels
1 cup chopped pecans
  (optional)

In a small bowl combine flour, baking soda and salt; set aside. In a large bowl combine butter, sugar, brown sugar and vanilla. Beat until creamy. Beat in eggs. Gradually add flour mixture and mix well. Fold in chocolate chips and nuts. Drop in desired size onto ungreased cookie sheets. Bake 9 to 11 minutes at 375 degrees.

Katy Ward, Dallas, TX

Christmas Holly Cookies

¼ cup margarine or butter
16 large marshmallows
¾ teaspoon green food
  coloring

¼ teaspoon vanilla
2½ cups corn flakes
Red Hots

Blend butter and marshmallows in a double boiler until melted. Stir in food coloring and vanilla. Fold in corn flakes until each flake is well coated. Drop cookies on waxed paper and form into a wreath shape. Top with three red hots. Let dry 24 hours uncovered. Store in an airtight container. Yields 16 2-inch cookies.

Faith Matthews, Farmerville, LA

Brownies

4 1-ounce squares
   unsweetened chocolate
½ cup butter (do not
   substitute)
4 eggs

2 cups sugar
1 cup sifted flour
1 teaspoon vanilla
1 cup chopped pecans

Preheat oven to 325 degrees. Melt chocolate and butter together and let cool. Beat eggs and add sugar, flour, chocolate mixture, vanilla and pecans. Mix with a wooden spoon until well mixed. Pour into a greased and floured 8 x 12-inch pan. Bake for about 30 minutes. Do not overcook. Yields 2 dozen brownies.

Jacqueline Hawkins, Dallas, TX

Blond Brownies

2 sticks butter
1 box of light brown sugar
2 eggs, well beaten
2 cups flour

2 teaspoons baking powder
2 teaspoons vanilla
1 cup chopped nuts

Melt butter over low heat; add sugar. Remove from heat and add eggs. Stir in flour, baking powder, vanilla and nuts. Put in a greased 9 x 13-inch pan. Bake in 350 degree oven for 30 minutes. Yields 2 dozen.

Lucille Stewart, Farmerville, LA

Graham Cracker Cookies

15 graham cracker rectangles,
  finely crumbled
2 cups chopped nuts
2½ cups small marshmallows
½ cup coconut

2 eggs
1 cup sugar
1 teaspoon vanilla
¾ cup margarine
Powdered sugar

Combine first 4 ingredients in bowl. Beat eggs, sugar, vanilla and margarine and cook over medium heat until thick, stirring constantly. Pour over cracker mixture and mix thoroughly by hand. Press firmly into a buttered jellyroll pan and refrigerate at least 2 hours. Cut in thin bars and roll in powdered sugar. Keep refrigerated.

Pat Russell, Farmerville, LA

Cowboy Cookies

2¼ cups sugar
2¼ cups brown sugar
2¼ cups margarine, softened
5 eggs
2¼ teaspoons vanilla
4½ cups flour

2½ teaspoons soda
1¼ teaspoons salt
4½ cups oatmeal
1 large package chocolate
  chips
2 cups chopped pecans

Cream sugars and margarine together. Add eggs and vanilla. Mix well. Add flour, soda, salt and oatmeal. Mix and add chocolate chips and nuts. Drop by teaspoonfuls onto a greased cookie sheet. Bake in 350 degree oven for 10 to 12 minutes. Do not overbake. Yields 160 cookies.

Mimi Woody, Dallas, TX

Soft Molasses Cookies

2½ cups flour
1 teaspoon soda
1 teaspoon cinnamon
1 teaspoon ginger
½ teaspoon salt
⅔ cup shortening

½ cup sugar
1 egg, unbeaten
½ cup molasses
½ cup buttermilk
1 cup chopped pecans

Sift together flour, soda, cinnamon, ginger and salt. In large mixing bowl combine shortening, sugar, egg and molasses. Beat for a minute on medium speed. Add buttermilk and chopped pecans. Gradually increase speed while adding flour mixture and beat until blended. This is best done by hand instead of mixer. Roll into small balls and press onto greased cookie sheet. Bake at 350 degrees for about 12 minutes. Frost with lemon glaze.

Bill Hollis, Farmerville, LA

Ice Box Cookies

2 cups sugar
1 pound margarine
2 eggs
1 tablespoon hot water

1 teaspoon vanilla
5½ cups flour
1 teaspoon soda
2 cups chopped nuts

Cream sugar and margarine. Add eggs and beat thoroughly. Add hot water and vanilla. Mix in flour and soda. Stir in finely chopped nuts. Chill for 2 hours or longer. Divide dough into fourths and roll into rolls about the diameter of a fifty cent piece. Refrigerate or freeze until baking. When ready to bake, cut dough into thin slices, place on ungreased cookie sheet. Bake at 350 degrees until light brown. Remove from cookie sheet and cool on waxed paper. Store in tightly closed container.

Delzie Courtney, Ruston, LA

Butter Cookies

1 box Duncan Hines Butter
  Recipe Golden cake mix
1 small package butter pecan
  instant pudding mix

1 cup Crisco oil
1 egg, beaten
1 cup chopped pecans or
  walnuts

Do not use an electric mixer. Stir together with spoon. Mix dry ingredients together. Stir the oil in. Add egg and mix thoroughly. Stir in nuts. Form into small balls and place on an ungreased cookie sheet about 2 inches apart. Bake in a 350 degree oven for 8 to 10 minutes or unitl lightly browned. Do not overcook.

Leslie Read, Farmerville, LA

Sour Cream Tea Cake Cookies

1 cup butter
1½ cups sugar
2 egg yolks
1 teaspoon vanilla extract
¼ teaspoon salt

1 teaspoon baking soda
1 teaspoon baking powder
1 cup sour cream
5 cups all-purpose flour

Preheat oven to 350 degrees. Lightly grease cookie sheets. Cream butter and sugar until fluffy. Beat in egg yolks, vanilla, salt, soda, baking powder and sour cream. Gradually add flour until all is blended. Roll dough into little balls about walnut size. Press down with fingers or fork onto cookie sheet. Bake 15 minutes, cool a minute or two on cookie sheet. Remove to wire racks or dish towels.

Variation: ¼ teaspoon nutmeg. Butter recommended for flavor and texture.

Bill Hollis, Farmerville, LA

Nun Better Cookies

1 cup margarine	1 teaspoon salt
1 cup butter	2 teaspoons soda
3 cups sugar	4 teaspoons cream of tartar
4 eggs	Cinnamon and sugar mixture
5½ cups flour	

Cream margarine, butter, sugar and eggs until fluffy. Combine flour, salt, soda and cream of tartar together. Gradually mix the dry ingredients into the creamed mixture. When dough is thoroughly mixed, refrigerate for a MINIMUM of 4 hours or until dough is chilled completely. Roll bits of dough into 1-inch balls. Roll each cookie ball in cinnamon and sugar mixture. Place 2 inches apart on ungreased cookie sheet. Bake in 350 degree oven for 8 to 10 minutes or until cookies are light golden brown. Yields 8 dozen.
Note: Dough must be chilled thoroughly or it will not be rollable.

Mary Francis, Boston, MA

Butter Nut Balls

1 stick butter	1 cup chopped pecans
3 tablespoons sugar	1 teaspoon almond flavoring
1 cup flour	Powdered sugar

Preheat oven to 350 degrees. Bring butter to room temperature. Using your hands, mix butter, sugar and flour thoroughly. Add pecans and almond flavoring. Mix well. Form a small amount into a ball and place on an ungreased cookie sheet about 1-inch apart. Bake for 15 to 20 minutes. Do not overbake. They should not become golden in color. Remove from pan and roll in powdered sugar. Store in an airtight container.

Judy Teaster, Monroe, LA

Snickerdoodles

1 stick butter
½ cup shortening
1½ cups sugar
2 eggs
2¾ cups sifted flour

2 teaspoons cream of tartar
1 teaspoon soda
½ teaspoon salt
2 teaspoons cinnamon
2 tablespoons sugar

Cream butter, shortening and sugar. Add eggs and beat well. Sift all dry ingredients except cinnamon and sugar; add to egg mixture. Mix thoroughly and put in the refrigerator overnight. Roll into balls the size of a walnut. Roll in cinnamon and sugar mixture. Bake on an ungreased cookie sheet at 375 degrees for 8 to 10 minutes. Let stand a minute before removing from cookie sheet. Makes 5 to 6 dozen.

Jannette Liner, Farmerville, LA

Thimble Cookies

1 egg
½ cup butter
¼ cup brown sugar
1 teaspoon vanilla

1 cup plus 2 tablespoons flour
1 cup finely chopped pecans
Strawberry preserves

Separate egg. Cream butter and sugar; add egg yolk, vanilla and flour. Mix well. Pinch off enough dough to roll into bite-size ball. Roll each dough ball in egg white then pecans. Place on ungreased cookie sheet. Use thimble to make indention in the center of each ball. Bake at 350 degrees for approximately 10 minutes. Remove from oven and transfer to waxed paper. Fill thimble indention with strawberry preserves. Yields 12 to 16.

Sandy Acerrano, Richmond, TX

Crazy Crust Apple Pie

1 cup all-purpose flour
1 teaspoon baking powder
½ teaspoon salt
1 tablespoon sugar
1 egg
⅔ cup shortening

¾ cup water
1 1-pound 5-ounce can apple
  pie filling
1 tablespoon lemon juice
½ teaspoon apple pie spice
  or cinnamon

In small mixing bowl combine flour, baking powder, salt, sugar, egg, shortening and water. Blend well. Beat 2 minutes at medium speed. Pour batter into 9-inch pie pan. Combine pie filling, lemon juice and spice then pour into center of batter. Do not stir. Bake at 425 degrees for 45 to 50 minutes. Yields 6 servings.
Note: Makes its own crust as it bakes. Mincemeat pie filling may be substituted for apple.

Alice Williamson, Palmyra, NY

Frozen Banana Split Pie

1 12-ounce container whipped
  topping, thawed
1 9-inch pie plate
1 quart strawberry ice cream,
  divided
1 8¼-ounce can crushed
  pineapple, drained

¼ cup chocolate topping
2 bananas, sliced
½ cup chopped nuts
10 maraschino cherries, well
  drained

Spoon 3 cups whipped topping into a 9-inch pie plate. With back of spoon, spread and shape into a shell; freeze until firm. Spread crust with ⅓ ice cream, top with pineapple. Spread another ⅓ ice cream over pineapple; top with chocolate topping. Spread remaining ice cream over chocolate. Freeze several hours or overnight. Before serving, top with bananas; spread with remaining whipped topping. Sprinkle with nuts; top with cherries. Yields 10 servings.

Alice Williamson, Palmyra, NY

Buttermilk Pie

1 9-inch pie shell, unbaked
½ cup butter, softened
2 cups sugar
3 tablespoons flour

3 eggs, beaten
1 cup buttermilk
1 teaspoon vanilla
Dash ground nutmeg

Prepare unbaked pie shell. Cream butter and sugar together with mixer. Add flour and eggs and beat well. Stir in buttermilk, vanilla and nutmeg. Pour filling into pie shell. Bake on lower rack of oven at 350 degrees for 45 to 50 minutes. Place on wire rack and let cool completely before serving.

Note: For a variation add ¾ cup of coconut.

Mary Pfeiffer

Lemon Cream Pie

3 eggs
¾ cup sugar
½ cup lemon juice
8 ounces cream cheese, softened

1 baked pie crust
½ pint whipping cream
1 teaspoon vanilla
2 tablespoons sugar

Beat eggs until fluffy then gradually add sugar and lemon juice. Cook in a double boiler with constant stirring until mixture thickens. Using mixer add cream cheese to thickend mixture and beat until smooth. Pour into baked pie crust. Refrigerate until serving. Just prior to serving whip the whipping cream, adding vanilla and 2 tablespoons of sugar after it has begun to thicken. Serve pie with whipped cream topping.

Melba Simmons, Bunkie, LA

Cream Pie

1 cup sugar
2 tablespoons butter or
  margarine
4 tablespoons flour
2 eggs

1 cup evaporated milk
1 cup milk
1 teaspoon vanilla
1 unbaked pie crust

Mix sugar, butter and flour. Add eggs one at a time; cream well. Add evaporated milk, milk and vanilla. Pour into unbaked pie crust and bake at 450 degrees for 10 minutes then 350 degrees for 20 to 30 minutes. Pie is done when the filling is set.

Jane Jackson, Alexandria, LA

Lemon Meringue Pie

¾ cup sugar
2 tablespoons flour
2 tablespoons cornstarch
¼ teaspoon salt
1¼ cups hot water

2 lemons, juiced
2 teaspoons grated lemon peel
3 egg yolks
1 tablespoon butter
1 cooked pie shell

Mix sugar, flour, cornstarch and salt. Add water. Cook over medium heat until thick. Add lemon juice and lemon peel. Then add beaten egg yolks. Cook until it comes to a boil. Remove from heat and add butter. Stir until cool. Pour into pie shell. Top with meringue.

Meringue:
3 egg whites
¼ teaspoon salt
1 teaspoon cream of tartar

⅔ cup sugar
1 teaspoon vanilla

Preheat oven to 375 degrees. Beat egg whites until foamy. Gradually add salt and cream of tartar. Continue beating until stiff, add sugar and vanilla and beat until a stiff peak forms. Pile on pie filling, sealing edges. Bake in oven for 10 to 15 minutes or until meringue is slightly browned. Yields 6 servings.

Charlotte Baham, New Orleans, LA

Lemon Tassies

Cream Cheese Pastry:

1 8-ounce package cream
  cheese

2 cups flour
2 sticks margarine

Combine ingredients. Make into walnut-size balls and chill. Shape into 1-inch balls. Place in tiny ungreased 1¾-inch muffin cups. Press dough against bottom and sides of cup. Bake until done in a 325 degree oven. Cool.

Filling:

3 eggs
¾ cup sugar
½ cup lemon juice

2 teaspoons grated lemon rind
1 8-ounce package cream
  cheese, softened

Beat eggs in cold double boiler until thickend and fluffly. Continue beating while adding sugar, lemon juice and rind. Cook over hot water until smooth and thick. Cool. Gradually blend cream cheese into custard. Fill pastries and top with whipped cream, if desired.

Beverly Johnson, Farmerville, LA

Fresh Peach Pie

1 9-inch baked pie crust
1 cup sugar
1 cup water
3 tablespoons cornstarch

3 tablespoons orange Jello
3 cups ripe peaches
8 ounces Cool Whip
½ cup chopped pecans

Bake pie shell and allow to cool. Cook sugar, water and cornstarch until thick and clear. Add dry orange Jello. Stir and set aside to cool. Cut up peaches and place in cooled pie crust. Pour cooled cornstarch mixture over peaches. Cover pie with Cool Whip and chopped pecans. Will keep several days in refrigerator.

Elizabeth Ardoin, Alexandria, LA

Pineapple Millionaire Pies

2 cups sifted powdered sugar
½ cup margarine, softened
2 eggs
⅛ teaspoon salt
¼ teaspoon vanilla
2 9-inch baked pie crusts

1 cup heavy cream, chilled
½ cup powdered sugar
½ cup chopped pecans
1 cup crushed pineapple,
drained

Cream together 2 cups sifted powdered sugar and margarine. Add eggs, salt and vanilla, beating until light and fluffy. Half mixture, spreading evenly into two baked pie crusts. Chill. Whip cream and blend in ½ cup powdered sugar. Fold in pecans and drained pineapple. Half the cream mixture, spreading over top of chilled base mixtures. Chill thoroughly. Yields 12 servings.

Alice Mathews, Alexandria, LA

Pumpkin Chiffon Pie

1 envelope unflavored gelatin
¼ cup cold water
3 eggs, separated
1 cup sugar
1¼ cups pumpkin (fresh
cooked or canned)
½ cup milk

½ teaspoon salt
¾ teaspoon cinnamon
¾ teaspoon nutmeg
½ teaspoon ginger
½ cup whipping cream
1 9-inch baked pie crust

Soften the gelatin in the cold water and set aside. Beat the egg yolks with ½ *cup* sugar until thick. Add pumpkin, milk, salt, cinnamon, nutmeg and ginger and mix thoroughly. Pour into a large saucepan and cook over medium heat stirring constantly until mixture begins to thicken. Remove from heat and add the gelatin mixture and stir until dissolved. Chill until mixture is thick but not set. Beat ½ cup whipping cream until thick and fold into pumpkin mixture. Beat the egg whites until soft peaks form and gradually add the other ½ cup sugar until straight, glossy peaks form. Fold gently into pumpkin mixture. Spoon lightly into baked pie crust. Chill until firm (about 2 hours). Serve with a dollop of whipped cream if desired.

Maude Thompson, Litchfield, IL

Fresh Strawberry Pies

3 pints fresh strawberries
1 cup water
1 cup sugar
3 tablespoons cornstarch

Red food coloring
1 pint heavy cream, whipped
2 baked pie shells
Sweetened whipped cream

Wash and hull strawberries. Crush 1½ pints of berries and add water. Heat to a boil and then boil for 2 minutes. Combine sugar and cornstarch, mixing thoroughly, and stir into berry juice. Cook until bubbly. If mixture is lumpy, put into blender and blend until smooth. Add red food coloring for desired color. Slice remaining whole strawberries and place into bottom of the two pie shells. Pour cooked sauce over sliced berries. Refrigerate until set. Top with sweetened whipped cream and serve. Yields 2 pies.

Mary Margaret Coyle, Conroe, TX

Old-Fashioned Yam Pie

2 cups hot mashed boiled
   yams
¼ cup margarine
1 cup sugar
½ teaspoon salt

1 teaspoon cinnamon
1 teaspoon vanilla
½ cup cream or whole milk
3 large eggs
1 large unbaked pastry shell

Mix hot potatoes and margarine until margarine is melted. Add sugar, salt, cinnamon and vanilla, stirring until mixed. Add cream. Beat eggs until foamy and add to potato mixture. Beat gently until blended. Pour into pastry shell. Bake in 450 degree oven for 10 minutes. Lower oven to 350 degrees and bake about 45 minutes or until knife inserted in center comes out clean.

Bill Hollis, Farmerville, LA

Chocolate Amaretto Pie

3 packages instant chocolate
pudding (3⅛ ounce)
2 packages Dream Whip
(3 ounce)
1 cup milk for Dream Whip

2 cups milk for pudding mix
½ cup Amaretto liqueur
2 teaspoons almond flavoring
2 ready-made chocolate crusts
1 medium Cool Whip

Mix 2 packages Dream Whip with 1 cup milk as directed (medium box) then add 2 cups milk and 3 packages chocolate instant pudding. Mix well, then add ½ cup Amaretto liqueur and 2 teaspoons almond flavoring. Whip until fluffy and pour into 2 ready-made chocolate pie crusts. Top with Cool Whip and garnish with chocolate curls.

Dot Sarver, Leesville, LA

Chocolate Chip Cookie Pies

2 sticks butter or margarine,
melted
2 cups sugar
1 cup all-purpose flour
4 eggs, well beaten

2 teaspoons vanilla
12 ounces chocolate mini
chips
2 cups pecan pieces
2 pie crusts

Combine melted butter and sugar. Add flour, eggs and vanilla and mix well. Fold in the chocolate chips and pecans. Divide between the two pie crusts. Bake at 350 degrees for 45 minutes. Yields 2 pies. Delicious served hot with vanilla ice cream.

Leigh Rachofsky, Dallas, TX

Fudge Chocolate Pie

6 tablespoons flour
1½ cups sugar
3 tablespoons cocoa
2 egg yolks

1½ cups evaporated milk
1 teaspoon vanilla
3 tablespoons butter
1 baked pie shell

Mix flour, sugar and cocoa together. Add beaten egg yolks and evaporated milk. Mix together well, then add vanilla and butter. Cook in a double boiler until thick. Pour into a baked pie shell. Top with meringue and bake at 250 degrees for 15 minutes.

Judy Read, Farmerville, LA

Chocolate Fudge Pecan Pie

4 ounces sweet chocolate
¼ cup margarine
1 can sweetened condensed
  milk
2 eggs
½ cup hot water

1 teaspoon vanilla extract
⅛ teaspoon salt
½ cup pecan pieces
1 9-inch unbaked pie crust
1 cup coconut

Melt chocolate and margarine over low heat. Set aside. In a medium mixing bowl, combine milk, eggs, hot water, vanilla and salt. Mix well. Add chocolate and margarine. Mix. Place pecan pieces in bottom of unbaked pie crust and pour filling over pecans. Sprinkle with coconut. Bake in a preheated 350 degree oven for 35 to 40 minutes or until knife inserted into center of pie comes out clean.

Bill Hollis, Farmerville, LA

Auntie's Chocolate Pie

1½ cups sugar
4 tablespoons cocoa (heaping)
6 tablespoons flour
¼ teaspoon salt
1 large can Pet milk

½ can water
3 eggs, separated
1 tablespoon butter
1 teaspoon vanilla
1 9-inch baked pie crust

Mix dry ingredients. Add Pet milk and water. Mix in top of double boiler. Add egg yolks (beaten). Cook on medium heat. When hot, add butter. Cook until mixture thickens, stirring to avoid lumps. Cool. Add vanilla. Pour into baked pie crust. Top with meringue using egg whites and 6 teaspoons sugar. Brown in 350 degree oven.

Jane R. Parnell, Newport, AR

Chocolate Pie

4 tablespoons flour	4 egg yolks, well-beaten
1 cup sugar	2 tablespoons butter
4 tablespoons cocoa	1 teaspoon vanilla
¼ teaspoon salt	1 baked pie crust
2 cups whole milk	

Mix and sift flour, sugar, cocoa and salt. Pour milk into saucepan and add sifted mixture. Stir over heat until very warm. Add well-beaten egg yolk. Cook until thick, stirring often. Remove from heat and add butter and vanilla. Pour into baked pie crust and top with meringue. Bake at 350 degrees for 12 to 15 minutes.

Vivian Mitchell, Cotton Valley, LA

French Silk Chocolate Pie

½ cup butter	2 eggs
¾ cup sugar	½ pint whipping cream,
2 squares semi-sweet	whipped
chocolate, melted	1 Meringue Shell
1 teaspoon vanilla	

Cream butter and sugar. Add melted chocolate and vanilla to butter mixture and beat. Add eggs one at a time, beating about 5 minutes after each egg. Stir in or fold in one half of the whipped cream. Pour into Meringue Shell. Top with remainder of whipped cream. Chill at least 2 hours before serving.

Meringue Shell:

3 egg whites	1 teaspoon vanilla
1 cup sugar	½ teaspoon vinegar
½ teaspoon water	¾ cup chopped pecans

Beat egg whites until thickened. Then add sugar, liquids and pecans and continue to beat until stiff. Place in a greased pie plate to form a shell. Bake at 250 degrees for 1 hour. WATCH TIME. Shell should be dried out and slightly brown. If shell cooks too fast, lower oven temperature slightly and cook an extra 5 to 10 minutes.

Gloria Evans, Clarksdale, MS

Oklahoma's Cream Cheese Pecan Pie

Crust:

1 cup all-purpose flour
¼ teaspoon salt
1 teaspoon sugar
⅛ teaspoon cinnamon

¼ teaspoon baking powder
⅓ cup plus 1 tablespoon
   shortening
⅓ cup water

Combine flour, salt, sugar, cinnamon and baking powder in a mixing bowl. Cut in shortening with pastry blender or two knives until mixture is uniform. Sprinkle with water, 1 tablespoon at a time; tossing lightly with a fork. When all water has been added, work dough into a firm ball. On lightly-floured surface, roll dough into a circle 1-inch larger than inverted 9-inch pan. Gently lift dough into pan. Trim ½-inch beyond edge of pie pan, then fold dough under to make a double thickness around rim. Flute edges.

Cream Cheese Filling:

½ cup sugar
1 egg, beaten
½ teaspoon salt

1 8-ounce package cream
   cheese, softened
1 teaspoon vanilla extract

Combine sugar, egg and salt in a mixing bowl. Add softened cream cheese and vanilla extract. Cream mixture together. Spoon into unbaked pie crust.

Pecan Topping:

1½ cups chopped pecans
¼ cup sugar
3 eggs, beaten (do not
   overbeat)

1 cup light corn syrup
1 teaspoon vanilla extract

Combine pecans and sugar in a mixing bowl. Stir eggs, corn syrup and vanilla into mixture. Pour over cream cheese filling. Bake in 375 degree oven for 35 to 40 minutes or until topping is browned. Cool and serve.

Dixie Harlan, Paris, TX

Osgood Pie

2 eggs, separated
1 cup sugar
½ cup butter, melted
2 tablespoons flour
1 tablespoon vanilla
½ teaspoon cinnamon

½ teaspoon ground cloves
½ teaspoon allspice
1 cup raisins
1 cup coarsely chopped
    pecans
1 unbaked pie crust

Beat egg yolks adding sugar a little at a time. Stir in butter, flour, vanilla and spices. Mix thoroughly. Add raisins and pecans and mix well. Beat egg whites until stiff and fold into mixture. Turn into unbaked pie crust and bake at 350 degrees for 1 hour.

Hazel Ward, Belton, TX

Sawdust Pie

1½ cups sugar
1½ cups graham cracker
    crumbs
1½ cups coconut
1½ cups chopped pecans or
    walnuts

½ cup chocolate chips
7 egg whites
1 unbaked 9-inch pie shell

Mix all of the above by hand and turn into an unbaked pie shell. Bake in 350 degree oven for 35 minutes or until center is firm. Do not cut until cool.

Dixie Harlan, Paris, TX

Millionaires Pie

1 can Eagle Brand milk
1 large can crushed pineapple,
    undrained
1 cup pecans

1 tablespoon lemon juice
1 large carton Cool Whip
1 graham cracker pie crust

Mix milk, pineapple, pecans and lemon juice. Blend in Cool Whip. Pour into crust. Chill for two hours before serving.
Note: Can be frozen and served later.

Susan Cartier Willis, Austin, TX

Key Lime Pie

½ cup Key lime juice
1 can condensed milk
3 egg whites
¼ teaspoon cream of tartar

Graham cracker pie crust
Whipped cream
Key lime slices

Mix lime juice and condensed milk together in large bowl. In separate bowl beat egg whites with cream of tartar until very stiff. Fold egg whites into lime and milk mixture. Pour into graham cracker crust. Refrigerate at least 2 hours. Top with whipped cream; add lime slices for decorations if desired.

Elby Lores, Miami, FL

Pecan Pie I

3 eggs
½ cup sugar
⅔ cup dark Karo syrup
1 teaspoon vanilla

4 tablespoons butter
1 cup chopped pecans
1 unbaked pie crust

Beat eggs well with fork. Then add sugar and Karo and mix well. Add vanilla, butter and pecans. Pour into unbaked pie crust. Bake at 425 degrees for 10 minutes. Reduce oven to 375 degrees and bake for 30 to 35 minutes. Serves 6.

Mrs. Marlene Roussel, Baton Rouge, LA

Pecan Pie II

4 eggs
2 tablespoons butter
1 cup sugar
1 cup Karo syrup (white)

1 teaspoon vanilla
1 cup pecans
1 unbaked pie shell

Slightly beat eggs. Add butter, sugar, Karo, vanilla and pecans and blend well. Pour into pie shell. Bake at 325 to 350 degrees for one hour and ten minutes.

Barbara Hanson, Cotton Valley, LA

Pecan Tassies

Cream Cheese Pastry:

2 3-ounce packages cream
   cheese

2 cups flour
2 sticks margarine

Combine all ingredients. Make into walnut-size balls and chill.

Filling:

3 tablespoons melted
   margarine
3 eggs, slightly beaten

1 teaspoon vanilla
1 box brown sugar
1 cup chopped pecans

Combine all ingredients. In miniature muffin tins place balls of pastry dough and shape into shells, I use my thumb. Pour filling into shells and bake at 300 degrees for 30 minutes.
Note: Takes two pastry recipes for this amount of filling.

Laura S. Scott, Natchitoches, LA

Divinity Nut Pie

3 egg whites
1 cup sugar
1 teaspoon vanilla
23 Ritz crackers, finely
   crushed

1 cup chopped pecans
1 carton whipping cream
3 tablespoons sugar
1 teaspoon Quick cocoa mix

Beat egg whites until very stiff. Add 1 cup sugar and vanilla. Continue beating until sugar has dissolved. Fold in Ritz crackers (that have been crushed into fine crumbs in a food processor or put between waxed paper and crushed with a rolling pin) and chopped pecans. Pour into a buttered 8 x 12-inch pyrex dish or deep 10-inch pie plate. Bake for 30 minutes in a 350 degree oven. Remove from oven and cool. When cooled, top with whipped cream that has been sweetened with 3 tablespoons sugar and cocoa mix. Keep in refrigerator. Yields 7 to 8 servings.

Judy Read, Farmerville, LA

Old-Fashioned Sweet Dough

2 cups flour
1 cup sugar
¾ cup Crisco shortening
2 teaspoons baking powder

1 teaspoon vanilla
1 egg
½ cup milk

Mix together flour and sugar. Cut Crisco into flour mixture. Add remaining ingredients and mix until dough is ready to roll. Divide dough into 2 parts. Place dough on floured surface and roll out one pie crust at a time. Place in pie plate and use as you would any pie crust. If using a custard filling, bake the pie crust before filling it. Can also be used for double-crust pie.
Note: Sugar makes it surprisingly different.

Joan Ledford, Loreauville, LA

Never-Fail Pie Crust

2 cups flour
1 cup Crisco shortening
⅓ cup milk

1 teaspoon vinegar
Dash of salt

With a pastry cutter or fork mix flour and shortening until blended. Add milk, vinegar and salt. Mix well and knead to form soft dough. Yields one 2-crust pie.

Maude Thompson, Litchfield, IL

Marvelous Meringue

1 teaspoon cornstarch
½ cup water
3 egg whites at room
  temperature

¼ teaspoon cream of tartar
⅓ cup sugar

Combine cornstarch and water in saucepan and bring to a boil. Stir mixture until clear. Set aside to cool. Beat egg whites and cream of tartar until foamy. Gradually add the sugar until soft peaks form. Add liquid mixture and beat until stiff. Spread evenly over pie and bake to golden brown. Yields meringue for one pie.

Jane R. Parnell, Newport, AR

Bishop Greco and Sister Antoinette Baroncini

HAPPINESS FIRST

To live in an atmosphere of happiness is the right of every child. Especially is this true of retarded children, whose power to create their happiness is so limited.

THE REMARKABLE LIFE
OF
THE MOST REVEREND CHARLES P. GRECO

As Christians, we are called to share in the ministry of our Lord, to serve others and to teach by example. Such a ministry was exemplified in the life of the Most Reverend Charles Pascal Greco, former Bishop of the Diocese of Alexandria, Louisiana. His life overflowed with an abundance of love and concern for his fellowman, and was filled with a deep desire to have Christ reign in the hearts of all. In his devoted, humble, loving faith and service he provided the inspiration for others to "love one another as I have loved you..." (John 13:34)

On October 29, 1894, in the town of Rodney, Mississippi, Charles Pascal Greco was born. He was the third of thirteen children, six boys and seven girls, born to Frank P. Greco and Carmel Testa Greco. His parents were from Cefalu, a city on the northern shore of Sicily. There they were married and had their first child, a girl whom they called Josephine. His mother was an accomplished seamstress and excellent cook, and his father was a stone mason and builder in the old country before he decided to come to America to establish a home.

The family came to Rodney and it was there that their second child, Sam, and their third child, Charles, were born. While Charles was still an infant, they moved to Waterproof, Louisiana, in the Diocese of Alexandria, where they remained for approximately six years. His father operated a cotton plantation and a general merchandise store during this time, until, ironically, they were forced to leave because of flooding. From Waterproof, they moved into an area in the French Quarter of New Orleans which was inhabited by Italian immigrants. Here his father operated a general merchandise store.

From his boyhood, under the watchful eye of his father, young Charles developed his talents to create beautiful things from wood. The Greco family was very close, and young Charles was often found at his father's heels. He would beg his father for the wooden merchandise crates from the store, and from these crates, he would build toys and furniture for his brothers and sisters.

Bishop Greco said, "In God's Providence we moved to New Orleans." It was there that he became acquainted with the Missionary Sisters of the Sacred Heart of Jesus, an order of Nuns founded by Mother Cabrini. A few years before the birth of Bishop Greco, Mother Cabrini established an orphanage, convent and chapel at 817 St. Phillips Street, the first of two orphanges which she founded in New Orleans.

She opened St. Mary's School and Sacred Heart School, and it was St. Mary's School in which young Charles was first enrolled, later attending Sacred Heart School. Following Mass in the chapel of the convent young Charles, who served as an acolyte at the age of eleven, met Mother Cabrini. When Mother was introduced to young Charles, she took his hand, squeezed it warmly, and after a few moments asked, "Charles, what do you want to be when you grow up?" It took a moment for Charles to compose himself and reply, "Mother, I hope to be a priest." She placed her hand on his head, as if in blessing, turned and departed with two Sisters and Father Vincent Ciolino. A short distance away she stopped, seemed to gaze into the distance, then said, "Yes, this boy will become a priest, and he will go far in the priesthood." This statement was revealed to Bishop Greco by Father Vincent and the two Sisters, Sister Philomena and Sister Angela, when they were all in their eighties, several years after Bishop Greco had been appointed to the episcopacy. Her remark had been interpreted by those in her company as a prophecy.

After two years in St. Mary's School, Charles went to Old Immaculate Conception College, a Jesuit school, on Baronne Street in New Orleans. It was then decided that he should go to St. Benedict's Seminary, near Covington, Louisiana, to study for the priesthood. "I had always wanted to become a priest, therefore I was delighted with this announcement."

Upon completion of his minor seminary work, he was selected by Archbishop James Hubert Blenk, S.M., of New Orleans, for further study at the University of Louvain in Belgium. He remained in Belgium from 1913 to 1914, when the outbreak of World War I closed the school.

The war placed the young seminarian in a real dilemma since he had not received any orders from the Archbishop, and he did not have financial means to return to America. He went to Milan where he was directed to go to Menaggio, Italy, a small town near Como, where there was an institution for retarded children. The young seminarian spent three months in Menaggio, Italy, and it was here that he became friends with Father Luigi Guanella. Some years earlier, Father Guanella had founded a school for retarded children as well as the Congregation of Sisters of Mary of Providence, to care for the children. Enthusiasm for a program such as this was instilled in the heart of this young, devoted seminarian; yet position, time, nor funds would become available to fulfill such dreams for many years. Attempts were made to inform the Archbishop and his parents of his whereabouts. Later he learned that not one letter he had written ever reached its destination. The young seminarian waited for some word as to where he was to find a school to pursue his studies. Most of the national seminaries in Rome did not reopen and those that did were filled with refugee seminarians. Finally, permission was given to contact the University of Fribourg in Switzerland. There young Greco completed his studies for the priesthood.

Having completed his studies and now a deacon, young Charles was ready to be ordained. Reverend John W. Shaw, just appointed Archbishop of New Orleans, directed the seminarian to return to New Orleans. The new Archbishop requested that before returning, the young seminarian first go to Rome and bring back the prelates' pallium, the symbol given by the Holy See to Archbishops in recognition of their rank.

As instructed, the young deacon went to Rome to obtain the pallium. He refused to leave Rome without the pallium and began to request assistance from whomever he could find in authority. He was sent to Archbishop Corretti, Secretary of Extraordinary Foreign Affairs, who took him to Pope Benedict XV. This was the first of seven Popes that would become personally acquainted with this soon-to-be-ordained young man. Within two hours of his audience with Pope Benedict XV, the long sought after pallium was in his hands. It arrived in a small box covered in red wax and imprinted with many seals, "...hardly large enough to have been of such concern."

Young Greco returned to New Orleans with his package in hand. On July 25, 1918, in the Academy of Sacred Heart, he was ordained by Archbishop Shaw. He would remain in New Orleans for a brief period at St. Mary's Church on Chartres Street, where he celebrated his first High Mass. His first Low Mass was celebrated at Mother Cabrini's chapel where he had seved as an acolyte.

In 1919, he became assistant Pastor of St. Francis de Sales Church in Houma, Louisiana, where he remained for five years as Assistant Pastor. He began his work with Catholic youth and formed the Junior Holy Name Society for boys and the Sodality of the Blessed Virgin Mary for girls. He was called back to New Orleans in December, 1923, and named Vice Chancellor and later Chancellor of the Archdiocese of New Orleans.

In 1926, Father Greco went to St. Maurice Church in New Orleans where he remained for nineteen years as the adminstrator and pastor. During this time there was a great deal of construction, a number of youth programs developed through the Catholic Youth Organization, and Father Greco was appointed to serve in many capacities of great authority. He served from 1926 to 1945 as Defender of Marriage Bonds and was presiding judge of the Matrimonial Court of the Diocese of New Orleans. He was appointed Archdiocesan Consultor in 1935, and was named Domestic Prelate by Pope Pius XI on Christmas Day, 1937, with the title "Right Reverend Monsignor".

Monsignor Greco was asked to write a column of comment which he entitled "Keeping the Record Straight" in the Archdiocesan weekly, *Catholic Action of the South*, shortly after it was founded. He continued to write this column for ten years. In 1945, he was given the responsibility of Editor-in-Chief of the weekly publication.

During the proceedings for the Beatification of Mother Elizabeth Seton, Monsignor Greco served as the presiding judge of the Pontifical Tribunal. His title was the "Devil's Advocate", which is the traditional name of the "Promoter of the Faith", whose duty is, in the cause of canonization, to raise objections and possible difficulties against approval of the cause. This task is much like that of a prosecuting attorney. The Beatification of Mother Seton was the final phase in the cause for her forthcoming canonization.

On April 12, 1945, after having served as pastor of St. Maurice for some twenty years, Monsignor Greco was appointed by Archbishop Rummel as pastor of Our Lady of Lourdes in New Orleans, and chairman of the Youth Progress Program Drive. He took the oath of office as Vicar General of the Archdiocese of New Orleans June 15, 1945, and in September of that same year he received news of the death of Bishop Desmond.

On January 11, 1945, Monsignor Greco found a special delivery letter lying in the middle of his desk, having the return address of "3339 Massachusetts Avenue, Washington, D.C.". It was addressed to the Reverened Monsignor Charles P. Greco, 605 St. Maurice Avenue, New Orleans, Louisiana, *"Strictly Personal"*. Inside this outer envelope, however, was another envelope which read: "to the Most Reverend Charles P. Greco," *"Strictly Personal"*. That was the title given to bishops.

The sixth Bishop of the Diocese of Alexandria was appointed publicly by Pope Pius XII, on January 15, 1946, the feast of Our Lady of Prompt Succor, Patroness of Louisiana. Monsignor Charles P. Greco, at the age of 51, was consecrated a Bishop in St. Louis Cathedral, New Orleans, Louisiana, on February 25, 1946. On March 19, 1946, he was installed as Bishop of Alexandria by Archbishop Rummel in St. Francis Xavier Cathedral, in Alexandria, Louisiana.

The year 1946 proved to be a most eventful period for Bishop Greco. After having been appointed Bishop, he traveled to Rome for the canonization of Mother Francis Cabrini. This holy woman had made the prediction that he would become a priest and "go far". There are many events concerning Mother Cabrini which parallel the life of Bishop Greco. She too, was one of thirteen children. She was buried in 1918, the year he was ordained; venerated in 1937, the year he became Monsignor; canonized in 1946, the year he became Bishop.

During this trip to Rome in 1946, Bishop became aware of the desire of Mother Zita Verni, General Superior of the Congregation of Our Lady of Sorrows, to establish her congregation in the United States. He happily accepted the Sisters of Our Lady of Sorrows, and the following year, a group of thirteen sisters arrived in the Diocese of Alexandria with their Mother Superior.

For the next forty years, Bishop served the diocese of Alexandria as their Shepherd. During these years, many titles and honors were bestowed upon him. He was elected to serve as a member of the United States Bishops' Committee, the Confraternity of Christian Doctrine in November of 1950, and became the chairman of the committee in November, 1959, and was re-elected to a three year term in 1966. In 1961, while serving as chairman, he was appointed as Consultor on the Preparatory Committee for the Second Vatican Council by Pope John XXIII. The Council opened October 11, 1962, and closed December 8, 1965. It should be noted that he was the only native-born, Southern Bishop in the

306

United States to be named to one of the Ten Commissions of the Second Vatican Council. He helped prepare the "Constitution on the Life and Ministry of the Clergy" and additional preparatory material for the Council.

In July 1954, he was named State Chaplain of the Louisiana Knights of Columbus, and on January 14,1961, he became the Supreme Chaplain of the National Knights of Columbus. He held an honorary life membership in the society and was Supreme Chaplain for life.

In 1954, Bishop Greco began to realize a dream of some thirty-eight years: the dream of the young seminarian to establish a school for mentally retarded children. On February 24, 1954, Bishop purchased the White Hotel in Clarks, Louisiana, laying the foundation for St. Mary's Training School for Retarded Children. The school remained in operation in Clarks for some twenty years before being relocated to a spacious, modern facility in Alexandria, Louisiana.

The President's Cup was presented to Bishop Greco for his work to establish a school for the mentally retarded. This award is the highest honor given by the President's Committee on Mental Retardation.

In 1970, Bishop became seventy-five years of age, at which time it is required that a Bishop submit his resignation to the Pope, and the Pope then sets the date for acceptance. Pope Paul, VI, postponed acceptance of his resignation for three years so that the Bishop's program for the mentally retarded might be in a stage near completion.

When Bishop Greco retired in 1973, he had served the Diocese of Alexandria for twenty-seven years. During this time he led his people in an extensive building program, resulting in thirty-three new parishes, and the construction of over 450 buildings. Included in these buildings are schools, churches, convents, rectories, health faciliites and two schools for retarded children. He was well known for his work with youth, the Confraternity of Christian Doctrine and the Knights of Columbus.

One of Bishop Greco's fondest achievements was the establishment of the two schools for retarded children: St. Mary's Training School and Holy Angels School. This was a fulfillment of a promise of many years and a dream come true.

This most dedicated man gave totally of himself and was ingrained in the lives of those with whom he came in contact over the many years. He was truly a servant of our Lord, the loving Shepherd he was ordained to become almost seventy years ago. It seems that he was always in the right place, at the right time, to meet the call of our Lord and of his fellowman. God was his constant companion, leading him in every step along the path of life. Few men have had a greater love, faith and devotion, and it was by these attributes that he exemplified the special human qualities which set him apart from and above the majority of mankind and caused people to revere him.

It is so appropriately written in the "Dedication" of this book, that

307

Bishop Greco was like a gardener, feeding and nurturing the children of Our Lord. He planted the seed which created St. Mary's and Holy Angels schools; nurtured it and watched it grown, never failing to provide what was needed most, LOVE. Bishop Greco dedicated himself to providing a quality life for these children from birth to death.

As *The Bishop's Bounty* was nearing completion, Bishop Greco was called to the presence of God on January 20, 1987. His dream had been to establish an endowment fund for St. Mary's Training School, to enable the work with "God's special children" to continue. He gave us much assistance in preparing this book and was anxious to see it published. Bishop instilled his love and concern for these children in our hearts, and it is for this, and in his loving memory that we carry on his cause.

INDEX

309

Index

Index

315

Index

Index

The Bishop's Bounty Cookbook
% The Amicus Club
P.O. Box 5245
Alexandria, Louisiana 71307-5245

Please send me____copies of   @14.95 each_____
  The Bishop's Bounty
Postage and Handling   @ 2.00 each_____
Louisiana residents add 4% sales tax   @   .60 each_____
                                              Total enclosed_____

Name_____

Address_____

City_____ State_____ Zip_____

Make checks payable to *The Bishop's Bounty*.
All proceeds benefit St. Mary's Training School for Retarded Children.

The Bishop's Bounty Cookbook
% The Amicus Club
P.O. Box 5245
Alexandria, Louisiana 71307-5245

Please send me____copies of   @14.95 each_____
  The Bishop's Bounty
Postage and Handling   @ 2.00 each_____
Louisiana residents add 4% sales tax   @   .60 each_____
                                              Total enclosed_____

Name_____

Address_____

City_____ State_____ Zip_____

Make checks payable to *The Bishop's Bounty*.
All proceeds benefit St. Mary's Training School for Retarded Children.

Reorder Additional Copies